COMPETITIVENESS, SUBSIDIARITY AND INDUSTRIAL POLICY

Edited by
Pat Devine, Yannis Katsoulacos and Roger Sugden

London and New York

First published 1996
by Routledge
11 New Fetter Lane, London EC4P 4EE

Simultaneously published in the USA and Canada
by Routledge
29 West 35th Street, New York, NY 10001

Routledge is an International Thomson Publishing company

Typeset in Garamond by
Florencetype Ltd, Stoodleigh, Devon

Printed and bound in Great Britain by
T.J. Press (Padstow) Ltd, Padstow, Cornwall

British Library Cataloguing in Publication Data
A catalogue record for this book is available from the British Library

Library of Congress Cataloguing in Publication Data
Competitiveness, subsidiarity, and industrial policy/edited by Pat Devine, Yannis Katsoulacos, and Roger Sugden.
p. cm. – (Industrial economic strategies for Europe)
Includes bibliographical references and index.
1. Europe – Economic policy. 2. Europe – Economic conditions – 1945–. 3. Europe – Economic integration. 4. Competition – Europe – Case studies. 5. Industrial policy – Europe – Case studies. 6. Subsidiary – Case studies.
I. Devine, P. J. II. Series.
HC240.C5676 1966
338.94–dc20 95–31900

ISBN 0–415–13985–6

COMPETITIVENESS, SUBSIDIARITY AND INDUSTRIAL POLICY

What does competitiveness mean? In recent years, much discussion of economic policy has become dominated by the notion of 'competitiveness' with little notion of how this concept can be extended beyond the individual firm, or of how it might coëxist with the wider interests of communities or nations. In this volume a group of leading international economists explore these and other issues.

The book includes chapters addressing different aspects of competitiveness, subsidiarity and policy issues. It focuses on theory, on cross-country comparisons, and on single country case studies. Issues addressed include:

- the relationship between competitiveness and community objectives
- the coexistence of diversity, subsidiarity and EU industrial policy
- the impact of European enlargement and further integration

Pat Devine is Senior Lecturer in Economics at the University of Manchester. **Yannis Katsoulacos** is Professor of Economics at the Athens University of Economics and Business. **Roger Sugden** is Director of the Research Centre for Industrial Strategy and Professor of Industrial Economics at the University of Birmingham.

CONTENTS

List of figures vii
List of tables viii
List of contributors xi
Introduction xiii
Chapter abstracts xix
Acknowledgements xxvi

1 COMPETITIVENESS AND THE OBJECTIVES OF COMMUNITIES 1
Pat Devine

2 SOCIAL OBJECTIVES, MARKET RULE AND PUBLIC POLICY: The case of ownership 12
Johan Willner

3 SUBSIDIARITY AND ITS SIGNIFICANCE 42
Patrizio Bianchi

4 COMPETITIVENESS, EU INDUSTRIAL STRATEGY AND SUBSIDIARITY 58
Christine Oughton and Geoff Whittam

5 THE PRICE OF DIVERSITY: Rival concepts of control as a barrier to an EU industrial strategy 79
Winfried Ruigrok and Rob van Tulder

6 EUROPEAN ENLARGEMENT, COMPETITIVENESS AND INTEGRATION 104
Kirsty Hughes

7 CREATING A DYNAMICALLY COMPETITIVE ECONOMY: Defining the competitiveness of a nation and a case study of the post-war economic policy which made Austria competitive 121
Karl Aiginger

8 COMPETITIVENESS AND INDUSTRIAL POLICY IN PORTUGAL 147
João Confraria

9 GREEK OUTWARD INVESTMENT, COMPETITIVENESS AND DEVELOPMENT 159
Christos Pitelis, Roger Sugden and Lena Tsipouri

10 THE EUROPEAN COMMISSION'S FRAMEWORK PROGRAMME SUPPORT: Impact on Greek organizations 172
Y. Katsoulacos, G. Strogylopoulos and P. Kritsalis

11 EU STRUCTURAL POLICIES AND INDUSTRIAL DEVELOPMENT: Application of the subsidiarity principle in the Italian case 199
Piera Magnatti

12 ECONOMIC CONVERGENCE OR CRISIS MANAGEMENT? Subsidiarity and local economic strategies in the UK 220
Steve Martin

Index 233

FIGURES

4.1	Internal and external economies of scale	65
5.1	A continuum of dependency relations in an industrial complex	85
5.2	Uneven distribution of relative influence	88
5.3	Dependency relations and the position of the five concepts of control	90
10.1	Concentration of projects in research areas	181

TABLES

2.1	Percentage cost inefficiency and demand elasticity	20
2.2	Relative efficiency of private and public ownership – a summary	32
5.1	Five bargaining characteristics related to five concepts of control	86
5.2	Five concepts of control and empirical approximations	89
5.3	Stylized views related to each concept of control on subsidiarity, competitiveness and objectives	92
5.4	Diverging bargaining arenas and shifting concepts of control in Europe, the USA and Japan	96
6.1	Main host countries for foreign direct investment in the transition economies	106
6.2	Total foreign direct investment in Central and Eastern Europe – Czech Republic, Hungary and Poland (cumulative 1990–September 1994)	106
6.3	Foreign direct investment in Hungary (cumulative to September 1994)	106
6.4	Foreign direct investment in the Czech Republic by source country (US $m cumulative)	107
6.5	Foreign direct investment in Poland (cumulative September 1994, investments > US $1m: expressed in US $m)	107
6.6	German foreign direct investment in the transition economies (capital outflows, % distribution)	108
6.7	German net overseas capital transfers (DM m)	108
6.8	EU exports to, and imports from, Central and Eastern Europe, by country (1993: ECUm)	109
6.9	Percentage share of EU exports to Central and Eastern Europe (1989, 1993)	110
6.10	EU exports to Central and Eastern Europe as % of total extra-EU exports (by country, 1993)	110
6.11	Net trade balance, EU (total) and EU member states with Central and Eastern Europe (ECUm)	112

6.12 US exports to, and imports from, Central and Eastern Europe (US $m) 112
6.13 Czech Republic: main trading partners (% of total imports and exports, 1993) 112
6.14 Hungary: main trading partners (% of total imports and exports, 1993) 113
6.15 Poland: main trading partners (% of total exports and imports, 1993) 113
8.1 Subsidies and transfers received from abroad (% GDP) 154
8.2 Gross fixed capital formation and savings (% GDP) 155
9.1 Greek direct investment in Bulgaria, Albania and Romania (number of establishments by sector) 162
10.1 Selected economic development indicators (annual percentage change) 173
10.2 Basic fluctuations of the output of various manufacturing sectors 173
10.3 Number of industrial companies and licensing agreements signed during the period 1960–87 174
10.4 Research and development in the business enterprise sector (BERD) 175
10.5 Classification of the sectors of Greek industry according to their technological and structural characteristics 176
10.6 Revealed comparative average 177
10.7 Project allocation 179
10.8 Regional allocation of projects 180
10.9 Concentration of projects and funding per category of organization 180
10.10 Significance of technology transfer (%) 181
10.11 Type of transferred know-how (%) 182
10.12 Research output/publications 182
10.13 Research output/new products and production methods 183
10.14 Research output/patents and licences 183
10.15 Co-operative behaviour/relations with partners 185
10.16 Co-operative behaviour/economic relation with partners 186
10.17 Co-operative behaviour/importance of partners 187
10.18 Co-operative behaviour/after the project(s) 188
10.19 Additionality/new research activities 189
10.20 Additionality/co-operation before and after funding 190
10.21 Additionality/changes in R&D budget 191
10.22 Additionality/changes in the number of research and scientific staff 191
10.23 Additionality in the implementation of the research works 192
10.24 Benefits from the participation 193
10.25 Barriers to exploitation/commercialization of research results 194

10.26 General evaluation of the participation cost-benefit (%) 195
10.27 Success on the goals set (%) 195
11.1 Disparities in GDP per head (PPS) in the Community, 1980–91 (EUR 12 = 100) 205
11.2 Regional incentive expenditure indicators 207
11.3 Major policy changes in regional incentive policy since 1980 in Italy 208
11.4 GDP per head: *Mezzogiorno*/Centre-North (%) 212
11.5 Unemployment rate (%) 212

CONTRIBUTORS

Karl Aiginger University of Linz and Austrian Institute of Economic Research

Patrizio Bianchi University of Bologna

João Confraria Catholic University of Portugal

Pat Devine University of Manchester

Kirsty Hughes Royal Institute for International Affairs, London

Yannis Katsoulacos Athens University of Economics and Business, CEPR (LONDON) and ÉĚĎĐ (Athens)

P. Kritsalis LOGOTECH S.A., Athens

Piera Magnatti Nomisma, Bologna

Steve Martin University of Warwick

Christine Oughton University of Glasgow

Christos Pitelis University of Cambridge

Winfried Ruigrok Erasmus University, Rotterdam

G. Strogylopoulos LOGOTECH S.A., Athens

Roger Sugden University of Birmingham

Lena Tsipouri University of Athens

Rob van Tulder Erasmus University, Rotterdam

Geoff Whittam University of Glasgow

Johan Willner Åbo Akademi University

INTRODUCTION

This is the third collection of papers[1] to have emerged from an on-going project focusing on industrial economic strategy. This particular collection is the result of activities partly funded by the Commission of the European Community's Human Capital and Mobility Programme under the title 'Industrial Economic Strategies for Europe: Preparing for the Turn of the Century'.

The project entails various initiatives, including the explicit discussion and analysis of ideas but also the training of 'young researchers' and the creation of an international *network* of scientists, 'young' and 'established'. The context within which it is unfolding has four salient aspects. First, a double process of economic integration is taking place, at the global level and at the level of trading blocs. Second, with the failure of the new right's free-market orientation to achieve full employment, global stability and sustainable growth, the 1990s have seen a rediscovery of the need for collective action and a sharpened interest in industrial strategy. Third, at the same time, debates within the European Union over alternative interpretations of the concept of subsidiarity have resulted in a heightened awareness of the fact that local, regional, national and supra-national communities and governments may have different objectives, partly complementary and partly competitive. Fourth, it is nevertheless now widely accepted that some degree of international competitiveness is a necessary condition for the achievement of the objectives of any dynamic modern community. All of these aspects feature prominently in the current volume.

The Network that is being developed in the project involves economists from across the European Union and beyond, enabling the project to draw on a wide range of different experiences and traditions. It is very diverse, embracing different methodological approaches and incorporating different analytic and technical skills. However, there is an evolving common ground that is broadly shared by the members of the Network, which both links the group together and differentiates it from other trends within the economics profession. The common ground may be encapsulated by acceptance of the following six points:

1 There is a crucial positive role for states in influencing industrial economic activity in open, market economies.
2 A state's role entails something more than the traditional concerns of industrial economic policy; it entails something different to rectifying or compensating for market failures, which is not to deny that it may include such initiatives.
3 Dispersed, decentralized decision-making within and across both firms and states is a potentially vital aspect of successful industrial strategies.
4 It is important to understand the possible role of co-operation between firms and between regions, and how this role may be influenced by states.
5 A crucial foundation for analysis – and thus for the design of successful industrial strategies – is an understanding of peoples' objectives; for example this influences both what is meant by 'competitiveness' and how competitiveness is achieved.
6 It is perhaps inappropriate to think of distinct public and private sectors; rather we should consider, for example, interrelationships between 'public' and 'private' institutions.

Again, these points feature prominently in contributions to the current volume.

One outcome of the Network's activities so far has been the identification of five *research themes*, which have been to a greater or lesser extent implicit in the first phase of the group's work and will more explicitly inform the next phase. These are:

1 Economic objectives, integration and convergence
2 Policies and strategies: definitions, comparisons and the significance of market failure
3 Bottom–up versus top–down approaches to industrial strategy
4 Public- and private-sector mix and interaction
5 Innovation strategies: empirical analysis of sectors and instruments

The distinctive nature of the research activities of the Network arises from the way in which the pluralistic backgrounds of its members and the shared characteristics of the group interact in the context of the substantive work undertaken around the evolving research themes.

The particular focus of this volume is the relationship between competitiveness, subsidiarity and objectives. In many ways the concern is the first research theme (on economic objectives, integration and convergence) but it should become clear that other themes are also relevant. What does competitiveness mean? How does it relate to the objectives and activities not only of firms but perhaps more importantly also of communities, regions, nations and trading blocs? What is the relationship between the competitiveness of transnational firms and the competitiveness of nations? If firms are competitive, will this promote the objectives of the communities in which they are located? Is there any benefit in designing industrial policies to increase the competitiveness of firms if they do not create employment or contribute to the achievement of other objectives of the communities in which they operate? If the constituent regions and member states, and the European Union itself, adopt strategies to improve competitiveness, what form should these strategies take and what content should they have? How should these strategies relate to each other, given the principle and practice of subsidiarity? These are the sorts of questions under discussion. If there is a unifying theme running through the volume it is that the concept of competitiveness can only be given real meaning, and the significance of subsidiarity can only be fully understood, if the underlying objectives of policy are clarified.

The first part of the volume (Chapters 1–6) consists of a series of papers discussing competitiveness, subsidiarity and objectives from different angles; the second part (Chapters 7–12) then focuses on the specific context of particular countries. The ordering of chapters within each part is to a large extent *ad hoc*. We have chosen not to attempt to draw together detailed conclusions. This is because the volume was not conceived as a coherent, systematic approach to a well-defined set of issues, with the intention of providing definitive results; rather, it was conceived as a stimulating, rich and varied set of contributions to an on-going and evolving debate. Hence, it is left to readers to select from the contents according to their interests, aided and guided, perhaps, by the following comments on each chapter and the detailed abstracts that appear at the end of this Introduction.

Pat Devine begins the substantive content of the volume with a chapter explicitly focusing on competitiveness and subsidiarity, looking at the relationships between each of these concepts and the objectives of communities. Different routes to achieving competitiveness are discussed, and hence there is an examination of the different approaches to industrial policy that have been pursued in various countries. Against this background, the paper goes on to consider alternative possible policy regimes for the European Union, specifically regimes founded on a market failure approach, protectionism, and intercommunity negotiation. Chapter 1 concludes with a clear indication of some future research needs.

The chapter by Johan Willner roots its discussion quite extensively in earlier contributions to the project. Given this it is perhaps not surprising that the paper also shows clear signs of points which we have suggested above link members of the Network together as a group and set them apart from others. It focuses on the influence of social objectives on conventional criteria of competitiveness. The paper takes a critical view of ' "competitiveness" in the sense of power to compete', in the first part looking quite generally at the role of competition in the light of social objectives, and then reviewing in considerable depth the (in) significance of the ownership status of firms for efficiency. Willner ends with a brief discussion of subsidiarity.

Patrizio Bianchi's contribution, Chapter 3, turns attention squarely on to subsidiarity, which he describes as 'the most abstract concept introduced in the recent political debate in Europe'. The significance of subsidiarity is explored and discussed in the context of the European Union's evolving institutional structure and decision-making processes, and in the context of evolving economic thought. The importance of bottom–up and top–down approaches are highlighted, for example it being argued that 'subsidiarity means not only to decentralize decisions . . . but also that the highest institutional levels create the conditions to enable the weaker members, both nation-states and regional governments, to play effectively in the collective game'.

The next chapter maintains the explicit concern with the research theme on bottom–up versus top–down approaches to industrial strategy. Christine Oughton and Geoff Whittam discuss competitiveness and subsidiarity in the context of recent European Union policy pronouncements. They consider competitiveness 'defined as long-run growth in productivity, and hence rising living standards, consistent with increasing employment or the maintenance of near full employment', and in this context examine policies towards small and medium-sized enterprises (SMEs), and implications for subsidiarity. The paper contributes to the analysis of dispersed, decentralized decision-making, and highlights the potentially vital role of cooperation amongst SMEs, rather than amongst large firms, as a means of enhancing industrial performance.

The relationship between competitiveness and subsidiarity is also an issue taken up by Winfried Ruigrok and Rob van Tulder in Chapter 5. They analyse difficulties in formulating an industrial strategy for the European Union, in comparison to the United States and Japan. The analysis highlights the different 'solutions' firms and governments have adopted to issues of competitiveness, subsidiarity and policy objectives. It is suggested that Europe has faced particular problems in designing industrial strategies because, at given points in time, by contrast with the United States and Japan, several different solutions have co-existed within the Union. These problems pose significant questions for researchers and policy-makers over the coming years.

Further problems are raised by Chapter 6's argument that a process of readjustment of economic relations and interests is under way in Europe, implying changes that on current trends will reinforce differences in competitiveness across European nations. Kirsty Hughes's paper presents data on foreign direct investment and trade involving Central and East European economies, especially the Czech Republic, Hungary and Poland. Her discussion of these data raises significant questions for future consideration, particularly for the research theme we have labelled as economic objectives, integration and convergence.

Whereas the experiences of various European countries and regions, and of Europe more widely, figure prominently in Chapters 1 to 6, each of the subsequent chapters concentrates more immediately on experience in particular countries. Karl Aiginger's contribution, Chapter 7, reviews and evaluates various definitions of competitiveness, and then proposes and explores the following: 'a country is said to be competitive if it sells enough products and services at factor incomes in line with the country's (current and constantly changing) aspiration level at macro conditions (of the economic and social system) seen as satisfactory by the people'. The references to aspiration levels and the satisfaction of people clearly reveal his explicit concern with the objectives of nations, a particular issue stressed time and again throughout this volume. Having outlined Austria's post-1945 development, Karl Aiginger then applies his competitiveness definition in the Austrian context.

Chapters 8 to 10 consider two of the so-called less favoured countries of Europe. Much of João Confraria's paper (Chapter 8) is in fact a general discussion of what is meant by competitiveness; in this light it could be usefully read alongside, in particular, the contributions from Pat Devine, Johan Willner and Karl Aiginger. Among other things Chapter 8 discusses competitiveness in relation to the structure/conduct/performance paradigm and in relation to the transnationality of firms. It is argued that 'the concept of competitiveness of a given community is related to the survival and economic prosperity of that community'. João Confraria then comments on Portuguese competitiveness in the light of his earlier discussion, and returns the volume to an issue raised by Kirsty Hughes: convergence.

The following two chapters focus on Greece. Christos Pitelis, Roger Sugden and Lena Tsipouri pursue the (un)importance of the transnationality of firms. Their particular concern is outward investment, and their central query is whether or not such investment will positively contribute to Greek international competitiveness and industrial development. The chapter's principal contribution to the volume is to highlight the distinction between a nation's competitiveness and a (group of) firms' competitiveness. In doing so it reports evidence on the extent and nature of Greek outward investment, and draws heavily on previous literature evaluating the advantages and drawbacks of outward investments.

In Chapter 10, Yannis Katsoulacos, G. Strogylopoulos and P. Kritsalis analyse the impact of European Community Framework Programmes on Greek participants in those programmes. It can be seen as in part a contribution to the research theme on innovation strategies: empirical analysis of sectors and instruments. It explores the determinants of a nation's R&D environment, which may itself be viewed as a significant determinant of competitiveness. The authors analyse the impact of the programmes in the context of a general overview of the Greek economy. The paper effectively returns to the concern with SMEs and co-operation seen in the earlier chapter by Christine Oughton and Geoff Whittam.

Queries about the role of smaller firms, about co-operation and about the impact of European Community Framework Programmes all also figure in

Chapter 11, by Piera Magnatti. This contribution sharpens the volume's focus on subsidiarity. It may be usefully studied alongside, in particular, the papers by Pat Devine, Patrizio Bianchi, Steve Martin, and Christine Oughton and Geoff Whittam. The chapter concentrates on Italian experience, which is explored and analysed in the context of evolving European Union initiatives. Among its conclusions is the positive suggestion that 'local government – even without legislative and financial autonomy – can play an important role in modernizing the industrial system through initiatives which do not require vast sums of money but which identify and meet specific local needs'.

The volume ends with a chapter by Steve Martin. This also explores the subsidiarity issue. It helps to clarify the relationship between subsidiarity, regional competitiveness and convergence. The points raised are discussed by reference to the experience of British local government. The early part of the chapter looks in relative detail at different approaches across Britain. The threads are then drawn together; while it is suggested that 'meaningful subsidiarity' has not yet been achieved in Britain, in certain respects Steve Martin's contribution – like that of Piera Magnatti – is positive and optimistic about future possibilities.

NOTE

1 The previous two are: Keith Cowling and Roger Sugden (eds), 1992 *Current Issues in Industrial Economic Strategy*, (Manchester: Manchester University Press); Patrizio Bianchi, Keith Cowling and Roger Sugden, 1994 *Europe's Economic Challenge. Analyses of Industrial Strategy and Agenda for the 1990s*, London: Routledge.

ABSTRACTS

1 COMPETITIVENESS AND THE OBJECTIVES OF COMMUNITIES

In an increasingly global economy, some degree of international competitiveness is likely to be a necessary condition for the achievement of the objectives of any dynamic modern community, irrespective of how those objectives are arrived at and defined. However, in both history and theory different routes towards international competitiveness have been followed or advocated, influenced at least in part by the relative strengths of the interests involved and the prevailing view of how the economy works. In the 1990s the failure of the new right's free market orientation to achieve full employment, global stability and sustainable growth has led to a rediscovery of the need for collective action and a revival of interest in industrial strategy. At the same time, debates within the European Community (Union) over alternative interpretations of the concept of subsidiarity have resulted in a heightened awareness of the fact that local, regional, national and supranational communities may have different objectives, partly complementary and partly competitive. Having developed this context, the paper argues that a socially efficient European industrial strategy can only be elaborated through a process in which an inter-community division of labour based on dynamic comparative advantage is achieved predominantly through negotiation among communities rather than through the operation of unregulated market forces. Such a process would combine competition and co-operation, among the different social partners and across the different levels of community, in a matrix that harmonized objectives, strategic orientation and policy instruments.

2 SOCIAL OBJECTIVES, MARKET RULE AND PUBLIC POLICY: THE CASE OF OWNERSHIP

Competition may, when feasible, provide a way to achieve decentralized economic decision-making. This suggests that mergers should be discouraged, not only because of their disputable impact on efficiency. Moreover, if competition does not emerge spontaneously, it has to be created, for example by allowing a non-profit maximizing firm to act as a disloyal competitor. However, in a number of cases, some of which have been overlooked, competition between many providers does more harm than good. This calls for public ownership. However, according to a now popular view, this would always cause inefficiency. We present an empirical survey which disputes this simplistic notion. On the other hand, social objectives concerning income distribution, the pace of work and service quality typically imply that cost minimization is not even necessarily desirable, as shown in a couple of formal models. The present tendency to privatize therefore seems to be based on prejudice. Finally, we argue that the EU policy might be too soft on mergers and that there is a case for adopting a more creative attitude towards public ownership, for example by requiring joint supervision of public firms operating in several countries.

3 SUBSIDIARITY AND ITS SIGNIFICANCE

Subsidiarity is a concept which plays an important role in the institution building of the European Union. Article 3B of the Treaty of Maastricht affirms that the Community shall take action, in accordance with the principle of subsidiarity, only if and in so far as the objectives of the proposed action cannot be sufficiently achieved by member states and can therefore, by reason of efficiency or necessity, be better achieved by the Community. This principle is used for establishing at what institutional level decisions concerning the development of Community action must be managed. The Treaty mentions the European and the national levels, but, by extension, it involves also the regional and municipal levels.

This concept tackles the core of the problem of the Union's development, that of sovereignty. This concept is, hence, a constituent principle for the Union and a powerful instrument for managing the relations among policy-makers. Nevertheless, this principle remains vague and not sufficiently defined. The wording used to describe it reflects the compromise reached among member states.

Thus, in order to understand the role and significance of subsidiarity, we must analyse the specificity of the European integration process and of the associated institution building in driving this mechanism of economic and political integration among nation-states.

4 COMPETITIVENESS, EU INDUSTRIAL STRATEGY AND SUBSIDIARITY

This chapter is concerned with industrial strategies designed to raise competitiveness and focuses, in particular, on small and medium-sized enterprises

(SMEs) with a view to advocating policy proposals designed to enhance the dynamism of this sector. The theoretical section of the paper considers the impact of internal and external economies of scale on industrial efficiency and competitiveness. It is shown that co-operation between firms can result in significant efficiency gains via the exploitation of collective external economies. Within the context of industrial districts, it is argued that certain institutional arrangements foster co-operation and trust and increase industrial efficiency and competition. The analysis has a number of implications for subsidiarity and the appropriate level at which to implement industrial policy. In particular, it is shown that policies designed to raise competitive external economies of scale are best carried out at the EU and national levels, while policies aimed at enhancing the dynamism of the SME sector through the exploitation of collective external economies are best enacted at the regional level through the establishment of appropriate institutions. Co-operation is more likely to be successful in institutional environments that are democratic, accountable and provide effective monitoring mechanisms.

5 THE PRICE OF DIVERSITY: RIVAL CONCEPTS OF CONTROL AS A BARRIER TO AN EU INDUSTRIAL STRATEGY

This chapter discusses why it has proved so difficult in the European Union to formulate a common industrial strategy, and argues that social and economic diversity have acted as major barriers to this objective. Diversity is interpreted in terms of *rival industrial complexes* adhering to *rival concepts of control*. An industrial complex consists of a *core firm* and five sets of *bargaining partners*: suppliers, distributors, workers, financiers and governments. A concept of control incorporates the core firm's vision on how to organize productivity and competitiveness and on the role its bargaining partners should play to secure the production or distribution of a given good or service. Five rival concepts of control are identified, each supporting different roles of national and supranational governments. Within the European Union, there are at least four concepts of control competing for dominance. This means that it is very difficult to reach consensus on fundamental issues of competitiveness and industrial policy. The European Union's main competitors do not suffer from this weakness: the United States and Japan only have one or at most two concepts of control in their industrial systems competing for dominance.

6 EUROPEAN ENLARGEMENT, COMPETITIVENESS AND INTEGRATION

This paper considers the implications for European integration and competitiveness of the changes in the economic relations of East and West Europe since 1989. It focuses on the *de facto* enlargement of the European economy that has occurred due to the transition processes in Central and Eastern Europe (CEE) and Western responses to these, rather than on the specific arguments concerning admission of the CEE countries to the EU. The paper analyses both trade and foreign direct investment data to assess the pattern of economic relationships that are developing. It argues that the pattern of internationalization associated with these developments does not imply that the European economy will become a large and more integrated entity. Rather, on current trends, there will be a much closer integration between the German economy and the other CEE economies. The implications of this for individual country competitiveness and for convergence within the European economy are assessed.

7 CREATING A DYNAMICALLY COMPETITIVE ECONOMY: DEFINING THE COMPETITIVENESS OF A NATION AND A CASE STUDY OF THE POST-WAR ECONOMIC POLICY WHICH MADE AUSTRIA COMPETITIVE

The paper newly defines the competitiveness of nations. The definition explicitly relates competitiveness to performance and to the democratically defined aspiration level of an economy. The policy implication of this definition is that cost-cutting and devaluation are usually not the best strategies for regaining the competitive edge, since these strategies lead away from an economy's goal of creating high and rising incomes.

The paper describes the economic policy of post-war Austria. Starting from a low-income position, regulated prices, and a lack of competitive firms, Austria chose a gradual transition process, with demand- and supply-side elements and a strong emphasis on investment and human capital. The process was different from that selected for use in the transition economies following the breakdown of 'state socialism' in the late 1980s. Today, Austria's per capita GNP surpasses that in the EC and in the majority of industrialized countries.

The process of catching up, as well as the current strengths and weaknesses of Austria's position today, are analysed with respect to the concept of dynamic competitiveness. The concept is then applied to other European economies, to the USA and to Japan, providing insights into the concept's usefulness and comparing Austria's accomplishments with the performance of other countries.

8 COMPETITIVENESS AND INDUSTRIAL POLICY IN PORTUGAL

Competitiveness seems to be a popular subject in the political debate and even in some academic work. Perhaps as an undesirable consequence of this, there are several ambiguities related to the concept and to its role in policy making. In the second section, we discuss some current concepts of competitiveness, highlighting their relation to more familiar concepts in industrial organization. These ideas are used in a third section, to make a comparison about the role of competitiveness in Portuguese industrial policy, in two different historical periods: before 1973, when some protectionist policies prevailed notwithstanding Portuguese participation in the European Free Trade Association; and after membership of the European Economic Community, in 1986. The fourth section discusses specific issues arising from the European Union concerning the evolution of the Portuguese economy and bearing in mind the role of the Community Framework Support.

9 GREEK OUTWARD INVESTMENT, COMPETITIVENESS AND DEVELOPMENT

Outward investment in the Balkans has recently been a topical issue in Greece. In many respects there appears to have evolved quite a widespread presumption that such investment is desirable. The chapter examines the extent of this investment, and its potential impact on Greek international competitiveness and industrial development. It addresses fundamental issues concerning competitiveness, what this term means and how the concept is related to social objectives. It is suggested that there need be no link between outward investment by Greek firms and Greek competitiveness as a nation.

Preliminary evidence is offered on the extent and nature of Greek outward investment. The discussion of the impact of such investment draws on a wide literature. It is suggested that outward investment is neither unambiguously good nor unambiguously bad, hence it is inappropriate to presume that it is *ipso facto* desirable for Greece. The crucial importance of private versus community costs and benefits is emphasized. It is suggested that, as a minimum, the Greek government should design an industrial strategy which only facilitates outward investment beneficial to Greece.

10 THE EUROPEAN COMMISSION'S FRAMEWORK PROGRAMME SUPPORT: IMPACT ON GREEK ORGANIZATIONS

The objective of this paper is to illustrate the impact of the *European Commission's Framework Programmes* (FPS) I (1984/1987) & II (1988/1991) on the Greek participating organisations, with special attention to the impact on Greek firms. It also presents some results concerning the impact on the Greek RTD environment. It is based on the research project 'Evaluation of the Impact of the Community's RTD policy in Greece'.

It concludes that the majority of the participating organizations are located in the area of Athens and that transfer of know-how was overall encouraging but did not lead to a significant number of new products or processes. The impact concerning publications and communications was important but not that concerning patents and licences. Also positive was the impact on the co-operative behaviour of the organizations but it is doubtful how strong has been the effect concerning further investment activities on RTD. Nevertheless, the two first *Framework Programmes* have acted as a stimulus for Greek firms to continue improving their networking and RTD infrastructure, and to promote further RTD collaborations.

11 EU STRUCTURAL POLICIES AND INDUSTRIAL DEVELOPMENT: APPLICATION OF THE SUBSIDIARITY PRINCIPLE IN THE ITALIAN CASE

The present stage of European integration is based on a substantial U-turn in the policy-making approach of the Community. The Single European Act represents the transition from a centralized model of public intervention to an approach mainly based on the co-operation of the various national and local authorities.

One of the most important aspects of this 'new phase' is that this new approach is greatly influencing the industrial policies adopted by the single member states; in particular, the new EU approach has started a process of change affecting the old practice of the national governments of providing subsidies to individual firms to compensate for structural imbalances.

Italy represents a relevant example of this change; in fact

a) after forty years, the Special Intervention in the *Mezzogiorno* has finished;
b) the local/regional level of intervention (in other words, the actions promoted not only *for* the regions, but also *by* the regions) is becoming more and more relevant; and
c) in general terms, the role of public development interventions is going to be revised.

In this perspective, the main objective of this paper is to start a reflection on:

1 the effectiveness of the new approach and the needs in terms of industrial policy within the EU;
2 the conditions for the implementation of such policies; and
3 the role of the Commission within this context.

12 ECONOMIC CONVERGENCE OR CRISIS MANAGEMENT? SUBSIDIARITY AND LOCAL ECONOMIC STRATEGIES IN THE UK

This chapter examines the impacts which closer European integration, particularly the availability of EU financial assistance, have had upon local economic strategies in the UK. It argues that a growing number of UK local authorities regard EU programmes as an important source of funding for their economic strategies and that control over the allocation of assistance has, to some extent, shifted from the national to the supranational level. There are, however, significant constraints upon the scope for subsidiarity within the UK context. The impacts of EU funding have been modest in relation to the major economic problems confronting many local economies, political power has increasingly been transferred from local level to central government departments in Westminster, traditional local authority roles have been fragmented and central government remains ambivalent to the achievement of an 'ever closer Union' and largely opposed to strategic economic intervention.

Seen in this context EU intervention might be regarded as little more than a short-term palliative; a form of crisis management rather than a genuine attempt to promote convergence. Nevertheless, there are signs that, in some areas, it has revitalized local economic strategies, encouraging greater intra-regional co-operation and leading to the involvement of a wider range of social and economic partners. Given the deep-seated rivalry between local agencies and the UK's history of *ad hoc*, market-driven initiatives, even these embryonic strategic and participative ('European') approaches to regional and sub-regional planning may come to be seen as a considerable achievement.

ACKNOWLEDGEMENTS

Early versions of most of the chapters in this volume were presented at *Workshops* (in Lisbon, Crete and Bologna) supported by the Commission of the European Community's *Human Capital and Mobility Programme*. Others have been commissioned in the light of discussions at these Workshops. We would like to acknowledge the support we have received under the *Euroconference Contract Number ERBCHECCT93014* and *Network Contract Number ERBCHRXCT940454*.

1

COMPETITIVENESS AND THE OBJECTIVES OF COMMUNITIES

Pat Devine

INTRODUCTION: COMPETITIVENESS AND OBJECTIVES

International competitiveness has become a necessary condition for any modern, dynamic economy. The alternative is autarky, which is unlikely to be sustainable in the long run and is in any case unlikely to be attractive to a modern community. However, since international competitiveness has become so universally and unquestioningly accepted as a desirable objective, and its pursuit is frequently used to justify unpopular policies, it is worth asking why and in what sense competitiveness is necessary.

For a community integrated into the global economy, international competitiveness is needed in order to avoid stagnation and relative decline. Singh's definition of an efficient (or, in our terms, competitive) manufacturing sector is relevant here:

> An efficient manufacturing sector (is) one which . . . not only satisfies the demands of consumers at home, but is also able to sell enough of its products abroad to pay for the nation's import requirements . . . at socially acceptable levels of output, employment and the exchange rate.
> (Singh 1977: 128, emphasis omitted)

In an economic system in which resources are allocated and reallocated primarily through the operation of market forces, communities with competitive economies benefit from a virtuous circle of cumulative causation, while those with uncompetitive economies suffer the consequences of being locked into a corresponding vicious circle. The relevant concept is dynamic competitive advantage or disadvantage, with static comparative advantage being largely irrelevant. However, international competitiveness in this sense, while a necessary condition for the achievement of a community's objectives, is not the underlying objective, unless of course that objective is identified unambiguously with the outcome of the operation of market forces on a global scale. Furthermore, in a process of dynamic competition and cumulative causation there will always be losers as well as winners, so that not all communities can be internationally competitive in Singh's sense at the same time.

It may be helpful to consider the reasons why a community, if it had a real option of choosing between self-sufficiency or engaging in inter-community exchange might choose the latter, leaving aside for a moment the issue of whether such exchange would be mediated through market forces or in some other way. Any list of potential benefits from inter-community exchange would probably include comparative advantage, variety, innovation, and cultural pluralism and dynamism. The realization of these benefits would require some degree of inter-community division of labour, although the desirable extent of this would depend on the values and objectives of the communities involved, not least the weight given to the increasingly pressing considerations of global and local sustainability. Looked at in this light, inter-community competitiveness can be thought of as *the conditions that have to exist for a community to be able to participate in an inter-community division of labour to the extent that it would like, given its objectives.* This approach has similarities with that of Pitelis (1994) who discusses international competitiveness in the context of the ability of a country to increase its welfare – measured by a subjectively chosen index – relative to that of other countries.

The next section of this chapter summarizes the different routes in pursuit of international competitiveness that have been followed historically, noting how these have been influenced at least in part by the relative strengths of the interests involved and the prevailing view of how the economy works. That is followed by a section discussing the concept of subsidiarity and arguing that it is necessary to recognize that different communities – local, regional, national and supra-national – may have different objectives, partly complementary and partly competitive. The concluding section considers the implications of the previous sections for European industrial strategy.

ROUTES TO COMPETITIVENESS

The Bretton Woods system inaugurated in 1944 created an international context which made possible the pursuit of distinctive national objectives, subject only to achieving and maintaining adequate international competitiveness as defined by Singh in the quotation above. The driving force behind the agreement was the avoidance of the mass unemployment and associated political tensions of the inter-war period. Differential national economic performance resulted in changes in the fixed exchange rates, albeit asymmetrically and insufficiently frequently, with rules of the game to prevent beggar-my-neighbour policies. The system was operated by international institutions but was dominated and largely financed by the United States. It worked until the onset of the US balance of payments deficit in the 1960s undermined the stability of the dollar as the reserve currency and the increasing evasion and relaxation of exchange controls permitted the growth of large scale capital mobility.

Within this international context nations were able to pursue distinctive routes to international competitiveness, compatible with their distinctive national values and objectives. For our purposes these distinctive routes may be summarized schematically in terms of two models. The Anglo-Saxon model relied on macro-economic management combined with largely unregulated market forces at the micro level; the European/Japanese model combined macro-economic management with industrial policy. In practice, of course, each country had its own distinctive policy regime, reflecting history and the prevailing balance of socio-economic forces, but the two-model simplification nevertheless focuses attention on the distinction between those countries which operated a more or less effective industrial policy and those which did not.

A recent study by Hart (1992) looks at changing international competitiveness since 1945 among five countries – the United States, Japan, Germany, France and Britain – based on an analysis of the steel, automobile and semiconductor industries. It comes as no surprise that Japan and Germany emerge as having been the most internationally competitive in all three industries, Britain and the United States the least competitive, and France somewhere in between. However, the author's explanation for this is interesting. He identifies three principal social actors (state, business and organized labour) and finds that in the successful countries influence in policy formation was shared between two of them. In Japan the leading social actors were the state and business, with the state providing industrial strategy as the framework for *keiretsu* competition – competition among industrial groups each supported by a major bank. In Germany business and labour shared influence, with bank-led industrial policy operating in a context of co-operation between business and labour that was made possible by the high average level of labour skill. In the three remaining countries, one of the social actors predominated. In France the state dominated business and labour, with the result that its active industrial policy was only partially successful, since the absence of an independent business sector was associated with weak competition among domestic firms which inhibited technological dynamism. In the United States business dominated, with the fragmented character of the state precluding effective industrial policy. In Britain the strength of organized labour enabled it to block technological change in the face of fragmented business and, again, a fragmented state. Thus, the author concludes that differences in international competitivenes are best explained by differences in state–societal arrangements – the ways in which the state, business and organized labour are linked – and the extent to which these arrangements promote or enable an effective industrial policy. What he does not emphasize is that the different state–societal arrangements, which reflect differences in the relative power of the social actors, also led to differences in the weight given to objectives other than international competitiveness, such as social solidarity and welfare.

The Bretton Woods system under US hegemony made possible the long boom of the 1950s and 1960s which eventually generated global inflationary pressure. This, together with the relative decline of the United States in the face of competition from Germany and Japan, caused the system to break down. The relentless globalization of capital markets that followed during the 1970s and 1980s steadily undermined the ability of nation states to pursue distinctive policies. At the same time the rise of the new right and its free-market monetarist doctrine ushered in an era of privatization and deregulation, reinforcing the free-market orientation of the Anglo-Saxon model countries and weakening the commitment to industrial policy of the European/Japanese model countries. However, the manifest failure of the new right's policies to achieve full employment, global stability and sustainable growth led in the mid-1990s to a gradual change in the intellectual climate. The G7 leaders began to discuss the need for a new world order, based on new international institutions, and there was a revival of interest in industrial policy and strategy.

Given the globalization of capital markets and the extent to which the structure of production has become internationalized, recent discussion of industrial policy has for the most part started from two assumptions. First, the scope for national policies in pursuit of national objectives in relation to particular industries or sectors is widely considered to be severely limited. Thus, in Europe attention is increasingly focused on supra-national (European Union) and infra-national (industrial district) policies. Second, the only really legitimate objective of industrial policy is conventionally seen as being the promotion of competitiveness in non-beggar-my-neighbour ways. Taken together these two assumptions create a tension. On the one hand, European policy is directed towards the creation of a supra-national level playing field within the European Union, in order to prevent national, regional or local governments from adopting policies that give enterprises in their communities a competitive advantage. On the other hand, national and infra-national governments precisely seek to pursue policies that do increase the competitiveness of the enterprises within their communities (see also Patrizio Bianchi in this volume). And, of course, exactly the same tension exists between global policies designed to achieve a level playing field for global competition and policies pursued by regional blocs such as the European Union designed to increase the competitiveness of their economies within the global economy.

The reason for this tension, and the actual and potential conflict it generates, is that (international) competitiveness is not ultimately sought for its own sake but for its contribution to the objectives of the relevant community. What those objectives are partly depends on the level at which the community is defined. It will be determined through the community's decision making processes and will reflect the relative influence of the different social actors in the community. Within the interlocking and overlapping network of communities that make up the nation, the regional bloc and the global economy, there are inevitably going to be differing objectives – some complementary, some competitive. What is needed is a discursive process through which communities can negotiate a transparent, mutually beneficial inter-community division of labour that is sufficiently consistent with their underlying objectives for it to be acceptable to them.

SUBSIDIARITY AND THE OBJECTIVES OF COMMUNITIES

Recent discussion of strategic trade policy (Krugman 1986, 1990), the new competition (Best 1990) or the competitive advantage of nations (Porter 1990), focuses on the factors that contribute to the international competitiveness of the communities that constitute nation states. The classical theory of static comparative advantage, which demonstrates that under certain conditions all countries will benefit from trade, was the basis for free-trade doctrine. Given that the necessary conditions are never met, the doctrine is one which in practice tends to benefit the strong (competitive) at the expense of the weak (uncompetitive). The newer theories, with their emphasis on dynamic cumulative causation, recognize that competition produces losers as well as winners, that not all countries benefit, and that strategic policies may affect the distribution of gains and losses. However, strategic policies, even if pursued by all countries or regional blocs, cannot turn all communities into winners. They cannot distribute the potential benefits from inter-community exchange in accordance with a set of agreed criteria drawn up in terms of equitable outcomes rather than permitted policies.

The same is true of European Union policies to achieve a level playing field. In dynamic competition some communities will necessarily be more successful than others and, once established, dynamic competitive advantage is cumulative. Furthermore, the harmonization of monetary, fiscal, education, training, R&D and other supply-side policies will have consequences for communities that are not confined to the effect it has on their competitiveness. In relation to the Social Chapter, for example, levelling up and levelling down, while logically equivalent in terms of their contribution to the creation of a level playing field, nevertheless have very different effects on the communities making up the Union. Similarly, if underlying community objectives are to be the focus of attention, then ways must be found to enable communities to influence not just the rate of growth and dynamism but also the structure of their economies.

Within the European Union, the principle of subsidiarity has become a contested concept as alternative visions of Europe lay claim to it and place their own interpretation on it. The evolution of the Community from the initial stage, in which the Commission acted as a central bureaucracy to implement policies agreed unanimously by the member states, to the present stage, in which its principal function is to promote the harmonization of national and local policies through the principle of reciprocal recognition adopted within a framework agreed by majority decision, has been summarized by Bianchi (1992) – see also Chapter 3 of this volume. Subsidiarity is now interpreted to mean that the central authority intervenes only in relation to activities that are beyond the scope of effective action by any one local authority. Bianchi argues that this represents an approach 'based on the co-operation of various national and local authorities, all with the power to formulate norms and implement policies which must conform with those enforced by other authorities' (Bianchi 1992: 198).

However, a co-operative approach depends for its success on an acceptance by the various communities that the process is one from which all will benefit. This has resulted, on the one hand, in the adoption of competition policies to prevent or contain market dominance and to prevent discrimination in favour of national or local champions. On the other hand, there has been a recognition that intensified competition tends to benefit the strong and developed regions at the expense of the weak and less developed regions. In order to deal with this problem structural policy has been reformed and reinforced, based on a partnership between the Commission, national governments and regional governments. However, because the Community's underlying economic philosophy is that of free trade, structural intervention is only acceptable if it can be presented as contributing to the improvement of competitiveness. Support for individual firms has been replaced by support for less developed, less successful regions, in order to enable them to compete more effectively with the more successful regions.

This emerging framework for Community support for local community initiatives offers much potential scope for local communities to define their own objectives. However, tensions and contradictions remain. First, the success stories – the industrial districts such as Emilia-Romagna and Baden-Württemburg – are historically evolved organic communities and their experiences are unlikely to be readily transferable. Furthermore, it is still unclear whether the success of these industrial districts will turn out to have been transitory, as the dominant transnational corporations assert their power and competitive strength, or whether they have achieved a permanent structural transformation. Second, just as in the case of competition between firms there are always losers as well as winners, so also in the case of competition between regions they cannot all be equally successful. In fact, regional disparities in the European Community/Union have been increasing, not decreasing, over recent years (Bianchi 1992). Third, communities may have objectives which are unconnected with improvements in their competitiveness. They may wish to engage in exchange with other communities on a limited basis, retaining control over the structure of their economies and the social and cultural institutions and ways of life associated with it. Yet if competitiveness in the context of free trade is privileged as an objective, communities are coerced by the necessity of surviving in the regional, national or global economy. In such a context resources are allocated and reallocated primarily by market forces, irrespective of underlying community objectives, and rules of the game severely limit the ability of communities to have more than a marginal impact on this process.

Finally, the way in which competitiveness is pursued and the weighting given to different objectives is shaped by the distribution of power and the institutions through which decisions are made in a community. Hart's study of the relative influence of the different social actors in the United States, Japan and Western Europe has already been cited. A different example is the structure of the organic communities in the successful industrial districts. While this has enabled an effective balance to be achieved between co-operation and competition, this may in part have been due to the hierarchical and patriarchal character of the social structure, with obvious consequences for social and gender relations and the determination of community objectives. Efficient social decision making, which takes into account the objectives and knowledge of all those affected by decisions, needs to be based on relationships of equality and participatory democracy (Devine 1994).

The relationship between subsidiarity and community objectives is therefore complex. Localities, regions and nations will have their own distinctive objectives. These may be complementary but in the context of the European Union and its free market philosophy they are just as, or even more, likely to be in competition with one another. Indeed, the potential for conflict may be increasing with the end of the post-war trade boom. Sinclair (1993) has presented data that show a sharp fall in real export growth since 1980. In general, trade is now growing more slowly than output. He estimates that the volume of intercontinental trade has probably begun to decline and that although trade within regional trading blocs, including the European Community, is still expanding, the rate of growth has fallen sharply. Of course, it may well be that a reduction in the extent of inter community/international division of labour is desirable in the interests of local community autonomy and global sustainability. However, if this results from the interaction of effectively uncontrollable market forces and competitive protectionism, rather than negotiation on the basis of agreed principles of equitable distribution, the outcome is likely, as always, to favour the strong at the expense of the weak.

IMPLICATIONS FOR EUROPEAN INDUSTRIAL STRATEGY

The conclusion of the discussion so far is that there is an underlying tension evident in the revival of interest in industrial strategy in Europe in the 1990s.

On the one hand, the emphasis has been on the Commission developing policies to promote a level playing field for competition between communities by harmonizing their use of national or regional powers and policy instruments. On the other hand, the Commission and national and regional governments have developed schemes designed to enhance the competitiveness of the less developed, less successful regions. Both sides of the tension, however, are defined in terms of competitiveness and are set within a theoretical framework that takes it for granted that the operation of market forces should be the principal mechanism determining the allocation of resources. Thus, industrial strategy is normally justified in terms of market failure of various sorts, by contrast with protectionism which is seen as capitulation to vested interests. However, as Cowling and Sugden have argued, we need to go beyond 'preserving the rules by which market forces are allowed their full expression or preserving the activities that market forces have already deemed appropriate for a particular community' (Cowling and Sugden 1993: 84). Instead, we need to develop alternative sets of rules, institutions and discursive processes which enable local communities to interact with one another, and with regional, national and supra-national communities, in order to agree on a negotiated international division of labour that enables them to achieve their democratically determined objectives.

We can distinguish three possible regimes for industrial policy corresponding to these three perspectives: market failure, protectionism and inter-community negotiation. The market failure approach is considered in Johan Willner's contribution to this volume, although he recognizes that industrial policy may have objectives other than allocative efficiency, such as dynamism or a more equal distribution of income and economic power. Within the market failure framework Willner comments on the current state of knowledge with respect to deadweight loss, innovation, firm size, network externalities and mergers. Elsewhere, in a related paper, he also discusses in a similar context the phenomenon of social dumping – 'most European governments experience a pressure to degrade labour standards, reduce transfer payments and cut public consumption in a struggle for market shares and inward investments' (Willner 1994: 3) – which brings us to protectionism, the second potential industrial policy regime.

Protectionism is generally considered by economists schooled in the Anglo-Saxon tradition to be undesirable. Sinclair argues that the end of the world trade boom evident in the 1980s was associated with a pause in the GATT trade liberalization process, an increase in agricultural protection, greater use of quantitative import barriers, and the growth of regional trading blocs promoting intra-regional at the expense of intercontinental trade. He suggests two reasons for this growth of protectionism: the threat to jobs from cheap imports in the context of high levels of unemployment; and 'the meretricious idea that protectionism is justified by considerations of imperfect competition' (Sinclair 1993: 123). However, as a socio-political phenomenon, pressure for protectionism is more complex than the standard theoretical argument suggests. On the one hand, pressure for protection can be seen as the illegitimate attempt by groups of producers or communities to safeguard their vested interests or gain advantages at the expense of others. On the other hand, it may be seen as a legitimate attempt by communities to exercise some control over what happens to them when faced with market forces beyond their control and no alternative means of influencing the decisions that determine their future.

An alternative, third, regime for industrial policy would consist of rules, institutions and processes through which communities could negotiate an inter-community division of labour that was consistent with their objectives. Communities would have to be competitive in the sense defined in the Introduction – they would have to be able to offer something that other communities wanted in exchange for what they wanted from other communities. Cowling and Sugden have stated clearly what is needed:

> In Europe industrial policy must be regional policy, inspired and created within the regions, but regional policy must be coherent as a whole, at the inter-regional level, and common desires across regions should be pursued collectively.
>
> (Cowling and Sugden 1993: 96)

The rules, institutions and processes through which this coherence and collective action can be achieved are urgent matters for further research. However, there are some experiences and pointers to build on.

First, there is the experience of the Scandinavian model, characterized by Nielsen and Pedersen (1993) as the 'negotiated economy'. Although it has been widely argued that increasing integration into the international economy and growing international competition in the 1980s have undermined the Swedish model (see, e.g., Pestoff 1993), the concept of the negotiated economy is of great interest when thinking about possible future developments. Nielsen and Pedersen contrast the negotiated economy, in which the distinction between market and state, private and public, is increasingly blurred, with the mixed economy, based on a clear-cut division of labour between autonomous market agents and autonomous state bodies. In the negotiated economy,

> Decision making is conducted via institutionalised negotiations between various autonomous private, semi-public, and public agents. The state delegates powers and participates in decision making processes without full authority. Also the discretion of private agents is restrained by the results of the negotiations. Different rationalities are combined and private and collective interests are mixed as agents engage in direct cooperation.
>
> (Nielsen and Pedersen 1993: 91)

The negotiated economy is conceptualized as an evolving network of interlocking institutions which between them form policy, engage in discourse and negotiation, and allow for arbitration and sanctions. The outcome is a continuously changing common 'socio-economic framework of meaning', or set of values and priorities, within which negotiations over the changing institutional framework and over specific substantive issues take place. Thus, consensus is generated, compromise is encouraged, and flexible, non-confrontational adaptation is facilitated.

A second example is the emerging embryonic framework for partnership and co-operation between the European Commission, national governments and regional governments, in support of local community initiatives, as summarized by Bianchi (1992) and referred to in the previous section. This experience has been further analysed by Farrands and Totterdill (1993). It is worth quoting part of their conclusions on future possibilities for the development of a 'strategic-discursive mode of regulation' at some length. They emphasize:

> The enhanced significance of locality as an appropriate level of regulation, but within the context of supranational strategic frameworks. Priorities for the structural adjustment of key areas of economic activity may increasingly be established at European level in order to secure the competitiveness of community-wide industry in world markets. . . . For example, industrial sector strategies could be created by means of a dynamic partnership between European, national, regional and local administrations. Local and regional research and consultation would inform the determination of national and European strategic objectives and the distribution of associated resources. Each locality and region could submit its own sectoral development plan as a means of gaining access to these resources, allowing a high degree of autonomy at grass-roots level while ensuring broad compliance with the strategic framework.
>
> (Farrands and Totterdill 1993: 181)

While this approach still adopts European Community/Union competitiveness as the overriding objective, it nevertheless provides an interesting possible framework for a more general process of negotiation between localities, regions, nation-states and the Commission. Within this framework agreed Community-wide objectives, not confined to global competitiveness, could be negotiated in a process which enabled them to be harmonized with the particular objectives of local communities. Of course, for such a discursive decision-making process to be socially efficient, the social actors participating in the process would have to include all those affected by the decisions emerging from the process. Further research is therefore needed on

1 the appropriate rules, institutions and processes that would enable a negotiated inter-community division of labour to be agreed, based on an appropriate balance between co-operation and competition among communities, and
2 appropriate measures to redistribute power within communities in order to promote fully participatory, socially efficient community decision-making.

REFERENCES

Best, M. (1990) *The New Competition*, Cambridge: Polity Press.

Bianchi, P. (1992) 'Industrial Strategy and Structural Policies', in K. Cowling and R. Sugden (eds), *Current Issues in Industrial Economic Strategy*, Manchester: Manchester University Press.

Cowling, K. and Sugden, R. (1993) 'Industrial Strategy: A Missing Link in British Economic Policy', *Oxford Review of Economic Policy* (Autumn).

Devine, P. (1994) 'Industrial Strategy: Process or Content? Insights from the Austrians', in P. Bianchi, K. Cowling and R. Sugden (eds) *Europe's Economic Challenge,* London: Routledge.

Farrands, C. and Totterdill, P. (1993) 'A Rationale for an Appropriate Level of Regulation in the European Community', in R. Sugden, (ed.) *Industrial Economic Regulation*, London: Routledge.

Hart, J. (1992) *Rival Capitalists: International Competitiveness in the United States, Japan, and Western Europe*, Ithaca: Cornell University Press.

Krugman, P. (ed.) (1986) *Strategic Trade Policy and the New International Economics*, Cambridge, MA: MIT Press.

—— (1990): *Rethinking International Trade,* Cambridge, MA: MIT Press.

Nielsen, K. and Pedersen, O. (1993) 'The Negotiated Economy: General Features and Theoretical Perspectives', in J. Hausner, B. Jessop and K. Nielsen (eds) *Institutional Frameworks of Market Economies: Scandinavian and Eastern European Perspectives,* Aldershot: Avebury.

Pitelis, C. (1994) 'Industrial Strategy: For Britain, in Europe, in the Globe', *Journal of Economic Studies.*

Pestoff, V. (1993) 'Towards a New Swedish Model', in J. Hausner, B. Jessop and K. Nielsen (eds), *Institutional Frameworks of Market Economies: Scandinavian and Eastern European Perspectives*, Aldershot: Avebury.

Porter, M. (1990) *The Competitive Advantage of Nations*, London: Macmillan.

Sinclair, P. (1993) 'World Trade, Protectionist Follies, and Europe's Options for the Future', *Oxford Review of Economic Policy*, Autumn.

Singh, A. (1977) 'UK Industry and the World Economy: A Case of Deindustrialisation?', *Cambridge Journal of Economics.*

Willner, J. (1994) 'Competitiveness, Subsidiarity and Social Objectives: Issues for European Industrial Strategy', paper presented at the 1994 *Crete Workshop on Competitiveness, Subsidiarity and Objectives.*

2

SOCIAL OBJECTIVES, MARKET RULE AND PUBLIC POLICY

The case of ownership

Johan Willner

INTRODUCTION

The public sector is now under challenge as a provider of both private and collective goods. This trend is more or less universal, occuring in both industrial and developed countries as well as in Eastern Europe. Organizations like the IMF are recommending a set of structural adjustments which have in common a reduced role for the public sector.

In addition to general cuts in public provision and social security, this trend includes privatizing state-owned companies (SOEs) as well as restructuring public utilities, by means of managerial reforms, competition and often also divestiture. This chapter focuses on when and when not social objectives are best achieved by competition between profit maximizing firms, and gives a brief sketch of a more sensible approach.

The next section presents some comments on what competition can and cannot achieve and the objectives that have been put forward either for public ownership or for privatization. The third section analyses conflicts between different social objectives for public firms from a theoretical standpoint. In addition to the traditional trade-off between cost reductions and allocational gains, it addresses the distinction between an increase in efficiency and a regressive change in the functional distribution of income. Finally, it includes an analysis of quality in the particular case when part of what an industry should do is to maintain a capacity to produce a service, as in for example transport networks or health care. The fourth section surveys the empirical literature. In the light of the analysis of the third section, one might expect public firms to be more costly to run. However, this popular notion seems to be prejudiced. The concluding section tries to look at competition and ownership from a European perspective, with a focus on who (EU, the national government or the local authorities) is best suited to intervene. The chapter argues tentatively that the combined emphasis in Europe on market solutions and large scale leads to excessive market imperfections among large corporations and to competition only where non-profit-maximizing monopolies might do better.

The main part of the chapter is non-technical, but some of the points are clarified by formal examples which are separated from the main part of each section. The chapter makes frequent use of contributions presented at earlier workshops within the *European Network on Industrial Policy*.

COMPETITION, OWNERSHIP AND SOCIAL OBJECTIVES

The case for decentralized decision-making

Consider a perfectly competitive market for a private good such that externalities and other sources of failure are not present. It is well known that the allocation is then Pareto-efficient and there are no income inequalities caused by pure profits, but without perfect competition prices may exceed marginal costs. This not only redistributes real incomes at the expense of the rest of the society but also causes a deadweight loss from which the whole economy suffers. Even if there is some disagreement on its size, most economists would agree on the need to intervene. Interventions might include price caps, legislating against collusion, removing trade barriers, mixed oligopolies (see below) and nationalization.

However, it has sometimes been argued that decentralized decision-making and technical progress might conflict. According to this view, firms lack incentives to innovate without patent protection and firms under a certain size cannot afford R&D. There is no conclusive empirical evidence supporting this conventional view (Davies *et al.* 1989), but the market might underprovide R&D for other reasons.

Therefore, instead of merging or colluding, firms might be given incentives to co-operate in R&D, as in the case of Japanese research associations (Goto 1992). This is also to some extent practised in Europe, where the EC supports joint R&D projects. These may lead to subsequent co-operation as well (Katsoulacos and Nowell 1994). Co-operation may also take the form of networks including both firms and universities (Bianchi and Miller 1994), in which case excessive profit margins are not needed as a source of finance. Moreover, new ideas would not have to be kept secret. In other cases, public and private firms might reduce unnecessary duplication by competing in making an innovation (Delbono and Denicolò 1993), or they can build alliances to develop new products (Dorman 1994).

To encourage technical progress and to reduce profit margins would improve the performance of an industry as a whole. However, in everyday language competitiveness often denotes an ability to play a zero-sum game in a world of hostile take-overs and occasional price wars. Size and performance are believed to correlate, as when Europe is required to have a fair share of giant corporations (champions) as compared to Japan and the US (Ramsay 1992). This is not what competitiveness usually means for an economist. Moreover, to join fully utilized plants under a common administration does not generate economies of scale, and recent empirical research indicates that mergers do not make firms more efficient (Adams and Brock 1989; Schenk 1994).

The strategic decisions of oligopolistic firms may have wide-ranging economic, social and political consequences. This may be true locally even if firms are price takers on the world markets. Competition policy may therefore not only promote allocative efficiency, but also protect individuals and local communities from a concentration of power in a subset of the community. A competition strategy which has in mind the wider objective of decentralized decision-making is not the same thing as a general *laissez-faire* policy because of the many cases in which there remains a conflict between profitability and the interest of society. Therefore, some form of community planning must ensure that the preferences of the whole community are reflected in the behaviour of the firms (Cowling and Sugden 1992, 1994).

Decentralized decision-making does not mean that all firms are conventional profit maximizers. The objectives of the community may in many cases be best implemented under public ownership. As we shall see, this does not necessarily cause society prohibitive costs. Moreover, public ownership does not have to be an alternative to competition, but may even create it if there is a non-profit-maximizing firm on the market which forces its competitors to cut their profit margins. Such a market is called a *mixed oligopoly*. I have addressed this option in more detail elsewhere (see Willner 1992, 1994b, 1994c). Some of the literature is summarized in De Fraja and Delbono (1990).

Moreover, when competition works, it may be appropriate to encourage labour management, in particular in cases when the workers have strong preferences concerning working conditions or when the success of a firm depends on their knowledge. As shown by, for example, Bartlett *et al.* (1992), co-operative firms have turned out to work quite efficiently.

When does competition not work?

While the concern for technical progress and for 'competitiveness' in the sense of power to compete are scarcely reasons to accept market imperfections, there might be other situations in which competition is not feasible. I assume that the cases of public goods and the natural monopoly or oligopoly are well known, and therefore focus here on *network externalities* and *artificial competition.*

If there are network externalities, it is valuable for a customer that the commodity – or compatible versions – are used by a large number of people (Tirole 1988). There may be an indirect benefit from lower unit costs but there are also direct technical advantages, as when two researchers write a joint paper and are able to use the same word processing program. It is obvious that competition without intervention might result in insufficient standardization, while in other cases standardization can be achieved only if one firm gets a strong market position through a first-mover advantage. There are other potential market failures as well: firms may either issue halfway designs in order to be able to set standards or they may be too slow in adopting a new technology for fear of premature solutions setting the course of future development.

The term *artificial competition* refers to industries which are neither natural monopolies nor producing network externalities. However, their output would be easier to use with a single provider. For example, competing telecommunications systems can be set up at non-prohibitive costs. Under competition, customers have to compare costs and to use different codes for different systems, as in Finland, where the public telephone cards are in addition incompatible. Similar examples of artificial competition are provided by the deregulation of local public transport. The co-ordination necessary for making private provision perform adequately (through- and inter-ticketing, cross subsidization, common information, etc.) is likely to restrict competition and entry. Experiences from Britain show that privatization and competition not only reduce the amount of services but may also make the public transport system difficult to grasp and hence use.

The objectives of public firms

In an ideal democracy, the values of the citizens should be reflected in the behaviour of state-owned or municipal enterprises. This notion does not always exclude profit maximization, as in the case of lotteries in the Nordic countries. However, one might conjecture that revenue generating motives may have been too wide spread, as cases like the post and telecommunications in the Netherlands indicate. A concern for the well-being of the citizens is likely to require wider objectives of firms in common ownership, such as maximization of the total surplus in the industry.[1]

In most countries, the state or the local authorities produce more than purely public goods. There are few industries in which the conditions for the private sector to produce completely without failure are fulfilled, and public ownership then provides the authorities with an instrument of intervention. Firms might get excessive market power under private ownership, or markets might fail to perform accurately for other reasons. For example, state-owned enterprises (SOEs) may have been established because of lack of willingness in the private sector, as under Finland's first years as an independent nation, or in many developing countries. However, nationalization has in practice often been motivated by *ad hoc* reasons like saving an ailing company, rather than by a coherent industrial policy.

Firms in public ownership have often been required to conform to macro-economic objectives, for example by producing more than would be profitable in a recession, or keeping prices low in a boom. They may be required to support an active labour market policy, as when being over-manned on purpose during recessions in Britain before 1979. Employment was an important objective in Sweden, Austria, Ireland and France as well. In Finland, like in Italy, the location of firms was chosen with the impact on regional employment in mind. Nationalized firms in Britain were supposed not to increase prices if there were inflationary pressures; Robert Millward (1976) finds evidence for anti-inflationary pricing among British public firms 1965–7 and in the 1970s. In France, nationalization was even partly motivated by the need to control prices.

The price and investment policy of nationalized firms may also affect the balance of payments or even the exchange rate. For example, the SOEs in Finland were forced not to protect their foreign loans as the central bank tried to defend an overvalued currency against devaluation expectations. However, the policy failed and these companies made losses.

There might exist better macro-economic tools than price and employment policies operated by nationalized firms, but firms in public ownership might prove to be necessary from the standpoint of industrial policy. Not surprisingly, SOEs play an important part in rapidly growing economies such as South Korea and Taiwan. In Sweden, state-owned companies have been supposed to give the authorities insights about the industries in which they operate so as to make proper intervention posible. In Ireland, the SOEs have been instructed to work as development corporations. The emphasis on providing private producers in Finland with cheap energy, fertilizers and transport services can also be seen as part of an industrial policy; subsequent objectives have been more commercial.

According to a view that is presently less fashionable, public ownership is a powerful instrument for social justice, by ensuring that the workers get the fruit of their labour. As will be shown in the third section below, there may exist a link between ownership and income distribution. For example, the influence of SOEs was used in an attempt to reduce poverty by a number of Third World countries in the 1970s.

Excessive profit margins may also affect income distribution. The Social Democrats in West-Germany in the 1960s wanted firms owned by the federal or regional authorities (Ländern) to compete aggressively to reduce profit margins in cases of oligopoly, but there seem to exist few other examples where strong political parties have adopted a mixed oligopoly strategy. Another important objective may be to minimize environmental damage, as when nationalized firms were supposed to reduce the share of oil in energy consumption or when the supply and price of public transport is designed to reduce the use of private cars.

The present tendency to privatize and to emphasize commercial objectives means that important external effects of corporate decision-making are ignored. Some authors, such as Boardman and Vining (1989), argue that external effects, while not non-existent, are too difficult to measure and that profitability provides a guide to their shadow price. However, even if this were true, a public firm should not be condemned for failing to be profitable if it has been required to give first priority to employment in its region. Therefore, the only appropriate definition of the performance of a public enterprise is the extent to which it achieves the objectives which have been set for it (Rees 1984: 11).

Why privatization?

Privatization is often described as bringing about increased competition, and has therefore, together with deregulation, been seen as a way to achieve social objectives through the market mechanism. However, privatization has in some cases just transferred a monopoly from public to private ownership, as in the UK. It is far from obvious that a concern for decentralized decision-making should favour private ownership in such a case. In countries like Finland, the authorities tend to understand 'competitiveness' as the capability to compete, and privatization therefore takes place in order to abandon mixed ownership as being an obstacle to mergers ('Visio yksityistämisestä Suomessa', 1991).

The importance of privatization as part of present-day micro-economic policy is illustrated by the confusing use of the term in countries like Finland and Germany, as when SOEs or public utilities are restructured without abandoning majority ownership. Moreover, privatization can mean both divestiture and a reduction of public-sector shares through a share issue. In what follows, privatization means that the private sector takes over an activity, firm or organization. This includes cases when the position as a majority shareholder is lost, but not when an organization is only forced to adopt commercial objectives.[2]

The term privatization was actually first used by Ludwig Erhard in 1947 (Bös 1993), and some shares were sold in West Germany and Austria in the 1950s and 1960s. However, the present wave of privatization started when it became part of the Thatcher government's economic policy in the UK in 1983. Initially, only firms in mixed industries were privatized, but subsequently the policy was extended to public utilities like water and telecommunications. From 1983 onwards countries like Austria, France, Germany, Italy, the Netherlands, Portugal, Spain and Sweden have also been privatizing companies, but on a smaller scale.[3] Moreover, public utilities in these countries have in general been restructured rather than sold. The largest privatization operations outside the UK took place in Portugal and France, not long after a number of firms had been nationalized.

There are several reasons why SOEs are now being privatized.[4] Public ownership leads to less efficient production according to a popular view and the most prominent argument for privatization in industrial countries has been to improve financial performance. Accusations of inefficiency play an important part in the World Bank/IMF agenda for privatization in Third-World countries. Privatization is expected to increase efficiency not only via competition but also through better management.

Privatization can also be seen as a shift of economic power and it is therefore no surprise that it is advocated by governments which are eager to reduce the influence not only of the state but also of the labour unions. It is often argued that public-sector employees are better organized, but it is not necessarily true that they are stronger relative to their employer, as indicated by the coal strike in Britain in 1984–5

The aim of the early privatizations in Austria and Germany was to create a widespread system of share ownership, but the shares were soon acquired by large investors (Bös 1993). Similar motives were put forward in Britain, but typically the new shareholders are small, own no other shares and have no means of influencing companies' policies (Lashmar 1994). However, share ownership was believed to strengthen work motivation. There may also be strategic political considerations. A large number of middle-class voters became shareholders receiving short-term gains, which influenced voting behaviour because stock prices tended to reflect the Tories' electoral fortune (Vickers and Yarrow 1988).

Ownership is also associated with distributional objectives in another sense. Public utilities in particular used to charge lower prices for necessities used by less affluent consumers. As Vickers and Yarrow argue, the reduction of cross-subsidization in telecommunications in Britain has been likely to favour business customers. The combination of privatization and competition may even rule out cross-subsidization.

Finland is an interesting case in point because of the comparatively large proportion of public ownership. Before the present crisis, state-owned companies in Finland were responsible for about 20 per cent of domestic value added, as compared to 10–11 per cent in Britain. With the exception of some firms which performed badly under private ownership, the state did establish firms rather than nationalize. The most important reason for the need to establish firms was the lack of private risk capital. Thus, the SOE-sector was complementary to the firms in private ownership. However, from 1987 onwards governments have in principle supported privatization. In 1991 the Ministry of Trade and Industry issued a report setting an agenda for the sell-off of shares.

The commercial performance of SOEs in Finland was in general no worse than in similar private firms. Competition and efficiency have not therefore been important motives for their privatization. In fact, one reason why the report in question advocates privatization is that mixed ownership is seen as an obstacle to mergers. The authorities encourage competition only in the case of contracting out or reorganizing public services. The blueprint was written while there was still a public-sector surplus. As the depression generated a deficit in 1991, privatization tended to be advocated as improving the public sector's financial position, as in Britain.[5] During the worst phase of the crisis even a commercial bank was nationalized for a time, but privatization returned to the agenda in 1993.

PUBLIC OWNERSHIP AND CONFLICTING OBJECTIVES: A THEORETICAL DISCUSSION

The permissible range of cost inefficiency

Conventional wisdom claims that public production is 'inefficient', but it is not always clear what is meant by efficiency. For example, public firms are believed to be less profitable, but this is hardly surprising given that profitability is not always given the highest priority. Moreover, a public firm has often a strong market position, which means that both high and low profits can be interpreted to its disadvantage. Revenues, pricing policy or attitudes towards risk, which have been compared in some of the studies cited in earlier surveys, may be equally disputable criteria for the choice between public and private ownership.

If there are no considerable external effects, it is appropriate to focus on a partial analysis of allocative efficiency. The most efficient solution is then approximated by maximizing the total surplus, or the difference between the area under the demand schedule and the total costs. A necessary but not sufficient condition for such an optimum is that costs are minimized.[6] However, there is a trade-off in a natural monopoly or oligopoly if public ownership generates excessive costs while private ownership generates deadweight losses.[7]

In Britain, recent Tory governments have seemed to believe that private ownership is to be prefered even under monopoly. The conditions under which this is true can easily be explored by assuming iso-elastic demand and constant returns to scale. In Box 1 below we show how much more cost efficient a private firm has to be before the industry performs better than under public ownership.

The extent to which private profit maximization reduces welfare depends on demand elasticity. If demand is highly elastic, the market would prevent firms from setting excessively high prices. However, the model suggests that demand elasticity has to be extremely high and public production significantly less cost-efficient before private ownership yields higher allocative efficiency. Given that most industry studies about demand elasticity tend to suggest relatively low values, it seems that the differences in variable costs

BOX 1 PRIVATE AND PUBLIC OWNERSHIP UNDER NATURAL MONOPOLY

Suppose that an industry is a natural monopoly and that demand is iso-elastic, with the price elasticity e. Let p and x stand for price and quantity and let M be a positive parameter, so that demand can be written $x = M/p^e$. Further, suppose that marginal costs are c and $(1 + k)c$ under private and public ownership respectively; k is a positive coefficient. For simplicity, we assume that the fixed costs C are equal under private and public ownership and that that they are not so high that private production would be unprofitable.

A profit maximizing firm would charge $p^m + ec/(e - 1)$ which would yield $x^m = M/[ec/(e - 1)]^e$, provided that $e > 1$. If $e < 1$, the profit function would be non-concave and decreasing in x, in which case the profit margin is indeterminate. Given any allocation, the firm could increase its profit by increasing p^m and reducing x^m. A welfare maximizing public firm would charge $p^g = (1 + k)c$. The fixed costs are financed by the tax-payers. Output is then $x^g = M/[(k + 1)c]^e$. It is well known that allocative efficiency under public production is higher if the following condition holds true:

$$\int_{x^m}^{x^g} \frac{M^{1/e}}{x^{1/e}} \mathrm{d}x - (x^g - x^p)(k + 1)c - kcx^m > 0 . \quad (1)$$

We can solve for the maximum value $\hat{k}$ of k that is consistent with (1) as a function of e:

$$\hat{k} = \left(\frac{e}{e - 1}\right)^{e/(e-1)} \left(\frac{e - 1}{2e - 1}\right)^{1/(e-1)} - 1 \quad (2)$$

Table 2.1 shows the largest percentage efficiency difference ($\hat{k} \times 100$) under which public ownership would still yield higher allocative efficiency:

Table 2.1 Percentage cost inefficiency and demand elasticity

e	$\hat{k} \times 100$	e	$\hat{k} \times 100$
1.10	360.99	2.00	33.33
1.20	177.60	4.00	10.64
1.40	86.73	8.00	4.47
1.60	58.84	50.00	0.63
1.80	42.09	100.00	0.31

have to be large indeed before allocative efficiency would be higher under private production.

Ownership, efficiency and social justice

The absence of a share price, diffuse ownership and vaguely defined objectives (which are likely to change with the political situation) are popular explanations for why public ownership is believed to generate inefficiency.

For example, it is argued that a company which does not work as efficiently as it could is likely to be taken over. However, there exists a large number of efficient private firms the shares of which are not traded on the stock market. If takeovers would make firms more efficient, mergers would more often turn out to be successful. Moreover, it is far from certain that take-over threats will make firms more efficient in the long run rather than force them to adopt short-termist solutions (Vickers and Yarrow 1988; Bös 1991).[8]

As for the other reasons, the fact that the ownership of private firms may be diffuse does not seem to play any major role in their efficiency. Public ownership as such does not mean vague objectives (De Fraja 1993). Several authors, such as Estrin and Pérotin (1991), therefore argue that theory yields no unambiguous predictions about the relationship between ownership and efficiency.

The usual framwork for analysing how ownership might affect managerial efficiency is to set up a model in which the owner (the principal) cannot observe the actions of the manager (the agent). This informational asymmetry allows the manager to be lazy and to spend money on unnecessary items to his enjoyment (managerial slack). Is a profit-maximizing shareholder or a welfare maximizing government more efficient in reducing slack? According to De Fraja (1993), it is the nationalized firm which is likely to be more efficient, for the simple reason that welfare-maximization generates a stronger incentive to pay for higher efficiency. Less is at stake for a private firm, because only part of the total surplus matters. However, this mechanism does not work unless welfare (the total surplus) enters as a performance criterion and unless this affects the manager's compensation.

The literature on incentive schemes for public firms suggests that payment should be linear in the consumer surplus with a negative intercept and, under risk neutrality, a unit slope. According to Bös (1991), such a system is not applicable, because voters would never understand why managers should pay a fixed fee to the government in return for a sum equal to some obscure measure. However, it is misleading to describe a formula for taking social benefits into consideration as literally giving managers the whole consumer surplus after they have paid a fee. In analogy, a negative income tax scheme does not mean that the state literally gives us a fixed sum before we pay taxes. One might object to an excessive emphasis on economic incentives, but there is no reason to expect that welfare maximization could not be made operational.

Pint (1991) addresses a similar question as De Fraja, focusing on the optimal proportions between labour and capital. The firm in public ownership is assumed to maximize a weighted sum of the consumers' and the producers' surplus and the wages. It turns out that the public firm tends to be biased towards labour and the private firm towards capital.[9] The relative efficiency of a (regulated) private monopolist and a nationalized firm depends on the relative emphasis of the objectives. With appropriate weights, public ownership is likely to perform better. She suggests that the the reason why governments prefer private solutions is the search for electoral benefits. Moreover, privatization is difficult to reverse, and this restricts the actions of future governments.

Commercial objectives in a public firm may even be counter-productive. In a model which is described in more detail elsewhere (see Willner, 1994b), the wages and the managerial salaries and slack are determined by bargaining at the firm level. If the public firm is a profit-maximizing Stackelberg leader, it will get a larger market share than its private competitor(s) and thus get a larger surplus (gross profits) over the variable costs. The Nash bargaining solution yields wages, salaries and slack that are proportional to the gross profits, which implies that the leader gets lower profits per turnover and higher unit costs.

On the other hand, if the public sector maximizes welfare and if marginal costs are constant, the government must also decide on the proportion between public and private, because unconstrained welfare maximization would eliminate the private firms. A public firm which maximizes welfare subject to a constraint which prevents complete nationalization gets higher profits per turnover and lower unit costs than its profit-maximizing competitor.

Gravelle (1984) has modelled a bilateral monopoly with a labour union and a firm under public and private ownership. As can be expected, a strong union would desire too high labour intensity for the negotiated wage rate, but general conclusions about union strength under public and private ownership cannot be drawn. Experience seems to confirm that public ownership may both strengthen and weaken management relative to the unions. Nevertheless, the view that firms in public ownership are inefficient is often attributed to high wage costs caused by public sector unions. For example, Bös (1993) expects that governments within the EU might be forced to privatize because of higher wages making public firms unable to compete without a monopoly position.

If unionized firms are less profitable, this is often believed to depend on adverse effects on technical efficiency. However, some empirical studies tend to suggest that such differences reflect income distribution rather than efficiency. According to Katz and Summers (1989) and MacPherson (1990) in the US and Machin (1991) and Cable and Machin (1991) in the UK, there is an inverse relationship between profitability and the wage share of output. A wage increase is not completely offset by reduced employment, which means that unions tend to acquire part of the economic rent. According to Machin and Stewart (1990), the ability of unions to increase wages depends on the existence of rents caused by high market shares.

There seems to exist some systematic differences in wages between the private and the public sector. According to Gunderson (1979), public sector workers might earn 6.2–8.6 per cent more than in similar jobs in the private sector. In Haskel and Szymanski (1992, 1993), a reorientation towards more commercial objectives and privatization is shown to have reduced the wage differential between public and private sector employees. By studying a somewhat longer time period. Martin and Parker (1994) have been able to conclude that profits did indeed increase at the expense of wages, as a result of changed ownership. However, the effects on employment are less clear.

The notion of a trade-off between cost inefficiency and excessive price margins is over-simplified if unions influence the distribution of incomes. Profits and wages have been given a different treatment in the analysis of welfare losses. Excessive profits have been included in the social surplus, but excessive wages have, like other costs, been seen as a waste only. The reason why high profits can be seen as part of the surplus is that they can be taxed away, which means that they are at least a potential source of benefit to society. However, the same applies to excessive wages. Moreover, why should private sector firms always set the norm for what is normal and what is excessive?

Box 2 presents a model which treats wages and profits symmetrically and where the wage rate is set by Nash bargaining. The bargaining strengths of union and management are assumed not to depend on ownership, but the public firm is assumed to maximize the total surplus, including wages. As it turns out, such a hypothetical welfare-maximizing firm might then appear as less cost-efficient although it has been succesful relative to its objective.

BOX 2 WAGE BARGAINING AND OWNERSHIP

We consider again a monopoly under public and private ownership. To simplify, all variable costs are wages. Each unit of output requires one unit of labour. There is a labour union, which tries to increase the wage rate w. The private monopolist wants to set w at a level which maximizes profits, but under public ownership the firm would maximize the sum of the consumers' and the producers' surplus, which now includes the wage costs.

To make Nash bargaining work in a simple context, we assume linear demand. Let p denote the price and let a be a positive parameter. Choose units so that we get $p = a - x$. In a two-stage equilibrium, a profit-maximizing firm would then produce $(a - w)/2$ and set the price $(a + w)/2$, given w. A welfare-maximizing firm would produce $a - w$ and set the price equal to marginal costs, w.

Let α and $1 - \alpha$ express the bargaining strengths of the firm and the union; $0 < \alpha < 1$. The monopoly profits are $(a - w)^2/4$ and the fallback levels are assumed to be zero. The Nash bargaining solution then amounts to maximizing $B^m = [(a - w)^2]^\alpha w^{1-\alpha}$. It turns out that the wage rate in such a monopoly is $w^m = \beta a$, where β stands for $(1 - \alpha)/(1 + \alpha)$. The sum of the consumers' surplus, the profits and the wage incomes in the industry is then $S^m = (1 - \beta)\ (3 + \beta)\alpha^2/8$.

Suppose now that the management would pursue the new objective with equal efficiency under public ownership. If the total surplus includes the wage costs, Nash bargaining means maximizing $B^w = [(a-w)w + (a-w)^2/2]^\alpha w^{1-\alpha}$. The optimal wage rate is then $w^w = \sqrt{\beta a}$, which is larger than w^m. For example, if $\alpha = 1/2$, w^w exceeds w^m by a factor of 1.73. The total surplus $S^w = (1 - \beta)\alpha^2/2$, which is unambiguously larger than S^m.

The consumers' surplus is $(1-\beta)^2a^2/8$ under profit-maximization and $(1 - \sqrt{\beta})^2a^2/2$ under welfare maximization. Thus, the consumers are better off under public ownership under these circumstances. However, the the sum of profits and the consumers' surplus is larger under private ownership than the consumers' surplus under public ownership if $\alpha < 0.95$.

There are other reasons as well for interpreting cost differences carefully. The difference in wage rate between public and private employees is higher for low wage workers, which means that a convergence towards private-sector conditions would increase inequality (Gunderson 1979). This might affect, in particular, female employees. Zetterberg (1992) shows that the wage disadvantages of females within the public sector did increase in Sweden in the 1980s because of a shift from collective to individual wage bargaining. A private-sector firm is not more efficient if its cost advantage depends on paying lower wages to females.

Even genuine differences in cost efficiency may, on closer inspection, be ambiguous. It is often argued that unions care about both wages and working conditions, and these may in turn be related to efforts on the job. Union influence is believed to result in over-manning or other forms of 'featherbedding'. If public-sector unions are stronger, costs might therefore be lower in the private sector even if the wage rates are the same.

The conventional view of a firm is that of an organization which hires workers for jobs with a given description. The workers' preferences concern consumption and leisure only, and they accept a job unless their reservation wages are too high. However, most individuals spend a large proportion of their time at work and they are likely to value not only consumption and leisure but decent working conditions as well. It is a well-established notion in the literature on efficiency wages and effort bargaining that the employees' utility is affected by work intensity. If monitoring is costly, as in the efficiency-wage literature, employers are willing to pay in excess of the market clearing wage rate to provide incentives for harder work (see, for example, Shapiro and Stiglitz 1984, or Eaton and White 1983). In the effort bargaining literature, unions and employers jointly decide on the nature of the work contract, for example on the number of persons that operate a machine or the responsibilities of employees with a given job (see Johnson 1990; Clark 1990; or Rosén 1990).

The provocative implications of the notion that we have preferences about effort have not yet been fully explored. Is it then desirable that only employers set the effort targets? If not, what is the socially optimal work intensity if the workers' preferences are also taken into account? Can monitoring difficulties be socially beneficial? As explained elsewhere (see Willner 1994a), a competitive market economy may be Pareto-inefficient even under full information and full employment. The explanation is that too high efforts produce a negative externality even when the positive effect on consumption via lower prices is taken care of. In other words, the socially optimal utilization of manpower and machines differ, because machines have no preferences about how the work should be done.[10]

Costs and quality

Frequently running trains or buses provide mobility more efficiently than if services are infrequent and irregular. For example, an improvement of the rolling stock would not compensate customers for a deterioration of route network and schedules, as the experiences from bus deregulation in Sweden indicate.[11] If a public transport system is unsatisfactory, customers are likely to use private cars, as has been shown to be the case in a study about interaction between car ownership and public transport in South Yorkshire (Goodwin 1993).

Similar effects may be present in a number of other industries. For example, banks may save costs by increased queueing, because they do not have to pay for the customers' time, as when banks in Finland laid off employees after 1990. Frequent delivery of mail is likely to encourage a more intense use of postal services than non-frequent delivery.

A number of US studies show that non-profit-maximizing hospitals employ a larger staff per hospital bed, even when their total unit costs are lower (Arrington and Haddock 1990). Efficiency is often defined in terms of staff per bed, but at the same time hospitals are often criticized for being under-staffed. This seems to be the case in particular for the treatment of patients whose quality of life depends on the availability of nursing.

Thus, output (the amount of a service) should be distinguished from the capacity to produce. The latter is associated with factors like the frequency of mail delivery, the schedules of buses or trains and the size of staff in banks or hospitals. Thus, capacity represents an aspect of quality, and is therefore likely to affect demand, in particular if there exist substitutes. In evaluating the net welfare change of privatization, such a change in quality should be taken into account.

Most studies tend to show that the deregulation of the bus services in the UK in 1986 and their subsequent privatization have reduced operator costs. This may be an unambiguous reduction of waste, but it may also be a redistribution from the employees. In addition, fares have generally increased, which has led to a reduced patronage and hence to a loss of consumer surplus. A conventional cost-benefit analysis typically takes only these effects into consideration. For example, White (1990) reaches the conclusion that there has been a net welfare loss in the Shires and in Scotland, but net gains in London and the Metropolitan areas. However, as increased fares and cost cutting are likely to have shifted demand, such conclusions may be flawed.[12]

The adverse effects of privatization are naturally smaller if services are reduced prior to privatization to such an extent that it is no longer profitable to go further. In the UK, public firms in most industries were forced by the government to adopt more commercial objectives some years before being privatized (Haskel and Szymanski 1992). A similar strategy is adopted in Finland, and subsequent privatizations are likely. As Dodgson and Katsoulacos (1988) show, the size of the consumer surplus loss depends on the extent to which the objectives of the public firm were commercial before deregulation and privatization.

Thus, part of the cost reductions may be caused by a quality reduction which has not been taken into account. To understand the importance of this factor, we construct a model in which a firm determines its output (for example, passenger kilometres) and capacity. We compare the results of welfare and profit maximization respectively in the monopoly case, and we use the simplifying labels 'public' and 'private' although some public-sector firms maximize profits and there exist private firms which do not.

In Box 3 we present an example of a monopoly under public and private ownership in which firms have to choose capacity and where this choice affects demand. Capacity affects the extent to which the customer can rely on this market and not on some alternative service. Therefore, higher capacity means an outward shift in demand. Public and private ownership give access to the same technology, but a welfare-maximizing allocation nevertheless yields higher unit costs.

BOX 3 UNIT COSTS UNDER PUBLIC AND PRIVATE OWNERSHIP

Suppose that the inverse demand function is linear, and units are chosen so that its slope equals –1. Let a and b be positive parameters and let p and x represent price and quality. Let $\hat{x}$ denote capacity, which implies an outward demand shift because a high capacity implies that customers are less likely to use an alternative service the price of which is kept constant. Capacity affects demand in the simplest possible way, i.e. $p = a + b\hat{x} - x$.

We assume that marginal costs c_1 are constant and that an increased capacity increases total costs by a quadratic term with the coefficient $c_2/2$. We ignore all other fixed costs, although they may be important in the type of industry under consideration. Thus, the cost function is $TC = c_1x + c_2\hat{x}^2/2$. To get meaningful solutions, we have to assume that $c_2 > b^2$.

A private monopolist is assumed to maximize profits given $\hat{x}$. The first step of the calculation then yields $x^m(\hat{x}) = (a + b\hat{x} - c_1)/2$ and $p^m(\hat{x}) = (a + b\hat{x}c_1)/2$. Normally, the firm would choose no excess capacity because there is no uncertainty. Costs are increasing in $\hat{x}$ and it therefore adapts capacity to the profit maximizing level of output. It turns out that profits are:

$$\pi = \frac{(a + b\hat{x} - c_1)^2}{4} - \frac{1}{2} c_2\hat{x}^2 \qquad (3)$$

and the profit-maximizing level is $\hat{x}^m = b(a - c_1)/(2c_2 - b^2)$.

A welfare-maximizing firm would set prices equal to marginal costs c_1, so that total output is $x^g(\hat{x}) = a + b\hat{x} - c_1$. The total surplus is then:

$$W = \frac{(a + b\hat{x} - c_1)^2}{2} - \frac{1}{2} c_2\hat{x}^2 . \qquad (3)$$

Maximizing shows that the optimal capacity is $\hat{x}^g = b(a - c_1)/(c_2 - b^2)$. Thus, the welfare-maximizing firm would choose larger capacity.

Output is $\hat{x}^g = c_2(a - c_1)/(2c_2 - b^2)$ under profit maximization. Welfare maximization would yield a higher output, namely $x^g = c_2(a - c_1)/(c_2 - b^2)$. The unit costs are $c_1 + c_2\hat{x}^2/x$ and thus higher in a welfare maximizing firm.

The analysis can be reinterpreted to let $\hat{x}$ stand for quality in general, in which case a private monopoly would under-provide both quality and quantity. However, there may be cost differences even when capacity is not related to quality and hence does not shift demand. In Willner (1992, 1994c), a welfare-maximizing firm in a mixed oligopoly would choose a capacity level that gives it higher unit costs than its private competitors. Nevertheless, welfare is in general higher in the mixed oligopoly unless the number of firms is large and demand elasticity is low.

In the case of public transport, there are other aspects of quality that should be addressed. If the firm produces not only transport services but a network that brings about mobility, cross subsidization is not necessarily a distortion. The public authorities may be reluctant to support a sufficient number of unprofitable routes when competition eliminates this source of finance. Moreover, it may be more difficult to co-ordinate a service under competition than in a public monopoly. For example, it seems that splitting and privatizing British Rail would drastically reduce the number of stations at which through ticketing is available. The division which has already been made has reduced access to timetable information on other parts of the system. Similar effects can be seen as a result of bus privatization. As Tyson (1990) argues, such a quality reduction means that increased fares and reduced patronage give an incomplete picture of the welfare reductions.

AN OVERVIEW OF THE EMPIRICAL WORK

Although agency problems are not necessarily more difficult under public ownership, the previous analysis suggests that taking external benefits in consideration might lead to higher costs. In fact, there seems to exist a consensus that allocative gains which can be reached under public ownership must be traded off against higher costs increases.

The conviction that public production is inefficient has been sufficiently strong for empirical evidence to seem irrelevant. Succesful counterexamples do not make headlines. For example, the South Korean state-owned firm Pohang Steel Company may be the most efficient of its kind in the world (Singh 1992). If a large share of public enterprise is detrimental for economic growth, how can it be explained that rapidly growing economies, for example Japan, Taiwan and South Korea, have in general been highly interventionist, with a prominent sector of state-owned companies?

The empirical research has been unsystematic, but there exists by now a fairly large number of industry studies which throw light on the relative efficiency of public ownership. The studies concern different countries and different institutional settings and are not necessarily comparable.[13] However, if profits-maximizing private firms are always superior, we would expect this tendency to dominate despite different circumstances.

One approach is to estimate the production function of a public firm. If output is not on the production function, the company is technically inefficient. The advantage of this method is that technical efficiency in this sense is less ambiguous than costs. It has been applied to the post office in Belgium, and gives a fairly favourable picture (Deprins *et al.* 1984), and by Perelman and Pestieau (1988) on the railways and the postal services in 19 and 22 mainly European countries. There are large variations in technical efficiency between countries because of geographical and cultural factors. At least, the results suggest that SOEs are not inherently inefficient. Moreover, the number of efficient companies tends to be larger if the production function is not restricted to a particular functional form (Parris *et al.* 1987).

Another type of study focuses on the influence of ownership on costs in industries where both private and public ownership occurs. It is surprising that their number is not larger, given the importance of the notion of inefficient public ownership for the political agenda. The obvious limitation of this approach is the neglect of external benefits, but any view on what society has to sacrifice if firms reach other than commercial objectives should be based on facts, not prejudice.

This literature, which provides a fairly complex picture, has been reviewed earlier. Some of the surveys, like Bennett and Johnson (1980) and Boardman and Vining (1989), tend to conclude that private ownership is superior. On the other hand, Millward (1982), Boyd (1986), Yarrow (1986) and Vickers and Yarrow (1988) find from their surveys that public ownership does not lead to higher costs. Borcherding *et al.* (1982) is an intermediate case. Most of the studies they surveyed, including a number of non-academic reports, tended to favour private ownership. However, like other authors they warn against simplistic interpretations and suggest that competition might be more important than ownership. On the other hand, competition may not be crucially important for costs, because many sucessful public providers have been monopolies. The notion that competition is in general beneficial for public firm efficiency has recently also been disputed by Nelson (1990).

Table 2.2 (see Appendix) provides a new overview of the empirical literature, including 50 studies which explicitly refer to costs or productivity.[14] To give a more complete picture, it includes a limited number of second-hand sources as well, which are clearly distinguished with a reference to the survey in question. To reduce the risk of repeating earlier misinterpretations, each second-hand source is cited in at least two surveys and only if it is obvious what criterion of performance has been used.[15] However, it is worth mentioning that the proportion of reports favouring private ownership might have been reduced thereby, not least because of the fairly large number of non-refereed articles and reports in Borcherding *et al.*

In a majority of the cases cited, public production is either no worse than private production or is even superior. However, there are some notable differences between industries. Cost efficiency seems to be higher under private ownership in the bus industry, in housing, hospitals and health care and refuse, while ownership is irrelevant, or the reverse is true, in electrical utilities, insurance, railways and water utilities. In particular, evidence seems to suggest that the public sector performs at least as efficiently in electrical utilities and water, while refuse collection is cheaper if contracted out to private firms. The high frequency of industries in which private ownership is not cheaper suggests that there may be sources of private-sector inefficiency which have not been given due attention, but it may also depend on public firms giving a strong and possibly excessive emphasis on commercial objectives.

In the light of the analysis in the previous section, high costs might in many industries depend on non-commercial objectives rather than mismanagement or bad technology. For example, it is not surprising that bus services and hospitals often tend to be cheaper to run under private ownership.[16]

The effect of ownership on technical efficiency has also been approached by looking at the fate of privatized firms. In their analysis of early privatization in Britain, Vickers and Yarrow (1988) expect privatization to increase cost-efficiency in firms like Amersham, British Aerospace, Cable and Wireless, Enterprise Oil and Jaguar, which operate in fairly competitive industries, but they criticize the creation of private monopolies. Moreover, they argue that many objectives could have been reached without privatization as well.

Comparing the performance of the same firm under different forms of ownership may be misleading if privatization has taken place by the end of a recession. However, Martin and Parker (1993) have compared performance throughout the business cycle, taking into consideration that firms often tended to increase their productivity after the announcement of a privatization.[17] It turns out that six firms experienced a declining productivity growth in four years after privatization, while two other firms did not perform better. As they conclude, 'it is difficult to sustain unequivocally the hypothesis that private ownership is more efficient than nationalisation' (Martin and Parker 1993: 16).

Given Vickers' and Yarrow's (1988) conjecture on the impact of competition, it can be noted that of the firms working under competitive pressures, British Aerospace improved its performance, but it is doubtful whether the same can be said of Jaguar. Rolls-Royce experienced a relative decline in productivity growth as compared to the rest of the economy. Interestingly enough, a number of the firms even experienced a deterioration of profitability, although it could be expected that commercial objectives should lead to better performance in this respect.

SOME CONCLUDING REMARKS

Profit maximization may provide inadequate quality; cost differences may reflect income distribution or working conditions rather than technical efficiency. Therefore, it is often the case that firms should not minimize costs in a narrow sense. Given this potential contradiction between welfare maximization and cost minimization, we might expect overwhelming evidence showing that private ownership always leads to lower costs. However, this is not the case. The fact that public production is not unequivocally more expensive can mean that the price that we have to pay for considering non-commercial objectives has been exaggerated.

Unfortunately, the cost comparison may also reflect the fact that public firms are too often as commercial as private firms. This tendency may have been reinforced by the restructuring of public services in cases when they are not privatized. Depending on the nature of the external objectives, a public-sector firm or organization should be allowed to be either more or less autonomous. More could have been said on practical implementation, but it may be less utopian to get a well-educated and responsible management than to reverse the present trend to privatize.

The European Union is neutral towards privatization, and the Treaty of Rome acknowledges the fact that competition is not always feasible. On the one hand, firms from different countries should not be discriminated against, and public works of a certain size should be subject to competitive bidding. Outlawing long-term customer relationships might turn out to be an obstacle to a well-organized public service. Open and tacit collusion is forbidden, but co-operative R&D agreements are exempted. It may even be possible to agree upon joint exploitation of gains but not joint marketing. However, in practice, the policy of the European Union and its member states has been to encourage mergers in order to create giants supposedly strong enough to compete with Japanese and US firms. In Finland, which joined the EU in 1995, state-owned companies will be privatized with the explicit purpose to make mergers easier.

As our critical discussion shows, mergers are unlikely to improve performance. Moreover, the public- and labour-managed firms' unfavourable reputation is not supported by research. Therefore, to encourage mergers and to privatize is a misguided industrial policy with a bias which is reinforced by deregulation, reduced social security and cuts in public consumption. To merge large firms while local authorities or networks of small firms are forced to conform to inflexible rules about entry and bidding is to stand competition policy on its head.

The Single European Act represents a policy reversal as compared to the EC's earlier and more centralist approach to intervention. According to the principle of subsidiarity, the EU intervenes only when an issue cannot be decided at a lower level of authority (Bianchi 1992). This now means that a country can opt out from the Social Chapter while the EU still imposes, for example, competitive tendering on local authorities. However, it could be argued that local communities are strengthened by centralized decisions on social protection and standards about safety and the environment, but not by rigid rules which cause obstacles to public provision.

Another case for rethinking about the level at which decisions are to be made is provided by public-sector firms operating in several countries. For example, what is called privatization and deregulation in Finland will in fact make a bus company owned by the State Railways in Sweden one of the major operators. Even if such a company is accountable to the elected authorities in its home country, it is likely to operate as a private firm in Finland. To overcome such difficulties, multinational and democratically elected bodies should exert the ultimate control. In some cases, public firms operating on a European level might even be needed, because otherwise it may become increasingly difficult for public firms to pursue non-commercial objectives succesfully. In such cases, the EU should represent the owner.

APPENDIX

Table 2.2 Relative efficiency of private and public ownership – a summary

Author	*Country*	*G*	*ND*	*P*	*Source*
Airlines					
Davies (1971, 1977)	Australia	—	—	x	*
Forsyth and Hocking (1980)	Canada	—	x	—	*
Gillen, Oum and Tretheway (1990)	Canada	x	—	—	*
Bus Services					
Heseltine and Silcock (1990)	UK	—	—	x	*
Fazioli, (1992)	Italy	—	x		*
McGuire and Van Gott (1984)	US	—		x	*
White[b] (1990)	UK	—	—	x	*
Cement					
Cakman and Zaim (1992)	Turkey	—	x	—	*
Electrical Utilities					
Atkinson and Halvorsen (1986)	US	—	x	—	*
Färe, Grosskopf and Logan (1985)	US	x	—	—	*
Foreman-Peck and Waterson (1985)	UK	—	x	—	*
Hausman and Neufield (1991)	US	x	—	—	*
Meyer (1975)	US	x	—	—	*
Moore (1970)[c]	US		x	—	*
Neuberg (1977)		x	—	—	*
Pescatrice and Trapani (1980)	US	x	—	—	*
Peters (1992)[d]	US	x	—	—	*
Spann (1977)	US	—	x	—	*
Yunker (1975)	US	—	x	—	B, BV, M, Y
Hospitals and Health Care[e]					
Arrington and Haddock (1990)[f]	US	x	—	—	*
Becker and Sloan (1985)	US	—	x	—	*
Clarkson (1972)	US	—	—	x	*
Lindsay (1976)	US	x	—		*
Nyman and Bricker (1989)	US	—	x	—	*
Rushing (1974)	US	—	x	—	*
Sintonen, (1988)	Finland	—	x		*
Wilson and Jadlow (1982)	US	—	—	x	*
Insurance (Sales, Servicing and Processing)					
Finsinger (1984)	(W) Ger	x	—	—	*
Frech (1976)	US	—	—	x	*
Railways					
Caves and Christensen (1980)	Canada	—	x	—	*
Caves, Christensen, Swanson and Tretheway, (1982)	Canada and US	x	—	—	B, BV

Table 2.2 continued

Author	*Country*	*G*	*ND*	*P*	*Source*
Refuse Collection					
Bennett and Johnson (1979)	US	—	—	x	*
Collins and Downes (1977)	US	—	x	—	BPS, BV
Hirsch (1965)[g]	US	—	x	—	*
Kemper and Quigley (1976)[h]	US	—	x	x	BPS, BV
Kitchen (1976)	Canada	—		x	*
Pier, Vernon and Wicks (1974)	US	x	—	—	*
Pommerehne (1976)	Switzerland	—	—	x	B, BPS, Y
Savas (1977)	US	—	x	—	*
Spann (1977)	US	—	—	x	*
Stevens (1978)	US	—	—	x	*
Social Care					
Knapp and Missakoulis (1982)	UK	x	—	—	*
Knapp (1988)[i]	UK	—	x	—	*
Judge (1988)	UK	—	—	x	*
Water Utilities					
Bruggink	US	x	—	—	*
Byrnes, Grosskopf and Hayes (1986)	US	—	x	—	*
Crain and Zardkoohi (1978)	US	—	—	x	*
Feigenbaum and Teeples (1983)	US	—	x	—	*
Lynk (1993)	UK	x	—	—	*
Mann and Mikesell (1976)[j]	US	x	—	—	BPS, B, BV, Y
Teeples and Glyer (1987)	US	—	x	—	*
Universities					
de Groot, McMahon and Volkwein (1991)	US	—	x	—	*

Notes

Explanation of symbols: G = public production superior; ND = no difference or ambiguous results; P = private production superior. An asterisk refers to a first-hand source. B, BPS, BV, M and Y refer to articles cited by Boyd (1986). Borcherding, Pommerehne and Schneider (1982), Boardman and Vining (1979), Millward (1982) and Yarrow (1986) respectively.

a) The public firm (Air Canada) has lower unit costs, but more excess capacity.
b) This study shows that privatization has brought about lower costs, but it also reports that welfare has been reduced in some areas, and that the outcome has always been a reduction in the use of public transport.
c) Borcherding *et al.* (1983) interpret this source as less favourable for public production rather than neutral.
d) Strictly speaking, the original source is an unpublished report from 1992, which is cited by its author in Peters (1993).
e) In most American studies, the border-line is drawn between proprietary and non-profit institutions; the latter often seem less efficient, but only part of them are public. The British studies (see also under Social Care) tend to give a favourable picture of the efficiency of non-profit maximizing (voluntary) services, but they are counted among the private firms.

Notes to Table 2.2 continued

f) Average costs per bed are lower in non-profit hospitals, but on the other hand they have a larger number of employees per bed and longer average length of stay. On balance, non-profit institutions are reported to be superior in terms of benefits to society, but Herzlinger and Krasker (1987), which Arrington and Haddock (1990) criticize, reach the opposite conclusion.

g) Yarrow (1986) cites this study as favouring private ownership. However, as pointed out also by Bruggink (1982), Borcherding *et al.* (1982), Millward (1982) and Boardman and Vining (1989), he finds no significant differences in costs between private and public firms.

h) According to Borcherding *et al.* (1982), municipal collection is more expensive than contracting, but private non-franchise collection is more expensive than municipal collection. They interprete this as favouring private firms, but Boardman and Vining (1989) count this as an example of no difference or ambiguous results.

i) Knapp draws the *tentative* conclusion that private and voluntary child care employ more efficient 'technologies' of care, but the number of qualifications that he adds make us, hesitatingly, count the results as ambiguous.

j) Borcherding *et al.* (1982) give the opposite interpretation, but we follow Crain and Zardkoohi (1978), Boyd (1986), Yarrow (1986) and Boardman and Vining (1989). The original source is Mann, P.C. and Mikesell, J.L. (1976) 'Ownership and Water Systems Operation', *Water Resources Bulletin*, 12: 995–1004.

ACKNOWLEDGEMENTS

Comments from participants at the Crete Workshop on 'Competitiveness, Subsidiarity and Objectives: Issues for European Industrial Strategy' are gratefully acknowledged. The final version was prepared when the author was visiting the University of Warwick.

NOTES

1 A more detailed description of objectives imposed on state owned companies in some European countries can be found in Parris *et al.* (1987); for a discussion of Third World countries, see Singh (1992) and Ramanadham (1988).

2 This definition is not completely uncontroversial. With sufficient dispersion, it may be possible to control a firm without owning a majority of the shares. This raises the issue of what is the optimal degree of public ownership if the objective is to make an industry reflect the preferences of citizens. However, this question will be ignored.

3 As Bös points out, many public firms in Germany are actually owned by the regional authorities (Ländern), and they have been reluctant to privatize even when under Conservative rule.

4 A more detailed examination of the reasons for privatization, in particular in Britain, can be found in Vickers and Yarrow (1988), Yarrow (1986) and Cullis and Jones (1986). For a discussion of privatization in Third World countries, see, for example, Singh (1992). The reasons put forward in Finland are outlined in the memorandum *Visio yksityistämisestä Suomessa* (1991). The performance of the the country's SOEs are described in *Valtionyhtiöt markkinataloudessa* (1989).

5 This motive was not present at the beginning and was criticized by the former Conservative PM Harold Macmillan as 'selling the family silver to pay the servants' (Lord Stockton as quoted by Cullis and Jones 1987).

6 'Rees uses the term *managerial and technological* efficiency for what is often referred to as cost efficiency. In this sense, a method is technologically more efficient than another if, for a given level of output, it absorbs less of at least one input and no more of any other; or alternatively if, with the same input levels, it produces more output' (Rees: 1984: 14).
7 A discussion of this trade-off can be found in Vickers and Yarrow (1998) or Bös (1991).
8 The threat of bankruptcy is usually seen as another reason why managers are more disciplined under private ownership. However, if this is the case, the efficiency gain should be traded off against the costs of closures and redundancies as less efficient firms are not able to survive.
9 The media reports in the UK in 1995 about newly privatized public utilities show that they tend to reduce their work-force, which is consistent with these findings. On the other hand, they also suggest that top management is becoming more rather than less expensive than under public ownership.
10 A report by Göran Leijonhufvud (*Dagens Nyheter*, 4 May 1991) illustrates the point that some cost reductions may be expensive. After the oil price shock in 1974–5, firms in Japan required greater efforts, which increased the frequency of sudden death (*'karoshi'*) due to excessively demanding work.
11 There is also some evidence from Finland suggesting that long waiting times might be the most important factor deterring car owners from using public transport. The quality of the network as a producer of mobility should be distinguished from the quality of the equipment, on which, for example, Dodgson and Katsoulacos (1988) focus.
12 Strictly speaking, it is not always true that a reduced frequency means that bus kilometres have been cut. In some cases they have even increased, because of cream skimming: the supply has increased where services have already been acceptable and decreased on unprofitable routes.
13 For example, non-profit-maximizing but private organizations have been classified in different ways. In the US, they have been classified as private because of a focus on testing the property rights theory, in particular in health care. Most studies confirm its predictions that profit-maximizing firms are more efficient. By contrast, studies made after the first privatization initiatives in Britain tended to classify (comparatively efficient) voluntary organizations as private.
14 For example, we have omitted Boardman and Vining's (1989) own investigations because of their focus on profitability, which turned out to be higher under private ownership. Their comparison includes industries like petroleum, food or tobacco, paper or wood and chemicals, where profitability may reflect market power.
15 An example of the advantage of checking sources is provided by Kitchen (1976), who evaluates competition rather than ownership. It would not be fair to classify the study as favouring private refuse collection, as many surveys have done, without mentioning that it points out that cost minimization is not necessarily appropriate in the industry in question. Boardman and Vining (1989) describe Edwards and Stevens (1978) as favouring private ownership, although they only compare different ways of regulating firms which are or may be private. Note j in Table 2.2 seems to offer another example.
16 Boardman and Vining (1989) criticize the health care studies for not giving due attention to quality. This bias may work either way, because it may well be the case that the private providers specialize in giving a high-quality service for well-off patients. Moreover, after recent reforms, public-sector organizations in many countries may even be relatively more likely to cut costs at the expense of quality.

17 In a more recent study, Martin and Parker (1993) have analysed the development of value added per employee hour in 11 British firms (British Airways, British Airports Authority, Britoil, British Gas, British Steel, British Aerospace, Jaguar, Rolls Royce, National Freight, Associated British Ports and British Telecom).

REFERENCES

Adams, W. and Brock J.W. (1989) *Dangerous Pursuits. Mergers and Acquisitions in the Age of Wall Street*, New York: Pantheon Books.

Arrington, B. and Haddock, C.C. (1990) 'Who Really Profits from Not-For-Profits?', *Health Services Research*, 25, 2: 291–304.

Atkinson, S. and Halvorsen, R. (1986) 'The Relative Efficiency of Public and Private Firms in a Regulated Environment: The case of U.S. Electric Utilities', *Journal of Public Economics* 29: 281–94.

Bartlett, W. Cable J. Estrin, S. Jones, D.C. and Smith, S.C. (1992) 'Labour Managed Firms and Private Firms in North-Central Italy: An Empirical Comparison', *Industrial and Labour Relations Review* 46, 1: 103–18.

Becker, E.R. and Sloan, F.A. (1985) 'Hospital Ownership and Performance', Economic Inquiry, 23, 1: 21–36.

Bennett, J.T. and Johnson, M.H. (1979) 'Public vs. Private Provision of Collective Goods and Services: Garbage Collection Revisited', *Public Choice*, 34: 55–63.

—— (1980) 'Tax Reduction Without Sacrifice: Private-Sector Production of Public Services', *Public Finance Quarterly*, 8, 4: 363–96.

Bianchi, P. (1992) 'Industrial Strategy and Structural Policies', in K. Cowling, and R. Sugden, *Current Issues in Industrial Economic Strategy*, Manchester and New York: Manchester University Press.

Bianchi, P. and Miller, L.M. (1994) 'Innovation, Collective Action and Endogeneous Growth: An Essay on Institutions and Structural Change', paper presented at the 1993 Birmingham Workshop on Industrial Economic Strategies for EU.

Boardman, A. and Vining, A. (1989) 'Ownership and Performance in Competitive Environments: A Comparison of the Performance of Private, Mixed and Share-Owned Enterprises', *Journal of Law and Economics* 32: 1–33.

Borcherding, T.E., Pommerehne, W.W. and Schneider, F. (1982) 'Comparing the Efficiency of Private and Public Production: The Evidence from Five Countries', *Zeitschrift für Nationalökonomie*, Suppl. 2: 127–56.

Bös, D. (1991) *Privatization – a Theoretical Treatment*. Oxford: Clarendon Press.

—— (1993) 'Privatization in Europe: A Comparison of Approaches', *Oxford Review of Economic Policy*, 9, 1: 94–111.

Boyd, C.W. (1986) 'The Comparative Efficiency of State Owned Enterprises', in A.R. Negandhi (ed.), *Multinational Corporations and State-Owned Enterprises: A New Challenge in International Business*, Greenwich, CT and London: Research in International Business and International Relations, JAI Press.

Bruggink, T.M. (1982) 'Public versus Regulated Private Enterprise in the Municipal Water Industry: A Comparison of Water Costs', *Quarterly Review of Economics and Business*, 22, 1: 111–25.

Byrnes, P., Grosskopf, S. and Hayes, K. (1976) 'Efficiency and Ownership: Further Evidence', *Review of Economics and Statistics*, 68, 2: 337–41.

Cable, J.R. and Machin, S.J. (1991) 'The Relationship Between Union Wage and Profitability Effects', *Economics Letters* 37, 3: 315–22.

Cakmak, E.H. and Zaim, O. (1992) 'Privatization and Comparative Efficiency of Public and Private Enterprise in Turkey. The Cement Industry', *Annals of Public and Cooperative Economy*, 63, 2: 271–84.

Caves, D.W. and Christensen, L.R. (1980) 'The Relative Efficiency of Public and Private Firms in a Competitive Environment: The Case of Canadian Railroads', *Journal of Political Economy*, 88, 5: 958–76.

Clark, A. (1990) 'Efficient Bargains and the McDonald-Solow Conjecture', *Journal of Labor Economics*, 8, 4: 502–28.

Clarkson, K.W. (1972) 'Some Implications of Property Rights in Hospital Management', *Journal of Law and Economics*, 15: 363–84.

Cowling, K. and Sugden, R. (1992) 'Industrial Strategy, Regulation and Democracy', paper presented at the 1992 *Warwick–Birmingham Summer Workshop on Industrial Economic Strategy*.

—— (1994) 'Industrial Strategy: Guiding Principles and European Context', in P. Bianchi, K. Cowling and R. Sugden (eds), *Europe's Economic Challenge*, London: Routledge.

Crain, W.M. and Zardkoohi, A. (1978) 'A Test of the Property Rights Theory of the Firm: Water Utilities in the United States', *Journal of Law and Economics*, 21, 2: 395–408.

Cullis, J.G. and Jones, P.J. (1987) *Microeconomics and the Public Economy: A Defence of Leviathan*, Oxford: Basil Blackwell.

Davies, D.G. (1971) 'The Efficiency of Public Versus Private Firms: The Case of Australia's Two Airlines', *Journal of Law and Economics*, 14: 149–65.

—— (1977) 'Property Rights and Economic Efficiency: The Australian Airlines Revisited', *Journal of Law and Economics*, 20: 223–6.

Davies, S., Lyons, B., Dixon, H. and Geroski, P. (1989) *Economics of Industrial Organisation*, London and New York: Longman.

De Fraja, G. (1991) 'Efficiency and Privatisation in Imperfectly Competitive Industries', *Journal of Industrial Economics* 39, 3: 311–21.

—— (1993) 'Productive Efficiency in Public and Private Firms', *Journal of Public Economics* 50, 1: 15–30.

De Fraja, G. and Delbono, F. (1990) 'Game Theoretic Models of Mixed Oligopoly', *Journal of Economic Surveys* 4, 1: 1–18.

de Groot, H., McMahon, W.W. and Volkwein, J.F. (1991) 'The Cost Structure of American Research Universities', *Review of Economic Statistics*, 73, 3: 424–31.

Delbono, F. and Denicolò, V. (1993) '*Regulating Innovative Activity: The Role of a Public Firm*', *International Journal of Industrial Organization* 11, 1: 1–154.

Deprins, D., Simar, L. and Tulkens, H. (1984) 'Measuring Labor-Efficiency in Post Offices', in M. Marchand, P. Pestieau and H. Tulkens (eds), *The Performance of Public Enterprises. Concepts and Measurement*, Amsterdam: North-Holland.

Dodgson, J.S. and Y. Katsoulacos (1988) 'Quality Competition in Bus Services. Some Welfare Implications of Bus Deregulation', *Journal of Transport Economics and Policy*, 22, 3: 263–82.

Domberger, S. and Piggott, J. (1986) 'Privatization Policies and Public Enterprise: A Survey', *Economic Record*, 62, 177: 145–62.

Dorman, P. (1994) '*Innovation, Entrepreneurship and Industrial Districts*', in P. Bianchi, K. Cowling and R. Sugden (eds) *Europe's Economic Challenge*, London: Routledge.

Eaton, B.C. and White, W.D. (1983) 'The Economy of High Wages: An Agency Problem', *Economica*, May, 50: 175–82.

Edwards, F.R. and Stevens, B.J. (1978) 'The Provision of Municipal Sanitation Services by Private Firms: An Empirical Analysis of the Efficiency of Alternative Market Structures and Regulatory Arrangements', *Journal of Industrial Economics*, 27, 2: 133–47.

Estrin, S. and Pérotin, V. (1991) 'Does Ownership Always Matter?', *International Journal of Industrial Organization* 9, 1: 1–170.

Färe, R., Grosskopf, S. and Logan, J. (1985) '*The Relative Performance of Publicly Owned and Privately Owned Electric Utilities*', *Journal of Public Economics* 26, 1: 89–106.

Fazioli, R. (1992) 'Cost Structure and Efficiency of the Italian Regional Bus Companies', *Institute of Economics and Finance*, Ferrara University (mimeo).

Feigenbaum, S. and Teeples, T. (1983) 'Public versus Private Water Delivery: A Hedonic Cost Approach', *Review of Economics and Statistics*, 65, 4: 672–8.

Finsinger, J. (1984) '*The Performance of Public Enterprises in Insurance Markets*', in M. Marchand, P. Pestieau and Henry Tulkens (eds), *The Performance of Public Enterprises: Concepts and Measurement*, Amsterdam: North-Holland.

Foreman-Peck, J.O. and Waterson, M. (1985) 'The Comparative Efficiency of Public and Private Enterprise in Britain: Electricity Generation Between the World Wars', *Economic Journal*, 95, Supplement: 83–95.

Forsyth, P.J. and R.D. Hocking (1980) 'Property Rights and Efficiency in a Regulated Environment: The Case of Australian Airlines', *Economic Record*, 56, January 182–5.

Frech, H.E. (1976) 'The Property Rights Theory of the Firm: Empirical Results from a Natural Experiment', *Journal of Political Economy*, 84, 1: 143–52.

Gillen, D.W., Oum, T.H. and Tretheway, M.W. (1990) 'Airline Cost Structure and Policy Implications', *Journal of Transport Economics and Policy*, 24, 1: 9–34.

Goodwin, P.B. (1993) 'Car Ownership and Public Transport Use: Revisiting the Interaction', *Transportation*, 27, 1: 21–33.

Goto, A. (1992) '*Collaborative Research in Japanese Manufacturing Industries – Innovations in R&D System?*', paper presented at the 1992 *Warwick–Birmingham Summer Workshop in Industrial Economic Strategy*.

Gravelle, H. (1984) 'Bargaining and Efficiency in Public and Private Sector Firms', in M. Marchand, P. Pestieau and H. Tulkens (eds), *The Performance of Public Enterprises: Concepts and Measurement*, Amsterdam: North-Holland.

Gunderson, M. (1979) 'Earning Differentials Between the Public and the Private Sectors', *Canadian Journal of Economics*, 12, 2: 228–42.

Haskel, J. and Szymanski, S. (1992) 'A Bargaining Theory of Privatization', *Annals of Public and Cooperative Economics* 63: 207–28.

Haskel, J. and Szymanski, S. (1993) 'Privatization, Liberalization, Wages and Employment: Theory and Evidence for the UK', *Economica* 60, May: 161–82.

Hausman, W.J. and Neufeld, J.L. (1991) 'Property Rights versus Public Spirit: Ownership and Efficiency of U.S. Electric Utilities Prior to Rate or Return Regulation', *Review of Economic Statistics*, 73, 3: 414–23.

Heseltine, P. and Silcock, D.T. (1990) 'The Effects of Bus Deregulation on Costs', *Journal of Transport Economics and Policy*, 24, 3: 239–54.

Herzlinger, R. and Krasker, W.S. (1987) 'Who Profits from Nonprofits?', *Harvard Business Review*, 65, 1: 93–106.

Hirsch, W.Z. (1965) 'Cost Functions of Urban Government Services: Refuse Collection', *Review of Economics and Statistics*, 47, 1: 87–92.

Jacquemin, A. (1988) 'Cooperative Agreements in R&D and European Industrial Policy', *European Economic Review* 32, 2/3 (Papers and Proceedings): 551–60.

Jenkinson, T. and Mayer, C. (1988) 'The Privatisation Process in France and the U.K', *European Economic Review* 32, Papers and Proceedings: 482–90.

Johnson, G.E., (1990) 'Work Rules, Featherbedding, and Pareto-optimal Union–Management Bargaining', *Journal of Labor Economics*, January, 1990, Part 2 (Essays in Honor of Albert Rees), 8, S237-S259.

Judge, K. (1988) 'Value for Money in British Residential Care Industry', in A.J.

Culyer, and B. Jönsson, *Public and Private Health Services. Complementarities and Conflicts*, Oxford: Basil Blackwell.

Katsoulacos, Y. and Nowell, E. (1994) 'European Community R&D-support: Effects on the Cooperative Behaviour of Firms', in P. Bianchi, K. Cowling and R. Sugden, (eds) *Europe's Economic Challenge*, London: Routledge.

Katz, L.F. and Summers, L.M. (1989) 'Industry Rents: Evidence and Implications', *Brookings Papers*: Microeconomics, 209–90.

Kay, J.A. and Thompson, D.J. (1986) 'Privatisation: A Policy in Search of a Rationale', *Economic Journal*, vol. 96, 1, 18–32.

Kitchen, H. (1976) 'A Statistical Estimation of an Operating Cost Function for Municipal Refuse Collection', *Public Finance Quaterly*, 4, 1: 56–76.

Knapp, M.R.J. and Missiakoulis, S. (1982) 'Inter-sectoral Cost Comparisons: Day Care for the Elderly', *Journal of Social Policy*, 11, 3: 335–54.

Knapp, M.R. (1988) 'The Relative Cost-Effectiveness of Public, Voluntary and Private Providers of Residential Child Care', pp in A.J. Culyer and B. Jönsson, *Public and Private Health Services. Complementarities and Conflicts*, Oxford: Basil Blackwell.

Lashmar, P. (1994) 'Going for Brokers?', *New Statesman & Society*, 10 June: 24–5.

Leijonhufvud, G. (1991) 'Övertidsjobb till döds', *Dagens Nyheter*, 4.5.

Lindsay, C.M. (1976) 'A Theory of Government Enterprise', *Journal of Political Economy*, 84, 5: 1061–77.

Lynk, E.L. (1993) 'Privatisation, Joint Production and the Comparative Efficiencies of Private and Public Ownership: The UK Water Industry Case', *Fiscal Studies*, 14, 2: 98–116.

Machin, S.J. (1991) 'Unions and the Capture of Economic Rents', *International Journal of Industrial Organization* 9, 2: 261–74.

Machin, S.J. and Stewart, M.B. (1990) 'Unions and the Financial Performance of British Private Sector Establishments', *Journal of Applied Econometrics*, 5, 4: 327–50.

MacPherson, D.A. (1990) 'Trade Unions and Labor's Share in U.S. Manufacturing Industries', *International Journal of Industrial Organization*, 8, 1: 143–52.

Marchand, M., Pestieau, P. and Henry Tulkens (1984) 'The Performance of Public Enterprises: Normative, Positive and Empirical Issues', in M. Marchand, P. Pestieau and H. Tulkens (eds), *The Performance of Public Enterprises: Concepts and Measurement*, Amsterdam: North-Holland.

Martin, S. and Parker, D. (1993) 'Privatisation and Economic Performance Throughout the UK Business Cycle', Research Centre for Industrial Strategy, The University of Birmingham, *Occasional Papers in Industrial Strategy*, 16, November.

Mayer, C. (1989) 'Public Ownership: Concepts and Applications', in D. Helm, Dieter (ed.) *The Economic Borders of the State*, Oxford: Clarendon Press.

McGuire, R.A. and Van Gott, T.N. (1984) 'Public versus Private Economic Activity: A New Look at School Bus Transportation', *Public Choice*, 43: 23–43.

Meyer, R.A. (1975) 'Publicly Owned versus Privately Owned Utilities: A Policy Choice', *Review of Economics and Statistics*, 57, 4: 391–9.

Millward, R. (1976) 'Price Restraint, Anti-inflation Policy and Public and Private Industry in the United Kingdom 1949–1973', *Economic Journal*, 86, June: 226–42.

—— (1982) 'The Comparative Performance of Public and Private Ownership', in Lord E. Roll (ed.) *The Mixed Economy*, London: Macmillan.

Moore, T.G. (1970) 'The Effectiveness of Regulation of Electric Utility Prices', *Southern Economic Journal*, 37, April: 365–75.

Nelson, R.A. (1990) 'The Effects of Competition on Publicly Owned Firms: Evidence from the Municipal Electric Industry in the U.S.', *International Journal of Industrial*

Organization, 8, 1: 37–52.

Neuberg, L.G. (1977) 'Two Issues in the Municipal Ownership of Electric Power Distribution Systems', *Bell Journal of Economics*, 8, Spring: 303–23.

Norton, E.C. and Staiger, D.O. (1994) 'How Hospital Ownership Affects Access to Care for the Uninsured', *Rand Journal of Economics*, 25, 1: 171–85.

Nyman, J.A. and Bricker, D.L. (1989) 'Profit Incentive and Technical Efficiency in the Production of Nursing Home Care', *Review of Economics and Statistics*, 71, 4: 586–94.

Parker, D. and Martin, S. (1994) 'The Impact of UK privatisation on Employment, Profits and the Distribution of Business Income', Research Centre for Industrial Strategy, The University of Birmingham, *Occasional Papers in Industrial Strategy*, 18, April.

Parris, H., Pestieau, P. and Saynor, P. (1987) *Public Enterprise in Western Europe*, London: Croom Helm.

Perelman, S. and Pestieau, P. (1988) 'Technical Performance in Public Enterprises. A Comparative Study of Railways and Postal Services', *European Economic Review*, 32, 2/3, Papers and Proceedings: 432–41.

Pescatrice, D.R. and Trapani, J.M. (1980) 'The Performance of Public and Private Utilities Operating in the United States', *Journal of Public Economics*, 13, 3: 259–76.

Peters, L.L. (1992) 'For-Profit and Non-Profit Firms: Limits of the Simple Theory of Attenuated Property Rights', *Review of Industrial Organization*, 8, 5: 623–34.

Pier, W.J., Vernon, R.B. and Wicks, J.H. (1974) 'An Empirical Comparison of Government and Private Production Efficiency'. *National Tax Journal*, 27, December: 653–6.

Pint, E.M. (1991) 'Nationalization vs. Regulation of Monopolies: The Effects of Ownership on Efficiency', *Journal of Public Economics* 44, 2: 131–64.

Ramanadham, V.V. (1988) *Public Enterprise and Income Distribution*, London and New York: Routledge.

Rees, R. (1984) *Public Enterprise Economics*, London: Weidenfeld & Nicholson.

—— (1988) 'Inefficiency, Public Enterprise and Privatisation', *European Economic Review* 32, Papers and Proceedings: 422–31.

Rosén, Å. (1990) 'Bargaining over Effort', Mimeo, London School of Economics and Political Sciences, Centre for Economic Performance, July.

Rushing, W. (1974) 'Differences in Profit and Non-Profit Organisations: A Study of Effectiveness and Efficiency in General Short-Stay Hospitals', *Administrative Science Quarterly*, 19, December: 49–74.

Savas, E.S. (1977) 'Policy Analysis for Local Government: Public vs. Private Refuse Collection', *Policy Analysis*, 3, 1: 49–74.

Schenk, H. (1994) 'European Industrial Policy – an assessment of main elements', paper presented for the 1994 *Lisbon Workshop on Objectives of European Industrial Policy*.

Shapiro, C. and Stiglitz, J.E. (1984) 'Equilibrium Unemployment as a Worker Discipline Device', *American Economic Review*, June, 74: 433–44.

Singh, A. (1992) 'Industrial Policy in the Third World in the 1990s: Alternative Perspectives', in K. Cowling and R. Sugden (eds), *Current Issues in Industrial Economic Strategy*, Manchester and New York: Manchester University Press.

Sintonen, H. (1988) 'Comparing the Productivity of Public and Private Dentistry', in A.J. Culyer and Bengt Jönsson (eds), *Public and Private Health Services. Complementarities and Conflicts*, Oxford: Basil Blackwell.

Spann, R.M. (1977) 'Public versus Private Provision of Public Services', in T.E. Borcherding (ed.), *Budgets and Bureaucrats*, Durham NC: Duke University Press.

Stevens, B.J. (1978) 'Scale, Market Structure, and the Cost of Refuse Collection', *Review of Economics and Statistics*, 60, 3: 438–48.

Swann, D. (1988) *The Retreat of the State Deregulation and Privatisation in the UK and US*, New York: Harvester Wheatsheaf.

Teeples, R. and Glyer, D. (1987) 'Cost of Water Delivery Systems: Specification and Ownership Effects', *Review of Economics and Statistics*, 69: 399–408.

Tirole, J. (1988) *The Theory of Industrial Organization*, Cambridge, MA and London: MIT Press.

Tyson, W.J. (1990) 'Effects of Deregulation on Service Co-ordination in the Metropolitan Areas', *Journal of Transport Economics and Policy*, 24, 3: 283–95.

Valtionyhtiöt markkinataloudessa (1989) Helsinki: Liiketaloustieteellinen Tutkimuslaitos (LTT).

Vickers, J. and Yarrow, G. (1988) *Privatization: An Economic Analysis*, Cambridge, MA: MIT Press.

—— (1991) 'Economic Perspectives on Privatization', *Journal of Economic Perspectives* 5, 2: 111–32.

Visio yksityistämisestä Suomessa 1990-luvulla (1991) Kauppa- ja teollisuusministeriö, Teollisuusosasto.

Waterson, M. (1993) 'Developments in Privatisation in the UK', Proceedings of the University of Vaasa, Discussion papers 159.

White, P.J. (1990) 'Bus Deregulation: A Welfare Balance Sheet', *Journal of Transport Economics and Policy*, 24, 3: 311–32.

Willner, J. (1992) 'To Create Competition Without Regulation: a Mixed Oligopoly With Endogeneous Cost Differences', in K. Cowling and R. Sugden (eds), *Current Issues in Industrial Economic Strategy*, Manchester and New York: Manchester University Press.

—— (1994a) 'Can Firms Be Too Cost Efficient? A Simple Model to Determine the Optimal Effort Level', Mimeo.

—— (1994b) 'Wage Bargaining and Policy Objectives in Markets With Public and Private Ownership', Mimeo.

—— (1994c) 'Welfare Maximisation With Endogeneous Average Costs', *International Journal of Industrial Organization*, 12, 3: 373–86.

Wilson, G.W. and Jadlow, J.M. (1982) 'Competition, Profit Incentives, and Technical Efficiency in the Provision of Nuclear Medicine Services', *Bell Journal of Economics*, 13, 2: 472–82.

Yarrow, G. (1986) 'Privatization in Theory and Practice', *Economic Policy*, 2: 324–64.

Zetterberg, J. (1992) 'Effects of Changed Wage Setting Conditions on Male–Female Wage Differentials in the Swedish Public Sector', Department of Economics, University of Uppsala, Working paper 8.

3

SUBSIDIARITY AND ITS SIGNIFICANCE

Patrizio Bianchi

THE PRINCIPLE OF SUBSIDIARITY AND THE TREATY OF THE UNION

Subsidiarity is the most abstract concept introduced in the recent political debate in Europe. With the parallel principle of mutual recognition, subsidiarity was unknown in the previous Treaty of Rome; it emerges implicitly in the European Single Act (ESA), and becomes a central pillar of the constitutional definition of the Treaty of Maastricht.

Subsidiarity has played the most important role in the discussions at the two Community Summits at Birmingham and at Edinburgh, held to prepare the transition from the European Community (EC) to the Union (EU). From those discussions emerged the present definition of the basic principles of the new European Union, stemming from the previous experience of integration among European nation-states. Article B of the Common Provisions – Title I – of the Treaty of the European Union (TEU) expressly mentions that

> the objectives of the Union shall be achieved as provided in this Treaty . . . while respecting the principle of subsidiarity

This principle is implicitly defined in article 3B of Title II, 'Treaty Establishing the European Community. Part One Principles':

> In areas which do not fall within its exclusive competence, the Community shall take action, in accordance with the principle of subsidiarity, only if and in so far as the objectives of the proposed action cannot be sufficiently achieved by the Member States and can therefore, by reason of the scale or effects of the proposed action, be better achieved by the Community.
>
> Any action by the Community shall not go beyond what is necessary to achieve the objectives of this Treaty.

This principle is used as a central concept of the new Treaty, for establishing at what institutional level decisions concerning the development of the Community action must be managed. The Treaty mentions the European and the national levels, but, by extension, it involves also the regional and municipal levels.

Subsidiarity tackles the core of the problem of the Union's development, that of sovereignty. This means specifying the nature and significance of the relationship among different levels of institutional bodies, having the power of representing political, economic, ethnic, religious and cultural aspirations and interests and of deciding proper action.

This concept is, hence, a constituent principle for the Union and a powerful instrument for managing the relations among policy-makers. It has juridical value, because the decisions assumed within and throughout the Union cannot be in contradiction with article 3B of the Treaty. It is also a necessary principle, because its application cannot limit the power of the Commission, but also the Commission cannot decide on behalf of the national and regional governments, except for those areas that are explicitly listed as exclusively within the constituency of the European level institutions.

Nevertheless, subsidiarity is still an ambiguous concept. It is applicable every time a potential conflict emerges between the Community and the national levels; it concerns the constitutional nature of the Union and marks the difference between the new European Union and the previous European Economic Community.

Therefore, in order to understand the role and significance of subsidiarity, we must analyse the specificity of the European integration process and of the institutional construction that has been created to drive this process. We look into the meaning of the parallel principle of mutual recognition and at the constitutional nature of the transition from the previous Economic Community to the present Union.

THE EEC'S INSTITUTIONAL CHARACTERISTICS AND THE TREATY OF ROME

The European Community has institutional characteristics which do not directly correspond to either a federation of states or an international organization. This peculiar character has been confirmed also by the TEU. In fact it cannot be compared to a federation in which sovereignty is moved from the member states to the federation, and the federal institutions are given superior legislative, executive and judicial tasks, not only with reference to activity concerning relations among states, but also in relation to activities between individuals within countries participating in the federation. The EC also cannot be reduced to an international organization to which fully sovereign states attribute the power of co-ordination of specific international activities, but not authority with respect to relations between individual citizens within the member states.

In the EC there are present at the same time elements of a federation and of an international organization. In a federation there is the presence of a central authority of a supra-national character and some of the corresponding powers capable of developing and realizing its own body of laws valid within the borders of the member states. In an international organization, decision-making power is held by an intergovernmental body, and each member agrees to some general rules, but it maintains its own body of laws.

Both the European Single Act, and the TEU strengthen the role of the European Council by establishing the leading role of the Council of Ministers within a general framework of consolidating European institutions.

On the other hand, it is not only the procedural characteristics of a constitutional nature, as set out in the basic text, the Treaty of Rome and its amendments, and also the ESA, that create the principal source of community law. There are also evolutionary characteristics giving rise to substantial modifications in the institutional relations, that derive from the extension of powers of the Commission and the judicial interpretation of the norms of the Treaty which led to the modifications of the decision-making models internal to the community itself.

THE INSTITUTIONAL STRUCTURE AND DECISION-MAKING PROCESSES OF THE COMMUNITY

The original institutional profile of the EC was largely influenced by the preceding experiences of the European Coal and Steel Community (ECSC), the Organization for European Economic Cooperation (OEEC) and the Council of Europe (Urwin, 1991: 19, 27, 35). The historical reference thus retraces the idea of an international organization that nevertheless tends to become a federal state. The central structure of the Community's institutional apparatus is of 'French' derivation. Decisions are validated by the Council, a body which is representative of the national governments; national sovereignty is maintained through the role assigned to the Commission, a technocratic body, whose job it is to carry out and supervise the decisions of a central administrative structure.

It has to be noted that in the 'French' model there is no room for subsidiarity, because the power of representing the public interest and the governing is centralized at the highest institutional level. The sovereign can transfer some operational functions to the lower levels, but the source of legitimation remains attached to the institutional organ representing the nation-state. In some cases, the nation-state can transfer some powers to a supra-national organization, but this organization derives its legitimation and power from a specific delegation of the nation-states.

The High Authority of the ECSC and the Commission of the EC are organs of execution and supervision of the express wishes of the Council, that act as a collective president, while the Parliament remains the Assembly of an international organization and the Court of Justice remains a body of interpretation of the Treaty.

In designing the profile of the institutions of the European Community, the role of Monnet, first Commissioner of the French Planning Commission, was crucial. Monnet and the pioneers of the Europeanist Movement had clearly in mind that what appeared possible in terms of economic co-operation clearly was not possible in terms of political integration. Instead of advocating a complex project of political union, Monnet proposed a functionalist approach. His functionalist method sought to identify and isolate specific problems, to be tackled and solved through the creation of a specific institution, managed by a neutral, highly qualified bureaucracy, in order to internalize and settle specific conflicts among nation-states, and hence, induce the condition for positive political co-operation. Thus, steel and coal – the core of German rearmament – were managed by an international authority according to common rules; then, nuclear power, the nub of the new military and civilian power, was put under common control; agricultural production and farm incomes were also rapidly deemed matters of common decision, because it was thought necessary to stabilize the social basis of the Western European countries in the period of the Cold War; finally, the progressive rebate of customs tariffs was commonly regulated to avoid the possibility that structural adjustments connected to opening national markets might generate social disease.

Thus, the possibility of the easy assimilation of these bodies to those of a nation-state or those of a federal state fades away. The European Community was designed according to the French-style centrally administered unitary state, but the European Economic Community was neither a nation-state, nor a federal state, simply because it was not a state at all, but an economic initiative.

The Commission is not the 'government' of the Community, and its president is not a sort of Prime Minister of the Community, as Commissioner Hallstein asserted before the conflict with the French government in 1963. The Commission has power of initiative in Community policy-making, but the actions must be approved and thus ratified by the Council. The Commission is the 'Guardian of the Treaty', acting contemporaneously as both a proposing and consultative body to the Council of Ministers. It is an organ created by the Treaty that, after the compromise of Luxembourg, has the final say in decisive moments on single subjects. The Council of the Heads of State is a body not outlined by the Treaty of Rome, that assumes now the constitutional functions regarding substantial choices.

However, the Commission is endowed with the important power of initiative that pushed this body to continuously widen its sphere of action, multiplying the activities in a variety of interventions that were then destroyed by the White Book which in turn brought about the approval of the ESA.

Just as the Commission is not a government, but its activities arise from the combination of the actions and the interlacing of the two instances, supra-national and inter-governmental, neither is Parliament the simple transposition to the Community level of a national legislative body. The 'legislature' of the Community was defined as the inter-governmental body (the Council of Ministers), leaving to the Assembly, composed of delegates of the respective national parliaments, the functions of consultation, the censoring of actions taken by the Commission in exceptional cases, and control over the budget. The transformation into the European Parliament with direct election did not change this situation. It was only with the ESA that the recognition of powers of legislative interaction with the council emerged. On the other hand, this consultative role was shared with the Economic and Social Committee, which is the aggregation of explicit specific interests.

The institutional structure of the Community is in a certain sense 'misleading', because the supra-national function draws its legitimation from national sovereign powers still clearly exercised by the national governments. Yet in the context of limited, or better yet planned, delegated sovereignty, there were no clear sanctions against infringements or resistance to the common action that was agreed (Nugent 1991).

The transplanted vision of the 'French state' then proved to be fallacious because a hierarchy did not exist between the vertex and the inferior levels. The 'supra-national' organism does not have the exclusive power to exercise force within the administrative realm. The administrators even have the power of interdiction in relation to the action of the administrative leaders, in a mechanism of intersecting vetoes that block decisions and the recognition of initiative. Additionally, the long economic crisis of the 1970s highlighted once again the delicate relationship between representatives of collective interests and defence of economic interests at the national level.

The ESA introduced adjustments in this organizational structure and in fact took away from individual governments the powerful weapon of veto, exercisable in conditions of unanimous vote. But, above all, the ESA implicitly introduced the two principles, subsidiarity and reciprocal intervention, that reversed the general perspective of Community decision-making, passing from a 'French' vision to a 'German' vision. In a 'German' perspective, which is essentially federal-orientated, a centre endowed with strong initiative capabilities and foreign representation placed individual members in competition among themselves, favouring an evolutionary process in which the more efficient define the common norms. This vision places the emphasis on the characteristics of initiative and control of the Commission, establishing by definition an alliance among 'strong' subjects acting within the administrative territory.

Germany is the only federal country in Western Europe, and its experience has become a cornerstone for redesigning the institutional profile of the Community. In a federal state legitimation of public action stems from the bottom up. Powers are attached to the lower institutional levels, and the powers of the federal institutions are listed and exclusive. Also, in the case of existing federal states, subsidiarity does not play a constituent role, because allocation of functions among central, state and local governments is usually constitutionally defined and a supreme court assures the solution of potential conflicts among institutional levels (CEPR 1993: 28).

The crux of the institutional profile of the European Community is that it is a unique institution in which supra-national characteristics and institutions combine with inter-governmental characteristics and institutions (Nugent 1991: 383). It is an evolutionary institution, which is attempting to tackle the difficult task of going beyond the national institutions without overcoming the nation-states themselves.

For this peculiarity, the relaunching of the European integration that occurred in the mid-1980s needed to identify principles for favouring integration among different national institutions and co-ordination among different levels of decision-making.

Thus, we have two dimensions of normative integration:

1 horizontal: among nation-state institutions, and
2 vertical: among various levels of institutions from European to regional ones.

These two dimensions cannot be tackled by using the previous instruments given in the Treaty of Rome.

THE SINGLE ACT AND NORMATIVE INTEGRATION

The complex Community procedural mechanism has delineated through the years a system of reciprocal interdiction which has often resulted in a muddying of the common decision-making process. Obviously, the relationship between Community institutions and member states regarding the subject of normative harmonization is more delicate terrain; this is a necessary step in the passage from a customs union to a common market, in which not only goods, but also capital and people can move; clearly this normative harmonization is extremely complex because it involves adjustments in the institutional and administrative apparatus which different countries stratified over time, making them defining elements of their civil development.

The Single Act became the crucial moment of institutional reform of the Community because it acted on mechanisms of relations between community institutions and member countries. Consequently the ESA is not only a general programme to achieve the objective missed in the 1960s and 1970s – the passage from a customs union to an economic union – but it is rather a process of constitutional reform that reinforces the evolutionary nature of the process of integration.

The transition from a customs union to a common market is a very complex institutional change because it implies the weakening of the bond between the development of capitalism and the nation-state which characterized European history over the last two centuries.

The customs union is a policy mechanism for redefining economic relations among countries, allowing a country to open up to external trade while regulating the internal effects of this change; nevertheless it is assumed that the association of two or more countries, united by the common interest of excluding a third country with more efficient production processes, avoids the integration of the production structures which would lead to a loss of the respective national identities. The internal institutions not only remain unchanged, but in a certain sense they are reinforced in the determination of a principle of common centralized regulation within the respective national governments. Possible internal crises in the two countries reinforce this national character because the weak subjects of the two countries request protection from their national government against changes which have negative consequences for them.

Therefore, if the creation of a customs union demands the removal of tariff barriers, an economic union demands the removal of non-tariff barriers, which nevertheless are none other than the institutional differences accumulated in the different countries. These elements appeared with great clarity in the internal evolution of the Community from the crisis of the 1970s to the turnaround of the 1980s.

The transition to the economic union implies, then, a programme of harmonization in the norms that regulate the productive activity in the individual countries, which would permit the organization of production aimed at the market internal to the Community. The passage to the economic union implies not so much the transfer of productive activity from one country to another but a coherent reorganization of production with a reorganization of the extension of the market: the market becomes a single one, therefore production reorganizes itself within the territory of the economic union in reference to the market unified by the shared regulatory principle.

The process of normative harmonization can be conducted in two different ways: constitutionally or evolutionary. In the constitutional mode, the member countries agree among themselves a particular time to define and apply new common norms that override and substitute the national norms; a new central authority has to be established to manage the common rules and to control the observance of the common norms. In the evolutionary mode, general procedures are agreed among member states to induce the member countries to interact among themselves to affirm new common rules, and for successive adjustments, to reach the reciprocal assimilation of the existing national norms into a new common norm.

Article 100 of the Treaty of Rome referred to a constitutional mechanism. It affirmed:

> The Council, deciding unanimously on the proposal of the Commission establishes directives aimed at the reconciliation (bringing together) of the legislative, regulatory and administrative dispositions of the member states which have a direct incidence on the institutions or on the functioning of the common market.[1]

With the ESA it is recognized that the previous phase, based exclusively on constitutional procedures, did not work in that the individual member countries resisted normative integration, not only by using the right of veto in the areas of negotiation in which they felt weak, but also by not applying the actions defined at the community level.

It was then decided to render the 'constitutional' mechanism more rapid and efficacious, removing the unanimous vote and therefore taking away the right of veto, and moreover permitting the Commission to assume an initiative of vast range, defining a precise picture of directives of harmonization, to which the member countries had to adapt within the transition period which ended in 1992.

Nevertheless it appears evident that this reformatory action of the principle established by article 100 is not sufficient and with particular reference to the elimination of the technical barriers the principle of mutual recognition was adopted as the general principle. By introducing this principle to tackle the problem of horizontal integration, the procedural mode for integrating national institutions becomes more evolutionist. The White Book of the Commission of the completion of the internal market, arranged for the meeting of the European Council in Milan, 28–9 June 1985, states that: 'the Commission intends to design and implement its action, in general, no longer insisting on the concept of harmonization, but rather on that of mutual recognition and of equivalence' (CEE 1985: 7).[2]

The principle of mutual recognition signifies that a good, produced according to the laws of a member country, has free access to all the other member countries. This principle entered into Community law with the noted judgment Cassis de Dijon, discussed by the Court of Justice in 1978 (Al-Agraa 1990: 154), whose importance greatly surpassed the narrow realm of technical norms.

At the end of the 1970s the path of technical harmonization of products and services was entrusted to the capacity of the community bureaucracy to define European norms that the member countries had to unanimously accept. However, with judgments like that of Cassis de Dijon (Judgment of 20 February, 1979, Rewe-zentral AG c. Bundesmonopolverwaltung fuer Branntwein – causa 120–78) the Court of Justice recognized that the German authorities could not prohibit the import from France of an alcoholic drink, even if this is of a gradation inferior to that usually admitted in Germany, if this drink is legally produced and sold in another member state of the Community.

MUTUAL RECOGNITION AND QUALIFIED MAJORITY

The ESA fully assumed this principle of mutual recognition, establishing that 'the Council can decide that the norms enforced in a member country must be recognized as equivalent to those applicable in another'.

The principle is applied to the technical standards placed on goods, but is extended to services, like banks and services, professional activities, etc. Therefore, the importance of this approach is that controls are no longer exerted at the entrance into the national market to verify admissibility on the basis of national norms regarding consumer protection, or the environment, but are applied at the origin. This implies that in the single market products having different levels of quality compete with one another, and this results in the substitution of a spatial segmentation of the market with a qualitative segmentation of the market.

The possibility of placing on the national level an efficient public organization which defines technical standards and confirms the conformity of national products to such standards then becomes a very powerful means of collective competition for the firms of that country selling their goods in the single market and segmenting the market in their favour. The capability of a national organization to create the technical norms becomes, therefore, the instrument that activates an evolutionary process of technical standardization at the Community level. Thus, countries having a national industry capable of creating paths of technical innovation and through these of competition no longer based on price but on quality, become substantially advantaged if they have public organizations capable of creating national norms compatible with the interests of national industry, specifying norms that in fact assume prominence at the Community level.

Thus, a process of institutional competition has emerged, with individual governments and local authorities seeking to establish rules that favour the firms and the subjects that they recognize while participating in the process of normative definition at Union level. Therefore, a link between public authority and private interests is re-established even in a context of a common market.

Padoa Schioppa (1987), in the Report that outlined the strategy for the evolution of the economic system of the EC, specified that 'officially adopting the principle of reciprocal recognition suggested by the White Book, the Community achieved a very important change in its strategy of effective dismantling of the non-tariff barriers'. Moreover, it is added to underline the institutional scope of this assumption of the principle of mutual recognition:

> The White Book marks the passage from a monolithic conception of the process of integration, according to which the legislation and the national powers become fully substituted by community powers, to a pluralistic conception, pragmatic and federalist, in which the national legislation will become, not substituted but, framed within a common view such as to ensure the respect of several minimum criteria selected by the Community.
>
> (Padoa Schioppa 1987: 110)

The assumption of this principle of mutual recognition is accompanied by the removal of the unanimous vote for the majority of the decisions having a constitutional character, and the introduction of minimum standards on the subjects of security, health and environment that create the minimum limits within which the individual national legislatures can locate themselves.

Thus, we can assume that the capability of a country to assimilate the Community directives, and to carry out a sort of institutional competition through the issuing of its own ameliorative norms, must depend on the capacity of its internal productive and administrative apparatus to rapidly adjust itself to any new standards proposed. Thus, on the basis of the system of voting accepted, a general directive must be accepted by at least half of the productive and administrative structure of the Community which is ready to receive it.

In any case, the disposition of general rules which are ratified by the Commission and the Council establishes the inferior limits and creates an evolutionary process of institutional integration that nevertheless is guided by the most efficient countries, and powers of interdiction on the part of members who are slower in the adjustment process no longer exist.

As we have identified, a new procedure for normative integration among member states emerges, making it necessary to specify the power relations among different levels of decision-making. This allocation of functions cannot be given once and for all because of the evolutionary nature of the integration process.

THE ORIGINS OF THE PRINCIPLE OF SUBSIDIARITY

Just as Padoa Schioppa points out, the principle of subsidiarity is added to the principle of reciprocal recognition. The two principles are strictly interdependent and it is impossible to understand properly the former if we cannot understand the latter. Padoa Schioppa argues that subsidiarity means that

> the highest levels of government must exert only the functions that ensure public goods that cannot be supplied efficiently by lower levels.

> The list of these goods must certainly include unlimited access of all suppliers to the common market, minimum standards of security and stability, a minimum of protection for consumers and investors. Consequently, the Community must intervene only when it is the only level of government capable of supplying public goods that are such for the entire area of the community.[3]
>
> (Padoa Schioppa 1987: 111)

In this restricted definition the principle of subsidiarity is not at all new. It was already clearly specified in Smith, just as it is firmly rooted in the free-trade tradition.

For example, Smith recalled that the sovereign must guarantee the external and internal defence, just as the public works that make communication possible; yet Smith himself also introduces references to the public regulation of innovation, through patents and copyrights, and certification of the quality of products, over and above the controls against attempts of monopolization; in addition he asserted that education also had the characteristics of a public good (Smith, 1976, Part Four, and V, I, 1, 689; V, I, 708; V, 1, 723).

Along these same lines Lord Robbins recalled that there exists a continuity in English free-trade thought, from Smith to Keynes, that allows the State functions of intervention that overcome specific individual interests in the collective interest.[4]

Under the unitary state the extension of the activation and fruition of these public goods coincides with the area of extension of the sovereignty of the authority of government; thus the nation-state affirms itself, extending to all its territory common norms (exercised on the basis of its power of exclusive use of force) but also offering common services having the characteristics of public goods like defence or public order. On the other hand the political specificity of the governmental authority and its collective legitimation depend on the variety of public goods that the governmental authority is able to guarantee to its citizens.[5]

In a federal state the central apparatus of the federation assumes the general tasks that not only exceed the capacity of the supply of the individual citizen, but also that of the individual member states, like external defence, or the issuing of a common currency to facilitate trade within the entire federal territory. The supply of public goods extended to the whole federal territory implies, however, the identification of exclusive functions to the federal level in comparison to the state level, such that even if hierarchical links between the federation and states (or a direct chain of command among different governmental levels) are not established, a functional division of tasks is created that articulates the degrees of sovereignty of the different state and federal institutions.

The specification of the existence of a principle of subsidiarity defined as such (let us say in the liberal sense) on the part of the Community institutions implies the definition of functions on the Community level, renewing the functionalist vision of a European Community having its own *raison d'être*, over and above the unitary ideals, in the need for public goods at a level that exceeds the individual nation state.[6]

This principle is complementary to the preceding one of mutual recognition since it is agreed that certain public goods go beyond specific local interests and thus coincide with a larger area of sovereignty and find the authority capable of activating the public good under consideration in the community institution.

Nevertheless there is another reading of this principle that refers instead to the possibility that the higher authority substitutes for the local one if this is not able to interact in the evolutionary process of normative definition. According to other authors this principle goes back to the tradition of the social doctrine of the Church (Kapteyn 1991; Schaefer 1991).

Kapteyn argues for example that the principle of subsidiarity is defined in the identification of a *sussidio* that the central state presents to the authority at an inferior level to satisfy and sustain their initiative when these are not capable of acting autonomously.[7]

This formulation is found in the papal encyclicals and in particular in the *Quadrigesimo Anno* (1931) of Pius XI, and in later encyclicals (like *la Pacem in Terris*, 1983, and we believe also in the recent *Centesimo Anno*, 1991). In this conception there is undoubtedly a view of social organization in which the state is seen as an organic body in which the single parts must be integrated in the whole, and thus the function of the centre is to guarantee this integration, even substituting for local governments in cases in which they are not able to participate autonomously in the whole. This principle had few followers in Great Britain and France, where there existed a well-consolidated tradition of a unitary state whose legitimation was consolidated by the workings of a central government.

The major verification of this principle is found instead in the Constitution of the German Federal Republic, that is of a state which, after the war, had to redefine its legitimation beginning from the existence of a multiplicity of local states, in the explicit refusal of the centralization of power which came about under the Reich of Bismark and to an even greater extent under Hitler.

The role it played in the definition of the German Basic Law and later in the practical application by Adenauer largely explains how this principle, inspired by the social doctrine of the Church, entered among the foundations of the new Federal Constitution.[8] The central state intervened to guarantee the well-balanced development among the *länder*, acting where the local authorities could not respond because of their institutional limitations or administrative weaknesses.

This principle was linked in its German application with the Social Economy of the Market, derived from the '*Ordoeconomie*' that constitutes the German version of freetradism.

There resulted a general conception of the state founded on a principle of decisional decentralization, but also of strong institutional intertwining among the different private and public subjects, with criteria of codetermination and of decisional complementarity. Above these subjects is found a central authority able to intervene in cases where these mechanisms are not able to function in the general interest; a view thus strongly imbued with paternalism, but also gifted with efficient capacity of control over a very homogeneous and structured, even if articulated, society that can develop itself with its own internal norms, but in the realm of common rules supervised by a strong centre.

Thus, subsidiarity and reciprocal recognition are found in this view, of Catholic derivation, but they are substantiated in the German specification. In the ESA the reference to the principle of subsidiarity is limited to article 130R, which establishes that the Community can intervene in environmental subjects where the intervention makes more sense at the Community level rather than at the national or local levels.

Nevertheless, Kapteyn notes that this principle was used extensively by Delors (who represents a Catholic matrix while being a socialist): this principle, sufficiently ambiguous to be able to accumulate different motivations to the action of the Commission, is the basis of a strong push towards an evolution of institutional relationships within the EEC.

Moreover, this new formulation brings together not only the traditional Federal German formulation – remember that Germany is the only federal country in the EC – but also the recent push of the German *länder* which are seeking greater autonomy from their own central government by activating direct connections with the Commission (Schaefer 1991: 690).

Thus, this new approach creates an alliance among the most dynamic institutions which are interested in forcing the internal equilibria through the institution of a reformatory process of an evolutionary nature. On the other hand this approach is linked to the interests of big businesses that can redefine their productive organization within the entire territory of the Community, but installing their operative centres where the local norms are most appropriate to their interests in growth.

Therefore, a connection among interests of the local and national institutions and the development of firms is recreated and in a context which is nevertheless open within the ambit of the economic union.

Summing up, the matter of subsidiarity is not simply how much decentralization for Europe. But, it directly concerns the nature of the evolutionary mechanism. In an evolutionary context, rules emerge from the interaction, and the risk is that the weaker competitors will become even weaker, because they are not capable of playing the same game as the stronger contenders. Subsidiarity means not only the decentralization of decisions, and therefore the activating of a mechanism of reciprocal recognition among the members of the Union playing at different levels, but also demands that the highest institutional levels create the conditions to enable the weaker members, both nation-states and regional governments, to play effectively in the collective game.

EFFICIENCY, EQUITY AND STABILITY

Evolutionary criteria of norm definition extend the capacity of action of the individual members – at the level of national governments and local authorities – but also of the Commission, outlining a new approach to policy-making, that we have defined as a transition from a 'French' to a 'German' model.

The uniting element of the model is surely a reinforcing of the standards of efficiency, that is of the technical and organizational conditions for achieving a market context in which the firms most capable of competing create the new rules of competition; as a result the most efficient administrations (whether Community, national or local) are encouraged to create efficacious normative actions capable of guiding the process of completion of the internal market.

Nevertheless, if efficiency becomes the essential parameter with which to measure the progress of the Single Market and of the Union, the objectives of equity and stability that the Treaty links directly to efficiency become no longer protected by the right of veto of the national governments. It then becomes necessary to accompany this policy of completion of the internal market with the reinforcement of other policies whose function is to avoid the decay of the market as the mechanism of efficient allocation of resources, but also to activate policies which permit those who historically have been less efficient to adapt themselves to the new competitive and decision-making model. Thus, subsidiarity recalls not simply efficiency, but also the other two terms defining the role of sovereignty–equity among the members participating in the common venture and stability of this community because the members can equally participate in the common process.

In fact, there is a strong risk that the approach of efficiency translates into a strong concentration of market power of the strongest firms and furthermore that the weakest areas of the Community may become marginalized. By increasing disparities, the Community becomes unequal and therefore unstable.

Thus, competition policy was reinforced not only with regard to firms (developing regulation on concentrations) but also with regard to states (through stricter control of the national schemes of firm aid).

On the other hand, a reform was passed concerning structural funds, placing on the Community level the interventions to be realized at the local level with contributions of the national governments; this reform is then contextual to the affirmation of the new approach, but this is also centred on a 'German' view of economic life that presupposes a strong social structure and autonomous local authorities.

With the ESA and the TEU the peculiar characteristics of the Community institutions are therefore maintained and emphasized. Supra-national and inter-governmental powers tend to intertwine and balance one another with a strong accentuation of the evolutionary tendencies. The Commission strengthens its exclusive powers in some areas, such as competition policy regarding intra-CE trade, agricultural policy and commercial policy regarding tariff agreements.

The Commission also relaunched its role of initiatives in which individual members can participate (programmes dealing with technology, research, university mobility, etc., but also interventions of a structural nature). In these areas the decision-making model adopted by the Community requires a co-participation of various institutional levels, and therefore it is necessary to fix a guideline to avoid European authority limiting the lower institutional levels. Nevertheless, this view is not enough, and the enlarged interpretation of the subsidiarity principle requires that the upper levels generate the conditions for inducing the lower institutional levels to exert their role.

This evolutionary process would not be comprehensible without understanding the profound change in the decision-making process introduced by the ESA establishing the centrality of the principles of mutual recognition and of subsidiarity.

NOTES

1 Article 101 specifies that if a state does not adapt correctly and therefore maintains a normative disparity that distorts intra-community competition, the Commission must consult with that state with the aim of removing this obstacle, and only if the consultation does not produce results, the Council must decide unanimously on the directives needed to resolve the situation.

2 Furthermore it was added 'Moreover, the commitment directed toward the coming together of the legislative, regulatory and administrative dispositions of the member states will not diminish, in accordance with article 100 of the Treaty. Certainly, actions based on this article would be more rapid and efficacious if the Council would agree not to allow the requirement of unanimity block progress in the cases in which it is possible to find other solutions' (CEE 1985: 7).

3 It should be remembered that pure public goods have two crucial properties:

   1 the enjoyment of the benefits of public goods on the part of an additional individual does not cost anything; and
   2 it is impossible to exclude a single individual from the use of the public good.

4 See Lord Robbins (1978: 37–8).

5 According to some conceptions, for example, the state must furnish only several minimum services such as guaranteeing the validity of contracts between individuals, leaving then to individual citizens the liberty to activate or not relations of buying or selling of any good; according to other conceptions the state must instead guarantee a condition of well-being to all citizens, providing services to the collective and to individuals.

6 This view reappears in the English federalist tradition, represented by Lord Lothian and by Lord Robbins himself, which argues that the creation of common interests, and the construction of common organizations able to respond to these needs, requires a European federation.

7 Let us remember that in Latin *subsidium* means properly to offer help in the case of personal need.

8 It must be remembered that Adenauer's power lay in the support of the Catholic party, in the institutional roles of president of the Commission for the definition of the '*Grundgesetz*', and then as Chancellor.

REFERENCES

Al-Agraa, A.M. (ed.) (1990) *The Theory of Economic Integration in Economics of European Community*, New York: Philip Allen, 3rd edn.

CEE (1985) *White Paper on Completing the Internal Market*, Brussels.

—— (1987) *The European Single Act*, Brussels.

CEPR (1993) *Making Sense of Subsidiarity. How Much Centralization for Europe? CEPR Annual Report*, London.

Kapteyn, P.J.C. (1991) 'Community Law and the Principle of Subsidiarity', in *Affaires Europeennes*, 2: 35–43.

Nugent, N. (1991) *The Government and Politics of the European Community*, London: Macmillan.

Padoa Schioppa, T. (1987) *Efficiency, Stability, Equity*, Oxford: Oxford University Press.

Robbins, L. (1978) *The Theory of Economic Policy in English Classical Political Economy*, London: Macmillan, 2nd edn.

Schaefer, G.F. (1991) 'The Rise and Fall of Subsidiarity', in *Futures*, 7, Sept, 691–4.

Smith, A. (1976) 'An Inquiry into the Nature and Causes of the Wealth of Nations', in R.H. Campbell and A.S. Skinner (eds) *Works and Correspondence of A.S*, Oxford: Oxford University Press.

Urwin, D.W. (1991) *The Community of Europe. A History of European Integration since 1945*, London: Longman.

4

COMPETITIVENESS, EU INDUSTRIAL STRATEGY AND SUBSIDIARITY

Christine Oughton and Geoff Whittam

INTRODUCTION

Past decades have witnessed the parallel development of industrial policy at a number of levels – regional, national and European Union (EU). Despite the growing integration of the economies within the EU there has been little systematic consideration of how these policies relate to each other both in terms of objectives and effects. In many cases, elements of industrial policy, such as competition policy or regional policy, contain areas of overlap at European, national and regional levels. In addition, there are instances where the objectives of different strands of European industrial policy contain conflicting elements. This issue has come to the fore in relation to EU policy on research and technological development where recent studies (Kay 1991, 1993; Martin 1994) have pointed to possible contradictions between the EU's competition and technology policies. Indeed, this problem was highlighted in the EC White Paper on *Growth, Competitiveness and Employment*, which calls for 'the establishment of a concerted approach to strategic alliances, the uncontrolled development of which could result in the creation of oligopolistic situations prejudicial to competition.' (CEC 1993) A similar potential conflict emerges from the Commission's 1994 proposals on industrial competitiveness policy which identify both the promotion of industrial co-operation *and* the promotion of fair competition as key priority areas for policy action.

In this chapter we consider the latest EU industrial policy proposals in the context of industrial strategies designed to raise competitiveness. Here, competitiveness is defined as long-run growth in productivity, and hence rising living standards, consistent with increasing employment or the maintenance of near full-employment.[1] This definition is commensurate with that adopted in both the 1993 White Paper, which aims to 'lay the foundations for sustainable development of the European economies, thereby enabling them to withstand international competition while creating the millions of jobs that are needed', (CEC 1993:3) and the Commission's 1994 policy proposals which state that, 'competitiveness is not an end in itself, but is an essential means of improving the population's living standards' (CEC 1994a: 9).

In the context of industrial strategies for competitiveness, this chapter is particularly concerned with policies for small and medium-sized enterprises (SMEs).[2] Our decision to focus on SMEs is governed by a number of factors, most notably, the increasingly important role that SMEs are playing in terms of their share of economic activity; their role in innovation; their rate of job creation and their contribution to the dynamism and growth of successful regional economies such as the *Third Italy* and Baden-Württemberg. In addition to these points, we argue that the incorporation of an integrated strategy for SMEs into current mainstream European industrial policy is necessary in order to prevent a conflict of interest between the Commission's twin objectives of the promotion of industrial co-operation *and* fair competition (CEC 1994a). Consideration and inclusion of an industrial strategy for SMEs point to a bottom–up rather than a top–down approach to industrial policy and this raises a number of issues concerning subsidiarity and the most appropriate level at which to implement policy (see also Piera Magnatti in Chapter 11).

The following section provides a brief outline of recent developments in European industrial policy, highlighting three factors that mark a change in emphasis in the 1990s. First, the clear recognition of the need to generate policies to promote full employment. Second, the greater consideration of the role of SMEs and third, new emphasis on the need to promote investment, particularly investment in intangible assets. A third section considers the ways in which SMEs may overcome the disadvantages they face *vis-à-vis* large firms that are able to exploit economies of scale. This discussion centres on the possibilities for attaining *internal* and *external* economies of scale. Here, our analysis introduces a crucial distinction between what we define as *competitive external economies* and *co-operative external economies*. Co-operative external economies of scale enable SMEs to pool fixed costs to overcome entry barriers and thus result in greater competition and efficiency. Hence, co-operation amongst SMEs enhances competition. This outcome can be contrasted with that arising from co-operation between dominant firms, which may increase the height of entry barriers and facilitate collusive pricing practices. The penultimate section draws out the implications of our analysis for industrial strategy in the context of the current debate on subsidiarity, while the final section draws some conclusions.

EUROPEAN INDUSTRIAL POLICY IN THE 1990s

Prior to the 1990s one of the difficulties underlying European industrial policy was that it was developed without a detailed statement of the precise nature and objectives of European industrial strategy. The publication of the Bangemann Report (CEC 1990), the EC White Paper (CEC 1993), the recent proposals for an EU policy on Industrial Competitiveness (CEC 1994a) and the EU's proposals for SMEs (CEC 1994b), have gone some way towards rectifying this problem. However, as we will show below, there are significant differences in emphasis between these policy documents in terms of their treatment of SMEs as well as a potential inconsistency between different elements of the new proposals for industrial policy. The latest policy proposals for industrial competitiveness (CEC 1994a) highlight four areas for priority action:

1 the promotion of investment in intangible assets;
2 the development of co-operation between firms;
3 the ensurance of fair competition; and
4 the modernization of public authorities.

Contrary to the integrated approach emphasized in the White Paper, industrial policy designed to capture the dynamism of SMEs is not fully incorporated into the latest policy initiative but is dealt with in a separate policy programme for SMEs (CEC 1994) which aims to:

1 simplify and improve the environment in which SMEs operate, and
2 provide a number of support measures for SMEs, including the promotion of *enterprise networks*.

Historically, the absence of a detailed discussion on the objectives of policy, together with the considerable changes that the EU has experienced in recent years – both internally and in relation to her main competitors – have meant that industrial strategy has been designed in a piecemeal fashion. The single, most consistent element of the strategy has been increased economic integration and an emphasis on the gains from trade and competition. This emphasis is most readily apparent in the EU's competition policy and the Single European Act.[3]

The theoretical framework underlining this strand of EU policy rests on the identification of a (unique) competitive equilibrium which maximizes efficiency. However, even within this approach there are both empirical and theoretical reasons that point to a role for industrial policy. From an empirical or practical point of view, the standard justification for policy intervention rests on three observations. The first is that the conditions required to ensure competitive equilibrium are simply not met in practice. In this sense the model becomes a benchmark and policy is based on the premise that greater conformity with the model is desirable – hence more competition is preferable to less, etc.[4] European competition policy and the Single Market Act both represent attempts to enhance the degree of free trade and free competition. Second, the EU has always recognized regional disparities in income per capita and has accordingly placed emphasis on the need to finance structural adjustments necessary to ensure convergence of economic performance. Hence, funds are devoted to structural adjustment designed to facilitate growth in the poorer nations and regions. Third, innovation raises the possibility of a trade-off between static and dynamic efficiency which provides a justification for European intervention in research, technology and development policy.

At a theoretical level, recent developments in economic theory have resulted in a more fundamental reassessment of the role of the standard competitive model as the foundation for economic policy analysis. These developments fall mainly into three interrelated categories:

1 hysteresis effects and multiple equilibria;
2 institutional economics; and
3 endogenous growth theory.

The analysis of out of equilibrium beliefs and behaviour has emphasized the possibility of multiple equilibria and this raises the question of equilibrium selection. Final equilibria are shown to be dependent on the beliefs of agents and on the nature of institutions (North 1991). Here, institutions are defined as 'any shared rule or set of rules which guide individual behaviour by supplementing the conventional 'utility' maximising calculation' – hence the market is a particular kind of institution.[5] At a macro-economic level, developments in this field have stressed the role of wage and price setting institutions for unemployment performance, or the implications of central Bank independence for monetary policy.[6] At a micro-economic level, it is evident that industrial structure *and* the institutional environment in which firms operate – for example, the extent and nature of inter-firm networks or other co-operative agreements – can have significant effects on economic efficiency and performance. The growing literature on industrial policy and institutional organization in Japan, the Asian tigers and the industrial districts of the *Third Italy* and Baden-Württemberg serve to illustrate this point.

Theoretical developments that incorporate explicit analysis of the adjustment path and the role of institutions have provided a different, more pro-active, justification for industrial policy. The link between institutional structure and competitive advantage suggests that industrial performance can be influenced by policy and that policy goes beyond ensuring competitive markets. This point has been explicitly recognized in the 1994 policy proposal (CEC 1994) that aims to promote inter-firm networks and industrial cooperation.[7]

Endogenous growth theory (Roemer 1990) has also provided a *rationale* for a more pro-active policy. New theories of economic growth have added weight to the view that policy should do more than simply promote free trade and free competition by illustrating that growth, including productivity growth, is determined endogenously by the level of investment in tangible and intangible assets, such as knowledge, human capital, training and management skills. Hence, policies designed to raise investment in fixed and intangible capital can significantly affect productivity growth and the competitiveness of economies.

The developments in economic theory outlined above are reflected in the key EU industrial policy documents published in the 1990s. For example, sustainable growth and full employment are two of the overriding concerns of the EC's White Paper on *Growth, Competitiveness, Employment* (1993) which states that it aims to:

> foster debate and assist decision-making – at decentralized, national or Community level – so as to lay the foundations for sustainable development of the European economies, thereby enabling them to withstand international competition while creating the millions of jobs that are needed.[8]

In addition to a new emphasis on the importance of adopting a competitiveness strategy designed to increase employment, the latest proposals for industrial policy also stress the need for a policy that promotes industrial co-operation and intangible investment.

It is also clear that the EU is starting to break away from its traditional emphasis on large firm economies of scale in order to give greater attention to the role played by SMEs. The 1993 White Paper highlights the significance of SMEs and suggests a number of areas for policy action. This switch in emphasis has been governed by several factors. First, SMEs have come to play an increasingly important role in European economies in terms of their share of economic activity and their rate of innovation. This change has been underlined by a movement away from mass production towards flexible small batch production techniques with an increased emphasis on quality (see Milgrom and Roberts 1990).[9] Analysis of the size distribution of firms shows that there has been a discernible trend towards deconcentration in a number of economies with SMEs accounting for a growing share of employment.[10]

Second, in terms of innovation there is a growing body of evidence to suggest that small firms are instrumental in introducing technical change. For example, studies of innovation in the US, Germany, the UK and Italy show that small firms have a higher proportionate rate of innovation than large firms.[11] There is also evidence to suggest that the spillover rate from University research to the small firm sector is higher than that to large firms (Audretsch and Vivarelli 1994).

Third, the EU's latest annual review of the role of small firms (CEC 1994c) shows that SMEs have provided a significant source of employment creation at a time when large firms have been shedding jobs. Finally, it is evident that the growth of the SME sector and associated deconcentration can increase the degree of competition. Viewed alongside the technological dynamism of the SME sector this suggests that the SME sector might provide an important source of competition to challenge the power of larger enterprises.

Despite these developments, it is important not to overstate the significance of the SME sector or to imagine that the recent expansion of this sector is unproblematic. For example, SMEs may face significant disadvantages *vis-à-vis* large firms in terms of training and managerial skills, marketing expertise/resources and the ability to raise finance for expansion and investment in fixed capital and research and development (R&D). Moreover, comparison of failure rates for small and large firms in the UK suggests that small firms are considerably more prone to failure than large firms (Storey 1994). It is important to stress that the UK experience is not representative of all SMEs and differs markedly from that of the small firm industrial districts of the *Third Italy* and Baden-Württemberg where small firm failure rates are relatively low. Nevertheless, the UK data suggest that in the absence of policy changes designed to increase survival rates, the shift towards the SME sector could result in an increase in economic instability. In addition, the switch in employment from large to small firms may lead to a deterioration in working conditions. Again, while employment conditions in the prosperous small firm industrial districts of the *Third Italy* tend to be above average, evidence from the UK suggests that wages and fringe benefits are lower in SMEs, and the health and safety record significantly worse. For example, the chance of work place accidents involving serious injury is estimated to be almost 50 per cent higher in small firms as compared with very large plants (Storey 1994: 91). Hence, the growth of employment in small firms raises issues for social, as well as economic, policy.

It is interesting to note that in the transition from the White Paper to the Commission's Industrial Policy proposals, policies for SMEs were hived off in to a separate policy proposal outlining an *Integrated Programme in Favour of SMEs and the Craft Sector* (CEC 1994b). The central objective of this programme is to integrate the large variety of initiatives taken at local, regional, national and EU levels into a global framework:

> The integrated programme is not intended to substitute for various actions taken at a national or Community level, nor to interfere in the decision making process of the different actions . . . it will above all mobilize actions and orient them in the most effective way by the identification and exchange of best practice. . . . Respecting the principle of subsidiarity, the European Union will limit its own actions to that of catalyst if it is not able to contribute directly by its own actions in order to achieve the common objective.
>
> (CEC 1994b: 7)

The *Integrated Programme* has the advantage of devoting a single policy document to the development of a coherent approach to SMEs but it has three disadvantages. First, industrial policy for SMEs is de-coupled from the Commission's overall industrial policy/strategy and, as we will show below, this is likely to undermine the Commission's stated intention of ensuring, 'the consistency of all measures which could enhance industrial efficiency' (CEC 1994b: 1), particularly, the simultaneous promotion of co-operation and competition. Second, separation of the policies for SMEs from mainstream industrial policy is likely to marginalize and thus lower the profile of strategies for SMEs. By implication, this runs the risk of perpetuating the Commission's undue emphasis on large firm economies of scale (Schenk 1994). Finally, the separation allows the main industrial policy proposals to gloss over the issue of subsidiarity. While EU interest in industrial policy for SMEs is legitimate, it none the less favours a bottom–up approach that requires consistent application of the subsidiarity principle. Inclusion of policies for SMEs into the main policy document would therefore require a detailed discussion of the levels at which different policy proposals would be implemented.

INTERNAL ECONOMIES, EXTERNAL ECONOMIES, COMPETITION AND CO-OPERATION

In this section we focus on the role of internal and external economies of scale and consider how some of the problems facing the SME sector may be overcome via a coherent industrial strategy designed to capture the potential dynamism of SMEs. In this respect we aim to address the specific objectives and problems concerning SMEs outlined in the 1993 EC White Paper. To quote,

> It is important . . . to underpin the dynamism of SMEs. It is clearly more difficult and relatively more costly for SMEs than for very large firms to find their proper place in the globalized economy, to have access to world technological capital and to avail themselves of the most sophisticated management techniques and business services. The policies in support of SMEs must, therefore, take account of these new constraints and be strengthened accordingly.
>
> (CEC 1993: 78)

To the extent that there are economies of scale in any of these activities SMEs may be disadvantaged as compared with large firms. In the discussion that follows we analyse the contribution of internal and external economies of scale to economic efficiency in order to show how SMEs that are below the critical size to exploit internal economies may, nevertheless, successfully exploit external economies of scale.[12]

The difference between internal and external economies was highlighted by Marshall. In his *Principles of Economics*, Marshall drew a distinction between *external* economies of scale – which he defined as those economies that were dependent on the overall development of the industrial environment in which firms operate and *internal* economies, which depend on the internal resources of the firm and the manner in which they are organized

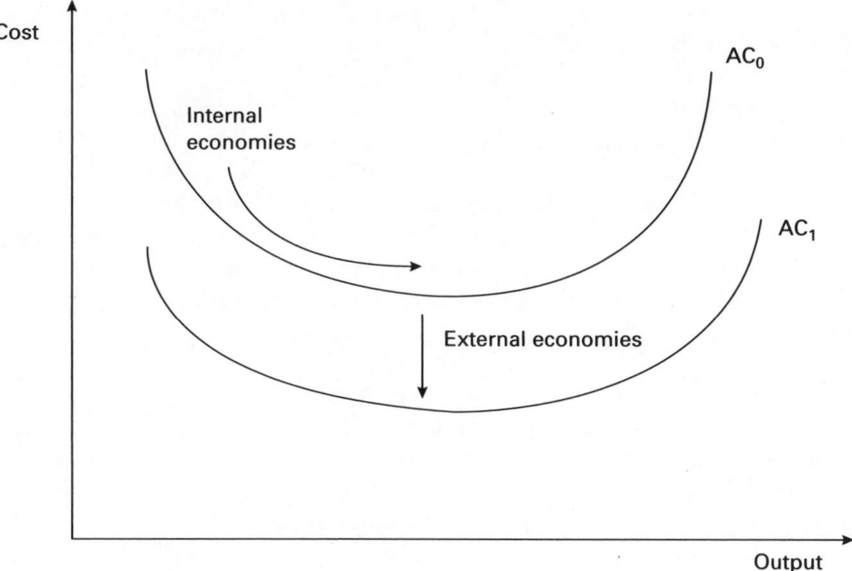

Figure 4.1 Internal and external economies of scale

and managed.[13] Internal economies are associated primarily with the scale of production and arise as a result of the spreading of fixed costs over a large number of units of output. As Lazonick (1993) has noted, the nature of internal economies is captured by the shape of the cost curve while external economies are reflected in a downward movement of a given cost curve as shown in Figure 4.1.

The crucial difference between the two types of economies identified by Marshall is that the first is specific to an individual firm while the second is available to all firms in the industry. Thus, while internal economies may result in considerable cost savings they may also introduce an impediment to entry. Consider a linear cost function of the form:

$$C = F + cq \tag{1}$$

where C denotes total cost, F, fixed cost, c, marginal cost and q, quantity produced. For a given industry price, p, profitable entry requires that the entrants output q_e is:

$$q_e \geq F/(p - c) \tag{2}$$

This anti-competitive element of internal economies contrasts sharply with the pro-competitive nature of external economies which result in cost savings for all firms in a particular industry or locality. Moreover, it is evident that to the extent that external economies have the effect of reducing fixed costs they also reduce the height of entry barriers.

The link between internal and external economies depends crucially on the degree of competition. Internal economies will result in external economies provided that industries are sufficiently competitive so that (at least a part of) cost reductions are passed on in the form of lower prices. In view of the role played by competition we define external economies that arise as a result of internal economies as *competitive external economies*. This distinction flows from the observation that competition is a necessary prerequisite for internal economies to lower prices and generate external economies. However, the difficulty with the concept is that internal economies also promote barriers to entry and limit competition.

The theoretical consistency of simultaneously assuming (perfect) competition and increasing returns to scale was questioned in Sraffa's (1926) seminal paper in which he showed that increasing returns result in natural monopoly and associated efficiency losses. Sraffa's analysis was based on the observation (which has subsequently been confirmed by empirical studies[14]) that firms are typically operating on the downward sloping part of their cost curve

> The chief obstacle against which [firms] . . . have to contend when they want gradually to increase their production does not lie in the cost of production – which, indeed, generally favours them in that direction – but in the difficulty of selling the larger quantity of goods without reducing the price, or without having to face increased marketing expenses.
>
> (Sraffa 1926: 543)

The essential point of this debate is that if internal economies are a necessary prerequisite for external economies but at the same time they lead to monopoly power, then that monopoly power will prohibit the passing on of lower costs to lower prices and undermine the significance of external economies. There are two main resolutions to Sraffa's argument. The first, which need not detain us here since there is already a considerable literature on this topic (Schumpeter 1954), emphasizes the dynamic rather than the static elements of Marshall's theory. That is, it stresses the historical nature of Marshall's analysis of industrial development and plays down the static equilibrium framework that was the aspect of his work which later received most attention. In a dynamic context, entry barriers are overcome by competitive forces which take the form of the introduction of product and process innovations and more efficient organizational forms.

The second response is based on the observation that there are some external economies that are unrelated to internal economies. In particular within industrial districts external economies may arise as a result of agglomeration economies reflecting the development of associated trades, financial services and infrastructure. Here it should be noted that public investment in transport and communications infrastructure and education and training are important contemporary sources of such external economies. Furthermore, Marshall introduced the concept of industrial atmosphere: a term which refers to external economies that arise as a result of spillovers in knowledge and skills. In his discussion of industrial districts it is evident that Marshall attached significant importance to the role of external economies. Since both agglomeration economies and industrial atmosphere have the effect of lowering the cost curves for all firms within an industrial district these economies can be realized without adversely affecting market structure – indeed to the extent that they lower firms' fixed costs they facilitate entry into an industry and enhance competition. We refer to these economies as *exogenous external economies*.

The role of exogenous external economies and Marshall's analysis of the growth of industrial districts has been extensively applied to explain the economic success of the small firm industrial districts of Emilia-Romagna and Baden-Württemberg. However, it is our belief that the nature of external economies attained in these regions goes beyond Marshallian external economies. In our view, the external economies realized in the small firms industrial districts of the *Third Italy* and Baden-Württemberg differ from Marshallian external economies in that they are realized through co-operation between firms. We define such economies as *co-operative external economies*. While these economies are external to the firm, it is important to note that they are internal to the network of co-operating SMEs. The distinguishing features of co-operative economies are that firms are actively, rather than passively, involved in the establishment and maintenance of institutional arrangements designed to exploit co-operative external economies of scale and that the realization of such economies does not necessarily increase, and is likely to decrease, market power.

The central proposition of this section of the chapter is that co-operative external economies can be realized through co-operation via the sharing of fixed costs. Moreover, such co-operation would be functional in that it would go some way towards solving the problem identified in the EC (1993) White Paper that SMEs are disadvantaged *vis-à-vis* large firms in terms of finance, marketing expertise, R&D and managerial skills/training.[15] As Geroski (1994) has pointed out, economies of scale in production 'are now generally fairly modest'; however, there are substantial sunk fixed costs in relation to marketing, advertising, R&D,[16] training and accountancy and finance. Consider the cost function shown in equation (1), where F denotes the fixed cost of establishing a marketing department, R&D department, accounting department, training department, etc. Assuming that SMEs form a competitive fringe and treat price parametrically, then SMEs will find it unprofitable to invest in these activities unless

$$q \geq F/(p - c) \tag{3}$$

However, by pooling fixed costs, SMEs can gain the advantages enjoyed by large U- or M-form firms. Obviously, the pooling of fixed costs requires co-operation among SMEs and this raises the question of how such co-operation is realized. In earlier studies (Oughton and Whittam 1994, 1995) we demonstrated that co-operation over non-price inputs can be viewed as a prisoner's dilemma problem and can be modelled using evolutionary game theory (Axelrod 1981). The concept of a collectively stable equilibrium is based on the notion of the survival of the fittest, i.e. a certain strategy can emerge as a stable equilibrium because firms find it the most profitable strategy to adopt. This approach shows that co-operation can evolve between self-interested firms provided that players have recourse to punishment strategies and attach sufficient weight to future plays of the game. Moreover, co-operation can evolve when a group of players adopt certain co-operative strategies (e.g. tit-for-tat) that are more profitable than other strategies: not only will these firms have a greater chance of survival but, provided that the cluster of co-operative firms is of sufficient size, other firms will find it in their interest to adopt the more profitable strategy. The crucial point for the present discussion is that institutions that are established to facilitate co-operation and enhance profitability will evolve and form collectively stable equilibria. Hence, in an institutional environment designed to foster co-operation and trust it would be possible for small firms to gain access to economies of scale by pooling fixed costs between them.

Examples of such institutions are found in the industrial districts of the *Third Italy* and Baden-Württemberg. These institutions provide a forum for co-operation and facilitate trust by virtue of their participatory and democratic nature. For example, the Business Service Centres of Emilia-Romagna, which provide real services to participating SMEs at competitive fees, were initially set up by the regional government in connection with local trade associations with a view to providing financial, marketing and technology services that SMEs could not produce in-house.[17]

Implications for Industrial Policy and Subsidiarity

The discussion of internal and external economies set out above has a number of policy implications that can be summarized as follows. The first is that given the conflict between internal and competitive external economies there is a clear need for anti-trust/competition policy and this should be carried out at national and EU level. Second, policies aimed at enhancing exogenous external economies are best carried out at the EU and national levels. Examples of such policies include the Single Market Act and the development of infrastructure, such as transport and communication systems. Finally, policies aimed at enhancing the dynamism of the SME sector through the exploitation of co-operative external economies are best enacted at regional or local level through the establishment of appropriate institutions. Co-operation is more likely to be successful in institutions that are democratic and accountable and provide effective monitoring mechanisms. Examples of such institutions are discussed below. This suggests a bottom–up approach to industrial policy both in terms of the level and nature of decision-making: i.e. decision-making should take place at local or regional level and be participatory in nature.

SUBSIDIARITY, INDUSTRIAL POLICY AND SMEs

The latest EU proposals for industrial policy and the *Integrated Programme* for SMEs raise a number of issues for subsidiarity. In this section we examine how the nature of industrial policy objectives influences the determination of the most appropriate level for the implementation of policy. The principal contention of this section is that policies designed to capture the dynamism of the SME sector are best enacted at local or regional level but that the EU has an important role to play as a catalyst or promoter of 'best practices'. Indeed, such a role is necessary to promote both efficiency and 'a level playing field'. In addition, we argue that the policy proposals for SMEs should be fully integrated into the EU's main proposals for industrial policy. Without this integration the Commission's proposals to encourage co-operation among firms are likely to increase the market power of large established firms.[18] In contrast, the promotion of co-operation amongst SMEs enables them to overcome entry barriers associated with fixed costs and economies of scale in marketing, finance, innovation and training and is likely to encourage entry and increase the survival rate of SMEs, thus promoting competition.

Subsidiarity and EU Industrial Policy

The issue of subsidiarity came to the fore in the policy debates surrounding the Maastricht Treaty. The term itself, however, has been around since at least the 1930s[19] (see also Patrizio Bianchi's contribution to this volume). The general meaning of the term has come to be that decisions should be taken at the lowest possible level. In the words of the Maastricht treaty:

> In areas which do not fall within its exclusive competence, the Community shall take action, in accordance with the principle of subsidiarity, only if and in so far as the objectives of the proposed action cannot be sufficiently achieved by the member states and can therefore, by reason of the scale or effects of the proposed action, be better achieved by the Community.
>
> (CEC 1992: Title II, article 3b; p. 14)

This statement identifies only two levels of decision-making, the European or the member state, however, it is clear that decisions are made at a variety of levels. In the implementation of regional policy for example, decisions are made at European, member state, regional and local levels. Moreover, 'policy' decisions are also taken and implemented by non-elected bodies (quangos) such as Scottish Enterprise.

The publication of the recent White Paper and the subsequent *Integrated Programme* for SMEs (CEC 1994b) raise the issue of subsidiarity in relation to the formation and implementation of industrial policy. The Treaty of European Union provides a legal basis for the implementation of EU industrial policy, which

> In line with the subsidiarity principle, is defined as a general obligation shared between the Community and the Member States for the 'strengthening of the competitiveness of Community industry' (Article 3 of the Treaty). . . . It is primarily up to Member States and the decentralized authorities to foster industrial competitiveness with the aid of a system of open and competitive markets. However, Article 130(2) adds that in order to attain these objectives the Member States 'shall consult each other in liaison with the Commission and, where necessary, shall co-ordinate their action'. The Commission is assigned the specific duty to 'take any useful initiative to promote such co-ordination.' To support this national action, the Community will generally help to achieve this objective of improving competitiveness by taking horizontal measures under a series of common policies (on research, cohesion, vocational training, networks and foreign trade), implemented by qualified majority vote in most cases, and by implementing competition policy.
>
> (CEC 1994a: 10–11)

As we have seen above, the EU's *Integrated Programme* for SMEs attempts to provide a global framework for co-ordinating the actions of all parties involved in the development of SMEs: 'Respecting the principle of subsidiarity, the European Union will limit its role to that of a catalyst if it is not able to contribute directly by its own actions in order to achieve the common objective' (CEC 1994b: 7). Operating as a catalyst the EU sees its role as identifying and highlighting 'best practice' for the support of SMEs. This will be done through a 'concerted effort' with the promotion of initiatives such as joint forums, so that member states can learn from each other. In line with this approach we consider cases of successful local and regional economies based on SMEs to provide examples of best practice. This analysis suggests that policies designed to capture the dynamism of the SME sector are based on a bottom–up approach to industrial policy that encourages co-operation between SMEs and the key players in the region, such as local government, chambers of commerce, trade unions.

Co-operation among SMEs

Successful regional economies based on SMEs, such as the *Third Italy* and Baden-Württemberg, have received considerable attention in the literature.[20] The previous section identifies two key factors that can enhance the performance of the SME networks, namely, the exploitation of co-operative and exogenous economies of scale. In an earlier paper (Oughton and Whittam 1994), we applied this analysis to explain the economic success of the small firm industrial districts of North Central Italy. Within successful industrial districts, such as Emilia-Romagna, SMEs are networked through democratic trade associations that work in conjunction with local government. In joint liaison, local government and trade associations have established *Collective Service Centres* that provide real services, such as accountancy, marketing, training, financial and advisory services. The services are provided at a fee that is below the market rate but is set in order to cover costs, i.e. the centres are intended to be self-financing in the long-run. The Collective Service Centres enable SMEs to gain access to co-operative external economies of scale and provide SMEs with access to business services on terms comparable with those available to a large firm conducting such activities in-house or exploiting monopsony power in the market place.

Similar co-operative external economies are realized through agencies designed to develop and diffuse new technologies, such as *CITER* (*Centro Informazione Tessile Emilia-Romagna*) which operates in the textile industry. *CITER* developed a computer-aided design system that significantly reduces the time taken to design and manufacture fashion garments. The investment in the hardware, software and training necessary to operate this system was financed jointly by the network of SMEs which enjoys co-operative external economies of scale.

Finance is provided to the small firm industrial districts of the *Third Italy* through loan guarantee schemes such as the Loan Guarantee Scheme of Modena. The scheme is funded by membership fees from the local trade association and by contributions from local, regional and national governments. Information asymmetries are closed down by the scheme as member firms operating in similar lines of activity vet each other's applications. In addition, the scheme is protected from abuse by the fact that firms that default can be prevented from reapplying for further finance.

One of the key reasons for the success of these schemes is that they operate at the regional level with the active co-operation of the key players involved. The decision-making takes place at the regional level in the context of a democratic institutional framework. While the *Third Italy* provides a clear example of best practice policy *vis-à-vis* support mechanisms for SMEs, a number of other cases can also be identified.

The German banking system operates a system of loan finance for SMEs that enables small firms to gain access to loan capital on the same terms as large firms that are able to exploit economies of scale in finance. The issue for SMEs, in terms of finance, is not simply the supply of funds, but the *terms* on which loans are made available for this sector (Hughes 1992). Given the lack of assets of SMEs and the paucity of information available about their performance compared with that available for public limited companies, the conditions necessary to secure loans are frequently more stringent for the small firms. The German banking system offers a formalized networking organization in an attempt to overcome these problems. The decentralized basis of the savings and co-operative banking system have ensured the availability of long-term finance for the SME sector (Vitols 1994). The structure of the system reflects the federalist form of corporatism typical of the organization of the German economy. Access to long-term, fixed rate funds (LTFR) for the smaller banks has been central to the provision of loans and finance to SMEs.

There are two processes at work. First, there is the establishment of relationships between the individual local banks with individual SMEs, which improves the information available to the bank and therefore reduces the risks in making a loan. Second, there is the confidence that the localized banks are not going to suffer a liquidity crisis, nor an increase in interest rates, due to their access to LTFR funds which can then be reloaned. Vitols (1994) identifies three mechanisms which assist the localized banks in providing long-term fixed-rate loans. The first is the role of financial intermediaries that issue bonds to refinance LTFR loans to SMEs, the second, risk pooling among the banks themselves, and the third, savings funds channelled through insurance companies via bank bonds. The combined effects of greater access to information regarding individual firms and access to LTFR, enables SMEs to secure loans at the same rate as large firms. These arrangements allow the small banks and the SMEs to achieve co-operative economies of scale in terms of financing loans.[21]

In analysing the rise of the textile-machinery industry in Baden-Württemberg in Southern Germany, Sabel *et al.* (1989) emphasize the role of the trade associations in the earlier part of the century in formulating 'specialization cartels' to promote joint marketing and research. These trade associations evolved with trade unions and local authorities, playing a part to expand their activities into training and technical education. Sabel *et al.* (1989) argue that the textile industry in Baden-Württemberg was able to withstand the increased turbulence in the world markets during the 1970s due to the networking arrangements that had evolved. Primarily, the rise of subcontracting in the region allowed a more flexible response to changing market conditions, while joint investment in intangible assets enabled firms to exploit co-operative external economies of scale.

A similar explanation has been offered by Lorenz (1989) in his analysis of the subcontracting arrangements in the SME French engineering sector situated around Lyons. The subcontracting relationships grew as a response to the crisis of 1981-2 which severely affected manufacturing industry. It was found that subcontracting firms could operate specific machine tools cheaper than the larger client firms. In order to exploit this economy, the client firms often made investments in capital assets which would have been prohibitive to the subcontractor acting independently. The consequent subcontracting relationships which evolved contained long-term commitments on both the clients, and subcontractors, in their partnership arrangements. Once the investments were made, the client firm could face the prospect of a *hold-up* situation: since the investment represents a 'sunk cost', the subcontracting firm could attempt to increase the agreed payments for carrying out the work. Likewise, the client firm could behave opportunistically to the subcontracting firm by, for example, insisting upon impossible deadlines. While the contracts drawn up were standard order forms, the partnerships were much more than agreements on price and quantity.

> It seems rather to involve the following: in exchange for improved performance by the subcontractor on quality and delivery, the client firm will make every effort to guarantee a level of work; furthermore, any adaptations to price, quantity and delivery are to be made in a non-opportunistic way by both sides.
>
> (Lorenz 1988: 206)

Plainly, the arrangement is more informal than the situation in Baden-Württemberg and Emilia-Romagna, but there exists, nevertheless, an institutional framework which transcends strict market transactions. The arrangements are designed to encourage co-operation rather than opportunism: 'The rules are designed to facilitate exchange in a situation otherwise open to exploitation' (Lorenz 1989: 190). It is arguable that what holds these informal networking partnerships together is the need to establish a reputation for trustworthiness. Both client and sub-contractor will have reputations to consider in dealing with each other. If one or the other gains a reputation for opportunistic behaviour then it will endanger their chances of securing future contracts.

Institutional co-operation and the role of the EU

This overview of four quite distinct and different institutional arrangements provides a brief insight into the manner in which co-operative external economies of scale may be realized by SMEs. Formal and informal networking arrangements between firms are the norm not the exception. In its role of catalyst the EU should attempt to foster institutional arrangements that facilitate the exploitation of gains from co-operation. One of the EU's stated objectives is to support the SME sector in the promotion of co-operation. However, the suggested method for doing this is rather vague. The White Paper (1993) and the subsequent *Integrated Programme* envisage the development of *enterprise networks* designed to 'introduce flexible specialized production systems' (CEC 1994b: 31). The kind of network being proposed is not specified in detail. The above case studies offer examples of 'best practice' of different types of networking arrangements.

The key to the success of the cases mentioned above is that decision-making is undertaken by the actors involved; the firms themselves, the regional authorities, the local financial sector, the trade unions, etc. Furthermore, the initiatives of the more formalized institutional arrangements have been developed in a localized economic framework. Bianchi (1994) offers an outline of the approach required for the promotion of networking arrangements to cultivate co-operation:

> The industrial micro policies are thus essentially networking actions, or policies aimed at reconstructing a network of relationships, that consolidate mechanisms of integration among individuals, permitting the evolution of a productive system based on reciprocal recognition, the sense of adherence to a group, the identification of public goods, and thus of externalities, and of therefore the suitability of collective action, with the capacity to sanction free riders.
>
> (Bianchi 1994: 34)

Where well-established institutional frameworks have evolved, accountable and enforceable arrangements frequently evolve to overcome potential free-rider and opportunistic practices. This is quite formal in the context of the German banking system and the industrial districts of the *Third Italy*, but less formal in the context of the engineering firms of Lyons. The further implications for subsidiarity are that industrial policy for the SME sector should be a bottom–up approach with the key players in the regions being actively involved in the formation and implementation of industrial policy.

Competition, co-operation and EU industrial policy

The networking arrangements outlined above are functional in that they allow small firms to exploit co-operative external economies of scale and gain access to business services on terms similar to those available to large firms. Moreover, to the extent that there are fixed costs associated with marketing, investment and R&D, co-operation has the effect of reducing the height of entry barriers and promoting competition. Hence, by facilitating the entry and survival of SMEs the promotion of co-operation in the SME sector is consistent with the promotion of competitive market structures. The economies that are realized through networking arrangements are external to the firm but internal to the network, hence SME networks can confer comparative advantage to particular localities/regions. In order to ensure fair competition and a level playing field, the EU has an important role to play to promote the widespread adoption of SME networks across regions and member states. The foregoing analysis indicates that networks that are accountable and democratic are likely to maximize the chances of successful co-operation. In order to ensure open competition it is necessary that networks should be open to SMEs operating in particular industries/ localities.

CONCLUSION

The EU's proposals for an industrial competitiveness policy outline a number of measures designed to raise productivity growth and employment. These include the promotion of industrial co-operation; the ensurance of fair competition; investment in intangible assets; and measures designed to capture the dynamism of SMEs. The theoretical section of this chapter illustrates that the appropriate level at which policy should be implemented depends on the nature of productivity gains or the type of economies of scale. For example, competition policy at the national and European level is necessary to ensure that internal economies of scale are transformed into external economies. Similarly, the nature of exogenous economies of scale associated with infrastructure and levels of education/training points to a role for both national and European intervention. By contrast, policy measures designed to promote co-operative economies are best enacted at regional level. Moreover, in order to avoid a conflict of interest between co-operation and competition, co-operation should be promoted within the SME sector. Entry and survival of SMEs can be facilitated by policy measures designed to capture co-operative external economies of scale. In this way the promotion of co-operation is likely to maintain or increase the degree of competition within industries. Moreover, to the extent that SMEs form a competitive fringe of price-taking firms, co-operation over input activities will be prevented from spilling over to co-operation (collusion) in product markets.

This positive association between co-operation and competition does not hold for all firm sizes or types of co-operation. Promotion of co-operation between large dominant firms is likely to increase economies of scale (that are external to the firm but internal to the partnership/group) but runs the risk of dampening competition. The anti-competitive effects of co-operation between large firms can arise for two reasons. First, co-operation between large firms that individually operate above current levels of minimum efficient scale will raise entry barriers rather than lower them.[22] Second, co-operation between firms that already control a significant proportion of the market is likely to increase the prospects for successful collusion in the product market. The possibility of price collusion is significantly less for networks of small firms that form a competitive fringe. Moreover, if SME networks are successful at encouraging entry and increasing the survival rate of SMEs then, *ceteris paribus*, firm numbers and the degree of competition will be increased. Accordingly, in order to preserve 'the consistency of all measures which could enhance industrial efficiency' (CEC 1994: 1) it is important that the Commission's objective of promoting of co-operation is aimed primarily, but not necessarily exclusively, at SMEs. This would require the active incorporation of the *Integrated Programme* into the EU's latest proposals for industrial policy (CEC 1994a) and greater emphasis on external rather than traditional economies of scale. That is, instead of concentrating on the promotion of large firm economies of scale, industrial policy should be more concerned with promoting co-operative external economies of scale in the SME sector. As we have seen, the nature of co-operative external economies suggests a bottom–up approach to industrial policy that would limit the role of the EU to the promotion of best practice, rather than the direct enactment of policy.

ACKNOWLEDGEMENTS

We are grateful to the participants of the 1994 *Lisbon Workshop on Objectives of European Policy* and the 1994 *Crete Workshop on Competitiveness, Subsidiarity and Objectives* for valuable comments and criticism. Any errors or opinions are attributable solely to the authors.

NOTES

1 As is apparent from the analysis of competitiveness in Devine's chapter the definition used here is relatively broad-based and could be achieved by a number of different routes.
2 SMEs are defined as enterprises employing fewer than 500 employees.
3 Although even here the consistency and effectiveness of EU policy is questionable: little is done to control dominant firms, indeed, RD joint ventures have been encouraged and competition and mergers policy have been lax (Schenk 1994).
4 Of course, this view is open to criticism on the grounds of the theory of the second best.
5 Hargreaves Heap (1994: 36).
6 See Hargreaves Heap (1994) for a survey of this literature.
7 Of course, the point is readily evident in actual policies even in economies that take a free-market approach – consider the case of the UK, where small firms receive significant government subsidies.
8 Commission of the European Communities (1993) *Growth, Competitiveness, Employment: The Challenges and Way Forward into the 21st Century*, p 3.
9 In itself this shift does not necessarily signal the demise of large corporations since large firms can undertake flexible multiproduct production, however, it could lower entry barriers by reducing the minimum efficient scale of production.
10 See Sengenberger *et al.* (1990) and Storey (1994).
11 Audretsch, D. and Vivarelli, M. (1994) 'Small Firms and R&D Spillovers: Evidence from Italy', *Centre for Economic Policy Research Discussion Paper Series*, 927: 6–7.
12 A more detailed discussion of co-operative economies of scale can be found in Oughton and Whittam (1994, 1995).

13 *Principles*, p. 441 and p. 266, pp. 314–317.
14 A number of studies have found evidence of L-shaped cost curves – see, for example, Pratten (1971).
15 For a detailed discussion of the argument see Oughton and Whittam (1994, 1995)
16 Indeed, Sutton (1991) has shown that, in the presence of fixed costs in advertising, marketing and R&D, increases in market size are associated with increased concentration and not reduced concentration as might be expected in the absence of non-price variables.
17 Note that the cost of attaining such services on the market is often prohibitive for small firms that lack monopsony power. Of course, if the market for business services is perfectly competitive then the only savings associated with co-operative provision would be transactions costs.
18 Firms employing more than 500 employees.
19 McCrone (1992) argues that the principle of subsidiarity has its origins in an encyclical letter of Pope Pius XI in 1931.
20 See, for example, Brusco (1982), Piore and Sabel (1984), Best (1990), as well as the chapter by Magnatti in this volume.
21 Note that in this context we define economies of scale in finance as reductions in the cost of finance related to the size of the firm's assets and the size of its borrowing requirements.
22 In the case of co-operation over R&D, EU policy permits R&D joint ventures provided that the combined production of the firms does not exceed 20 per cent of the market. If co-operation is to be encouraged on grounds that extend beyond the static efficiency/dynamic efficiency trade-off argument, then, plainly, the EU needs to introduce new guidelines to cover other types of co-operative agreements.

REFERENCES

Axelrod, R. (1981) 'The emergence of cooperation among egoists', *American Political Science Review*.

Audretsch, D. and Vivarelli, M. (1994) 'Small Firms and R&D Spillovers: Evidence from Italy', *Centre for Economic Policy Research Discussion Paper Series*, 927.

Best, M. (1990) *The New Competition: Institutions of Industrial Restructuring*, Cambridge: Polity.

Bianchi, P. (1994) 'Industrial Strategy in an Open Economy', in P. Bianchi, K. Cowling and R. Sugden (eds) *Europe's Economic Challenge*, London: Routledge.

Brusco, S. (1982) 'The Emilian Model: Produtcive Decentralisation and Social Integration', *Cambridge Journal of Economics*, 6: 167–84.

Commission of the European Communities (CEC) (1990) *Industrial Policy in an Open and Competitive Environment: Guide-lines for a Community Approach*, Brussels. COM(90) 556 Final.

—— (1992) *Treaty on European Union*, Brussels.

—— (1993) *Growth, Competitiveness, Employment. The Challenges and Ways Forward into the 21st Century*, White Paper.

—— (1994) *The European Observatory for SMEs: Second Annual Report*, Brussels.

—— (1994a) *An Industrial Competitiveness Policy for the European Union*, Brussels.

—— (1994b) *Integrated Programme in Favour of SMEs and the Craft Sector*, Brussels.

—— (1994c) *The Second Annual Report of the Small Firm Observatory*. Brussels.

Cooke, P. and Morgan, K. (1992) 'Industry, Training and Technology Transfer: The Baden–Württemberg System in Perspective', *Regional Industrial Research Report* No. 6, Cardiff.

Geroski, P. (1994) 'Entry and Market Share Mobility', in J. Cable (ed.) *Current Issues in Industrial Economics*, London: Macmillan.

Hargreaves Heap, S. (1994) 'Institutions and (Short-Run) Macroeconomic Performance', *Journal of Economic Surveys* 8, 1: 35–56.

Hughes, A. (1992) 'The "Problems" of Finance for Smaller Businesses', Working Paper No, 15, *Small Business Research Centre*, Cambridge.

Kay, N. (1991) 'Industrial Collaborative Activity and the Completion of the Internal Market', *Journal of Common Market Studies*, 29: 347–62.

— (1993) 'Mergers, Acquisitions and the Internal Market', in K. Hughes (ed.) *European Competitiveness*, Cambridge: CUP.

Lazonick, W. (1993) *Business Organization and the Myth of the Market Economy*, Cambridge: CUP.

Lorenz, E.H. (1988) 'Neither Friends nor Strangers: Informal Networks of Subcontracting in French Industry', in D. Gambetta, (ed.) *Trust*, Oxford; Blackwell.

— (1989) 'Neither Friends nor Strangers: Informal Networks of Subcontracting in French Industry', in G. Thompson (ed.) (1991) *Markets, Hierarchies and Networks*, Milton Keynes: Open University Press.

McCrone, G. (1992) 'Subsidiarity: Its Implications for Economic Policy', *National Westminster Bank Quarterly Review*, November 46–56.

Marshall, A. (1930) *Principles of Economics*, 8th edn, London: Macmillan.

Martin, S. (1994) 'Public Policies Toward Cooperation in Research and Development: the European Union, Japan, the United States', Mimeo, Department of Economics, European University Institute, Florence.

Milgrom T. and Roberts T. (1990) 'The Economics of Modern Manufacturing', *American Economic Review*.

North, D. (1991) *Institutions, Institutional Change and Economic Performance*, Cambridge: Cambridge University Press.

Oughton, C. and Whittam, G. (1994) 'Competition and Cooperation in the Small Firm Sector', *University of Glasgow Discussion Papers in Economics*, 9401.

— (1995) 'Competition and Cooperation in the Small Firm Sector', forthcoming in *Scottish Journal of Political Economy*.

Piore, M. and Sabel, C. (1984) *The Second Industrial Divide*, New York: Basic Books.

Pratten, C. (1971) *Economies of Scale in Manufacturing Industry*, Cambridge: CUP.

Roemer, P. (1990) 'Endogenous Technological Change', *Journal of Political Economy*, 98, 5, pt 2: S71–S103.

Sabel C., Herrigel, G. Deeg, R. and Kazis, R. (1989) 'Regional Prosperities Compared: Massachusetts and Baden–Württemberg', *Economy and Society*, 18, 4: 16–36.

Schenk, H. (1994) 'Industrial Policy: An assessment of Main Elements' paper presented at the 1994 *Lisbon Workshop on Objectives of European Industrial Policy*.

Schumpeter, J. (1954) *Capitalism, Socialism and Democracy*, 3rd edn, New York: Harper and Row.

Sengenberger, W., Loveman, G. and Piore, M. (1990) *The Re-emergence of Small Enterprises: Industrial Restructuring in Industrialized Countries*, Geneva: International Labour Organisation.

Sraffa, P. (1926) 'The Laws of Return under Competitive Condition', *Economic Journal*, December: 535–50.

Storey, D. (1994) *Understanding the Small Firm*, London: Routledge.

Sutton, J. (1991) *Sunk Costs and Market Structure: Price Competition, Advertising, and the Evolution of Concentration*, Cambridge, MA, MIT Press.

Vitols, S.I. (1994) 'The Institutional Infrastructure of Regional Development: Lessons From German Banking For Small-Firm Financing', paper presented at the 1994 *Lisbon Workshop on the Objectives of European Industrial Economic Policy*.

5

THE PRICE OF DIVERSITY

Rival concepts of control as a barrier to an EU industrial strategy

Winfried Ruigrok and Rob van Tulder

INTRODUCTION

Why has it proved so difficult to formulate a common industrial strategy for the European Union (EU)? This chapter suggests that social and economic diversity – treasured by most EU citizens, and for good reasons – has been a major hurdle towards a joint EU industrial strategy. The central argument here is that both within and between EU member states, large core firms tend to adhere to rival visions ('concepts of control') on how the industrial, financial, social and political networks around them should be organized. Understanding of these rival visions and the organization of these networks helps to explain the different types of 'solutions' firms and their national governments present on the issues of competitiveness, subsidiarity and policy objectives, and the barriers they pose to a common EU industrial strategy.[1]

THE INDUSTRIAL COMPLEX: CENTRES OF GRAVITY IN THE INDUSTRIAL RESTRUCTURING RACE

The central concept of this chapter is the *industrial complex* as a specific type of network.[2] An industrial complex has the following characteristics:

1 it is relatively stable, i.e. the actors do not meet accidentally;
2 the interaction is aimed at the exchange of goods, capital, technology, information, skills and/or people; and
3 it is aimed at the allocation of *values* (for instance on how the interaction should occur) (cf. Galtung 1964, 1971; Wallensteen 1974: 32).

The third element points at the power relations between the constituent parties.

It is assumed here that all large firms with major production and technology activities aspire to position themselves at the *core* of supply and distribution networks, as well as of political and financial networks, in order to play a leading role in the creation of added value and in restructuring. This does not necessarily mean that the *core firm* does all this itself. A core firm aspires to be the spider of an industrial web. A core firm is the principal actor as well as the director of the play. In certain types of networks, a core firm may have to give up its role as the sole director, yet it will always remain the leading actor, and, if possible, will try to regain control. A core firm has direct access to domestic and foreign end markets and/or customers and owes its relative independence to its financial strength and to its control over a series of core technologies and other strategic competencies particular to an industry or industrial activity. Most importantly, a core firm has an explicit vision on

1 the organization and management of the value chain, including the internal labour process; and
2 the role that external actors (such as banks and governments) should play to facilitate the creation of added value and the (re)structuring of the network.

An illustration of the significance of core firms can be read in the work of Lundvall and others, who, although using a different terminology, documented how large, technologically leading firms through the 1980s were able to impose a global restructuring trajectory upon other firms. These core firms, which Lundvall and his fellow researchers labelled *user-producers*, not only produced new products and production technologies, but were also among the leading users of these technologies. This endowed them with greater power and a better bargaining position than other, particularly smaller firms. In this way, these large firms have reduced the prospects for new entrants and have influenced the creation of substitutes (Lundvall 1988; Andersen and Lundvall 1988).

An *industrial complex* then can be defined as *a bargaining configuration organized around a core firm, consisting of (groups of) actors which are directly or indirectly engaged in the production and distribution of a given product*. An industrial complex is made up of *five types of bargaining relationships*:

1 relations between a core firm and its suppliers;
2 relations between a core firm and its workers;
3 relations between a core firm and its dealers;
4 relations between a core firm and its financiers;
5 relations between a core firm and its government(s).

FIVE CONCEPTS OF CONTROL

Each of the relationships between the core firm and a bargaining partner can be understood as a *dependency relation*, representing a *control problem* to the core firm. The management of each core firm has to decide whether, how and to what extent it is willing and able to control its bargaining partners. Usually, a decision to control one (set of) bargaining partners has direct implications on other bargaining relations. For instance, if many companies decide to limit their dependence on external suppliers by producing essential inputs themselves, this may lead to the 'degradation of work' and to the destruction of crafts (cf. Braverman 1974), while confronting these companies with larger capital requirements (affecting their bargaining relations with financiers) and with organized labour. This is indeed what happened during the rise of *Fordism*: one type of uncertainty was replaced by another. The strength of organized labour exposed vertically integrated companies' vulnerability to strikes, forcing their top management to enter into direct negotiations with labour unions over higher wages and secondary labour conditions. On the positive side, this mechanism helped to create mass consumption and a customer base for the mass producers. Since the 1930s this 'productivity-wage' coupling mechanism facilitated the *virtuous growth* cycles of the Fordist production organization in the United States and with some alterations also in Western Europe.

The dynamics and ultimately the crisis of Fordism can be understood as the result of the continuing efforts to resolve one set of control problems leading to the inevitable rise of another set of control problems. In the medium run, capitalist production and accumulation can only expand after the various control problems have been *resolved simultaneously and in an encompassing manner*. To this end, the top management of a core firm has to develop a coherent vision on internal company structures and external preconditions for longer-term growth. This requires a comprehensive vision on how to resolve the five control problems, i.e. on how a core firm aspires to control its five bargaining partners, including a definition of the 'national' or 'common' interest. Such a view will be dubbed a *concept of control*.[3]

As the history of Fordism suggests, no resolution of control problems, and therefore no comprehensive concept of control, will function forever. In fact, history suggests that any settlement of control problems will eventually provoke new contradictions and thus lead to new control problems. One can distinguish five rival concepts of control contending for hegemony in modern capitalism.

The first concept of control is based on *(networks of) small and medium-sized firms aimed at industrial craft-orientated production for small to medium-scale markets*. This type of industrial organization has been called 'flexible specialization' (Piore and Sable 1984; see also Christine Oughton and Geoff Whittam in this volume). Flexible specialization networks may of course also succeed in producing for larger markets. This would only increase the possible hegemonic aspirations of the concept.

The second concept of control is labelled *industrial democracy*. Industrial democracy only emerges as a result of social and political strategies developed by other actors than core firms, such as governments or trade unions. On an international scale some minor attempts have been made towards formulating international codes of conduct for transnationals, while trade unions' thinking on how to enforce a compliant bargaining attitude on the part of firms has been limited to theories of 'associative democracy' (Mathews 1989). Swedish core firms (in the 1970s) have probably been closest to the concept of industrial democracy.

The next category has been aimed at creating mass production in *vertically integrated firms*, on the basis of formal hierarchies producing for mass markets. This production organization strives for 'economies of scale' and has been called 'Fordism' (Gramsci 1980). In fact, this category needs to be divided into two concepts of control. The third concept of control can be dubbed *macro-Fordism* (cf. Mjøset 1987) and represents a situation in which core firms are confronted with relatively strong bargaining partners, such as national trade union federations and stronger national governments. Under such a regime, actors share the highest degree of interdependence (in the sense of mutual and equal dependence). The core firm will be forced to strike deals with others actors which most closely resemble a *coalition*. Under such circumstances it can be relatively attractive for the core firm to transfer its interest representation to a national employers' organization that bargains with governments and trade unions in a national context. In many of the smaller industrial countries this has led to tripartite corporatist bargaining institutions.

The fourth concept of control is called *micro-Fordism*, and represents the 'ideal typical' Fordism pioneered by Henry Ford. In micro-Fordism, *large, vertically integrated core firms* are aiming at economies of scale through a company-internal division of labour. High levels of vertical integration lead to relatively adversarial bargaining relations with suppliers and distributors/dealers. Deals with workers are struck at the level of the firm or of the industry at most. Its updated version could be called 'neo-Fordism'. Under neo-Fordism, core firms would also be able to serve medium-sized (and sometimes even small-sized) markets, due to the use of more flexible technologies and the introduction of less rigid organizational structures.

The fifth concept of control evolves around *large vertically de-integrated firms*, overseeing relatively *informal hierarchies* producing for medium-scale markets at first, but later also for mass markets. When analysing the German shift from Fordism to 'automated Fordism' or 'ultra-Fordism', Dohse *et al.* (1984) observed the rise of a confronting concept which they dubbed 'Toyotism'. Toyotist firms are aimed at 'economies of scope', which implies shorter production runs than Fordist firms. Toyotism, therefore, is better equipped than Fordism to produce for smaller-scale and niche markets. Others have proposed the term 'Japanization' or 'Fujitsuism' (Oliver and

Wilkinson 1988; Kenney and Florida 1988; cf. Jacot 1990). However, Toyotist firms are not necessarily Japanese, and Japanese firms are not necessarily Toyotist. For instance, Japanese companies such as Honda, Canon and Sony are probably closer to the micro-Fordist concept of control, due to a lack of structural control over their supply and distribution base, and their isolation on the industrial and political scene affected by more established companies.

These five concepts represent ideal types of how – temporarily – to resolve the five basic control problems of capitalist production and accumulation. Each of these ideal types has emerged in a very specific economic, social and political setting, and has flourished in a particular international context. Therefore, after it has emerged, the 'purest' form of the concept of control will long be found in the country of origin. However, the principles of each concept of control are *universally applicable*, provided that the proper economic, social and political environment is available or is created at the same time. The latter condition is very difficult to realize. Thus concepts of control are at the same time *unique* in the sense that they require a specific infrastructure and governance structure to emerge, and *general* in their *potential* as a model for capitalist production and accumulation.

BARGAINING AND POWER IN INDUSTRIAL COMPLEXES

As indicated, the interaction within an industrial complex can be analysed in terms of *bargaining*. A central element in the bargaining process is the concept of *power*. According to a traditional US definition, power represents 'the authoritative allocation of norms and values over society' (Parsons 1957). Dahl (1957) defined power as 'actor A's ability to make B do something he would not have done otherwise'. Political scientists have further distinguished between power and influence.

> [I]nfluence is applicable to a situation where A affects individual B, without B subordinating his wishes to those of A. . . . That is to say, A has influence over B, and over the making of a decision, but it is B that has the power finally to decide.
>
> (Pateman 1979: 69–70).

The question of how to use these concepts in analysing restructuring and corporate strategies is far from evident. According to Williamson and Ouchi, the 'distribution of power within the firms [is] endogenous and determined by the efficiency needs' (1981: 363–4). Although Williamson admits that regulation regimes are sensitive to bargaining processes and relations between business and government, he is not very impressed by the results of political scientists' research on firm behaviour. In his view, the notion of power 'is often used in ways that are either tautological or confuse power outcomes with efficiency' (1990: 8). In spite of this, 'delimiting the uses of power reasoning and establishing when and how the concept of power adds to rather than confuses our understanding of economic organisation would be major contributions' (1990: 8).

Several authors have argued in favour of introducing the role of power into economic theory. Rothschild (1971) argued that 'economics is a social science', that 'the economy is guided not only by the search for gain, but also by that for power' (1971: 7), and called upon economists to fill this deficiency in economic theory. Mainstream economic theory seems to have made little progress in this respect. In the management literature, Andrew Pettigrew (1973, 1992) and Jeffrey Pfeffer (1992) have tried to introduce the concept of power in the analysis of organizational behaviour and decision-making.

Obviously, it is often difficult to point out exactly how and why firms are exercising power. The act of doing business does not allow business people to talk openly about their strategies of playing off one supplier against another, or influencing a local government. However, this lack of reliable information may be circumvented in a similar manner as political scientists have done when analysing 'pure politics'. It is possible for instance to measure decisions to put certain issues on the agenda, or voting behaviour, even if these only show the *outcome* and not necessarily the actual process of exercising power. Likewise, one may interpret the outcome of a bargaining process between a firm and another actor as an indication that power has been exercised, even if we lack detailed information on the very 'whys' and 'hows' of this. If we define the core firm as actor A and its bargaining partner as actor B, we may assume (even without detailed information on the respective agendas of A and B) that B does not manoeuvre itself voluntarily into a position in which the core firm largely dictates to B what to do, i.e. in which B depends on A. If a bargaining process between A and B nevertheless *does* create such dependency of B on A, this can be attributed to A occupying a stronger bargaining position than B. Such an approach implies an *ex post* reconstruction or 'backward engineering' of A's and B's initial positions.

The next step then is to assess the effects of particular deals between two actors on their respective dependence, and to rank these deals on a scale ranging from 'no effect' on either actors' dependence to 'B becoming entirely dependent on A'. One can distinguish three basic positions *vis-à-vis* the core firm: (cf. Wallensteen 1973: 32)

1 independent
2 interdependent and,
3 dependent

Position of Partner ↓

INDEPENDENT	INDEPENDENT WITH INFLUENCE	INTERDEPENDENT	DEPENDENT WITH INFLUENCE	DEPENDENT WITHOUT INFLUENCE
[	][	][	][	]
CO-OPERATION OR COMPETITION	COMPLIANCE	COALITION	DIRECT CONTROL	STRUCTURAL CONTROL

Attitude ↑ of core firm

Figure 5.1 A continuum of dependency relations in an industrial complex

However, power may be exercised in two directions: from A to B and from B to A. Thus, even if B is more dependent on A than vice versa, B may still be able to exert some influence over A. Conversely, if B is independent of A, B may still be able to influence A. Therefore, the relative positions of actors A and B are shaped by their respective influence over each other. Figure 5.1 combines these two elements on a continuum, which shows parties' *relative bargaining positions* towards each other.

The upper categories in Figure 5.1 refer to the dependency relations in an industrial complex and to B's position in relation to core actor A. The lower categories refer to the attitude or strategy of the core firm. Based on the dimensions of dependency and influence, one can distinguish six basic bargaining attitudes of a core firm *vis-à-vis* the other actors:

1 cooperation
2 competition;
3 compliance;
4 coalition;
5 direct control; or
6 structural control.

The dependency scale shows two partners' relative bargaining position at a given instant. Although the scale represents the relative bargaining positions at a particular moment in time, these positions may of course shift over time. Figure 5.2 shows two lines approximating both partners' relative influence over each other in a qualitative manner. If at a given position one line is further away from the horizontal axis than the other, this should be read as one actor occupying a better bargaining position than the other. The five positions will be briefly discussed below:

- At the left extreme of the scale (*independent*), two actors may choose to interact or not, yet in either case they cannot exert any influence over each other. The distance A–a′ equals the distance A–a″;

Table 5.1 Five bargaining characteristics related to five concepts of control

Position partner	*Independent:*	*Independent with influence:*	*Interdependent:*	*Dependent with influence:*	*Dependent without influence:*
Core firm towards	*flexible specialization*	*industrial democracy*	*macro-Fordism*	*micro-Fordism*	*Toyotism*
Suppliers	• division of labour • flexible supply: high degree of substitution between suppliers • local deliveries • competitive and co-operative relations • no clear profit hierarchy	• minority share holding • supplier of strategic components, longer-term supply contracts favoured • many single sourcing relations • profit of supplier may surpass that of core firm	• division of labour in which (small number of) suppliers have also relationships with other core firms • local delivery • no clear pattern of profit distribution • single sourcing relations	• vertical integration • large numbers of competing suppliers • international deliveries (global sourcing) • antagonistic relations • profits tend to diverge, but not in a hierarchy • low level of black box engineering	• vertical deintegration • small number of prime contractors • local deliveries • control hierarchy with coalition between core firm and first tier suppliers • profits: only convergence with first tier suppliers • high level of black box engineering
Distributors/ dealers	• risk of becoming dominated by distributors is high • limited influence on ultimate price of product	• distributors can hold shares in core firm • core firms are confronted with many mega-dealers • dealers can earn larger profit margins than core firms	• converging profit margins • important function for importers • importers 'partners' of the core company: no large price differences around the world	• core firm tries to own the distributors and importers • low price at production site, higher prices abroad (due to higher transport costs)	• control (i.e. via data networks) • single franchise dealers • less importance for importers • higher prices in market of production site, lower prices abroad ('export residual')

Table 5.1 continued

Position partner	*Independent:*	*Independent with influence:*	*Interdependent:*	*Dependent with influence:*	*Dependent without influence:*
Core firm towards	*flexible specialization*	*industrial democracy*	*macro-Fordism*	*micro-Fordism*	*Toyotism*
Trade unions/ workers	● loose relation with (craft-orientated) unions or no unions ● nationally or internationally organized unions	● national union confederations ● representation at company council ● national productivity coalitions	● (multinational) company council, representing sectoral unions ● sectoral productivity coalitions	● firm-orientated or sectoral unions ● contrasting interests ● country by country productivity coalitions (weak co-ordination)	● plant/company unions ● firm loyalty ● decentralized productivity coalitions (centrally co-ordinated) ● rigorous selection
Financiers	● effort to autofinance ● family company ● distant relation with (limited number of) banks	● industrial bank with unilateral directorships and considerable shareholding in core firm ● institutional investors ● commercial bank having financed large part of company's debt	● financial group ● relationship with first tier bank issuing bonds or first tier bank issuing stock as head of underwriter syndicate ● coalition with bank	● direct control over own finances ● large number of small stockholders ● high degree of self-financing ● underwriter hierarchies ● adversarial relations with banks	● collaborative relation with first tier banks ● mutual shareholdings in other firms of the same conglomerate ● high degree of self-financing without this being used
Governments	● arm's-length relations ● government support of 'keep it small' policies ● Relatively strong supra-national governments	● strong national home governments, making use of a variety of instruments curbing the influence of individual firms ● nationalizations	● strong regional/state home governments ● loose coalitions ● active procurement policies ● subsidies sustaining diversity in the industrial structure	● *ad-hoc* coalitions with national/federal governments ● adaptive/independent from local environment ● active 'creation' of local environment in company towns	● local player status preferred ● focus primarily on local governments ● structurally dominant position ● no need to control the region directly

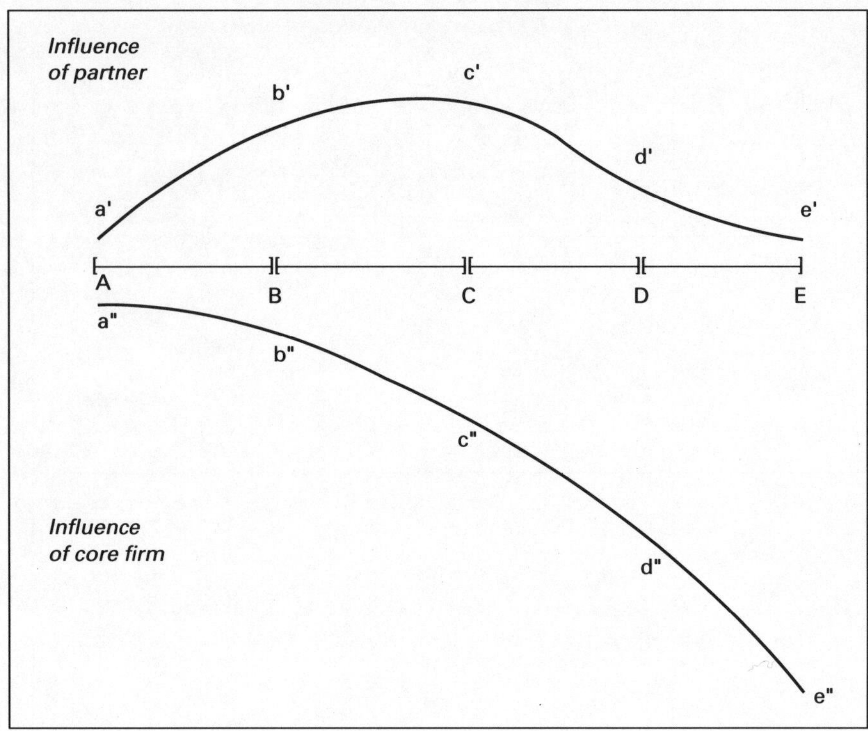

Figure 5.2 Uneven distribution of relative influence

- Moving to the right (*independent with influence*), the balance of influence shifts in favour of the partner. This is the only instance at which the core actor may be driven to act differently than it would have done otherwise, due to the pressure exerted by the other actor. Thus the distance B–b′ is larger than the distance B–b″;
- In the middle of the scale (*interdependence*), the balance of influence of both partners is restored again. The distance C–c′ again equals the distance C–c″;
- Moving further to the right (*dependent with influence*), the core actor clearly becomes the stronger partner. The line shows that the distance D–d′ is smaller than the distance D–d″. Note, however, that the D position is not simply a reversal of position B. At B, the core actor may have to comply with the other actor's strategies, but it maintains its independence. At D the partner has come to be in a dependent situation;
- Finally, at the right extreme of the scale (*dependent without influence*), the partner has lost virtually every possibility to influence the core actor's behaviour. At this position, the distance E–e″ is infinitely larger than the distance E–e′.

Table 5.2 Five concepts of control and empirical approximations

Concept of control	*Nature of industrial complex*	*Core firm's strategy towards bargaining partners*	*Approximations*
Flexible specialization	changing network of suppliers, different sizes and capabilities, no intervention by government (except in catastrophes)	*co-operation and/or competition*: one core firm is unable to control another	'Italian SME model': clothing, ceramics, shoe and leather industry; ancient 'British model' (Rolls-Royce)
Industrial democracy	core firm surrounded by strong and relatively independent suppliers, financiers, labour unions and governments	*compliance*: substantial concessions to bargaining partners	'Swedish model': Volvo, Electrolux
Macro-Fordism	partial vertical integration, supplemented by strong and relatively interdependent suppliers, financiers, labour unions and governments	*coalition*: established bargaining patterns with strong suppliers, trade unions and governments	'German model': Volkswagen; Mercedes-Benz; Siemens; Mannesmann; Bosch
Micro-Fordism	advanced vertical integration; suppliers, financiers, labour unions and governments unable to exert much influence over core firm	*direct control*: attempt to control bargaining partners via take-overs; play off governments; avert sectoral trade unions	'American model': Ford; IBM
Toyotism	vertical deintegration; vertical supply and distribution pyramid sanctioned by government	*structural control*: attempt to control legally independent bargaining partners via order portfolio control over technology, managing their financial room, company unions	'Japanese model': Toyota; Matsushita

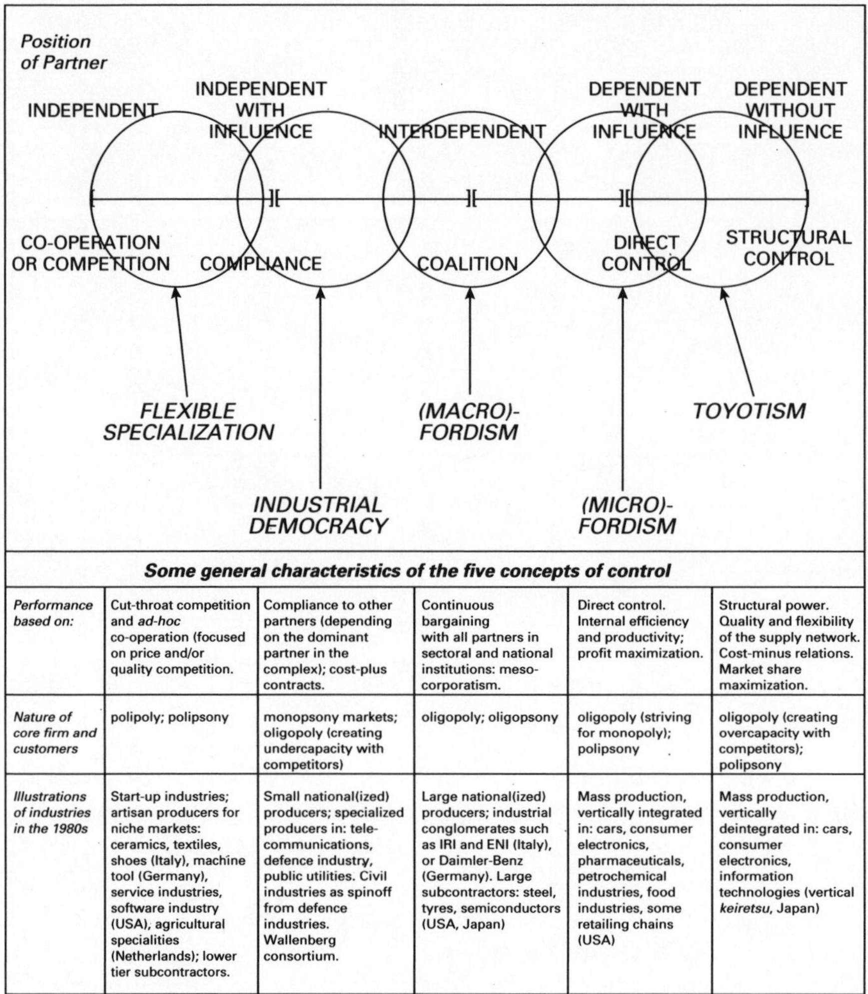

Some general characteristics of the five concepts of control

Performance based on:	Cut-throat competition and *ad-hoc* co-operation (focused on price and/or quality competition.	Compliance to other partners (depending on the dominant partner in the complex); cost-plus contracts.	Continuous bargaining with all partners in sectoral and national institutions: meso-corporatism.	Direct control. Internal efficiency and productivity; profit maximization.	Structural power. Quality and flexibility of the supply network. Cost-minus relations. Market share maximization.
Nature of core firm and customers	polipoly; polipsony	monopsony markets; oligopoly (creating undercapacity with competitors)	oligopoly; oligopsony	oligopoly (striving for monopoly); polipsony	oligopoly (creating overcapacity with competitors); polipsony
Illustrations of industries in the 1980s	Start-up industries; artisan producers for niche markets: ceramics, textiles, shoes (Italy), machine tool (Germany), service industries, software industry (USA), agricultural specialities (Netherlands); lower tier subcontractors.	Small national(ized) producers; specialized producers in: tele-communications, defence industry, public utilities. Civil industries as spinoff from defence industries. Wallenberg consortium.	Large national(ized) producers; industrial conglomerates such as IRI and ENI (Italy), or Daimler-Benz (Germany). Large subcontractors: steel, tyres, semiconductors (USA, Japan)	Mass production, vertically integrated in: cars, consumer electronics, pharmaceuticals, petrochemical industries, food industries, some retailing chains (USA)	Mass production, vertically deintegrated in: cars, consumer electronics, information technologies (vertical *keiretsu*, Japan)

Figure 5.3 Dependency relations and the position of the five concepts of control

In sum, the upper line of Figure 5.2 depicts what could be seen as an uneven distribution, whereas the lower line shows a progressively downward sloping line.

Each position on the dependency scale represents a different *mode of conflict management*. Since it is not possible in this chapter to discuss all five bargaining relations and their implications, Table 5.1 summarizes the indicators of all five bargaining constellations. The relation between these modes of conflict management and the rival concepts of control is shown in Figure 5.3. As an approximation of the five concepts of control, Table 5.2 mentions some examples of core producers in various industries (see also pages 94ff).

If a core firm has succeeded in organizing its relationships with *all* five domestic bargaining partners at one and the same position on the dependency scale, the bargaining arena of the industrial complex is characterized by a high degree of cohesion. *The higher the cohesion of the bargaining arena, the more the outcome of the bargaining processes represents one of the concepts of control.* In such a case, the institutional setting, i.e. the roles and policies of governments and the bargaining procedures (the rules of the game) between the core firm and its bargaining partners, are transparent to all participants (though not necessarily to outsiders). Conversely, the lower the level of cohesion, the more turbulent bargaining patterns within the industrial complex will be, and the more each bargaining partner will try to maximize its individual short-term profits.

Since national economies often contain more than one industrial complex, it is useful to distinguish between an industrial complex and the *national industrial system* (Lundvall 1988; Nelson 1993; De Banville and Chanaron, 1991). For instance, the German car system consists of the Volkswagen, Ford, Opel, Mercedes-Benz and BMW complexes. If a national system contains more than one industrial complex, different types of bargaining and different concepts of control may co-exist for a transient period. However, within national industrial systems, bargaining patterns have tended to converge along the lines of the bargaining rules set by the most cohesive complex, at the expense of the weaker complex(es).

Within the EU, convergence of such a common denominator is much less likely to emerge due to the national sovereignty of the individual member states. As a result, fifteen industrial systems and dozens of industrial complexes produce a cacophony of agendas competing for dominance.

RIVAL VIEWS ON COMPETITIVENESS, SUBSIDIARITY AND OBJECTIVES

Table 5.3 shows that the five concepts of control each present different visions on the issues of competitiveness, subsidiarity and objectives. While subsidiarity and policy objectives are normally outside the direct sphere of

Table 5.3 Stylized views related to each concept of control on subsidiarity, competitiveness and objectives

View on/definition of → *Concept of control* ↓	*Competitiveness*	*Subsidiarity*	*Objectives*
Flexible specialization	valued highly, to be achieved by market sector	no major issue	government abstention, yet generic tax measures, fierce competition policy (to avert concentration) and intellectual property rights enforcement
Industrial democracy	'fair' return to all bargaining partners (stakeholders) valued, not competition as such	potentially an issue, since supra-national authority may distort critical power balance among bargaining partners	government has legitimate role to play to support competitiveness of entire industry (not just national champions) and to promote social contract; relatively weak competition policy enforcement
Macro-Fordism	one of several objectives, competitiveness seen as vehicle to realize other bargaining partners' interests as well	no major issue as long as it does not outpace companies' internationalization	government (trade and/or industrial) support may be necessary but must be reassessed regularly; moderate competition policy and intellectual property rights enforcement
Micro-Fordism	leading motive, also in deciding whether to increase or decrease vertical integration	fear of rise of strong bargaining partner; internationalization as *runaway* from government power	fierce competition policy and intellectual property rights enforcement; averse from specific industrial and trade policies
Toyotism	of absolutely overriding importance, all other bargaining partners subjected to pursuit of competitiveness	major issue: fear of creating powerful supra-national body which could undermine core companies' control strategies	government has legitimate role in maintaining structural control over supply and distribution systems (esp. in build-up phase); weak competition policy and intellectual property rights enforcement

influence of core companies – albeit the object of articulated demands *vis-à-vis* governments – the competitiveness issue directly touches the core firm and its industrial complex. The quest for *competitiveness* is at best one out of several objectives in two concepts of control (industrial democracy and macro-Fordism). These two concepts of control have been dominant in leading continental EU economies, such as Germany, France and Italy – although in different degrees and at declining levels of cohesion. In these member states, core firms' bargaining partners have successfully bargained for their share of the profits: workers bargained for relatively high wages, holidays and fringe benefits, governments for relatively high taxes, and suppliers for high input prices, thus forcing companies to broaden the scope of their agendas[4] (see also Pat Devine in this volume).

In the other three concepts of control (flexible specialization, micro-Fordism and Toyotism), the absence of strong bargaining partners implies that competitiveness is an objective in itself for the core firm. Even more than for the other concepts of control, competitiveness is the key to the economic survival of the flexible specialization type of firm, since it often lacks financial reserves. The ultimate micro-Fordist company seeks to secure its competitiveness through a worldwide division of labour, exploiting comparative advantages all over the world. If it is faced with stronger bargaining partners at home, it will either seek to diminish their power or gradually *escape* its domestic bargaining arena. The Toyotist core firm also attaches utmost importance to the issue of competitiveness, but it seeks to obtain this by seeking to manoeuvre its bargaining partner into a position of severe and continuous pressure where they have no choice but to perform as best as they can.[5]

The issues of subsidiarity and (policy) objectives belong to the realm of government. *Subsidiarity* appears to be an issue in particular in the concepts of control of micro-Fordism and Toyotism, and perhaps to some extent in industrial democracy. In the former two, the core firm's aim is to dominate, or otherwise be invulnerable to, its bargaining partners, including the national government. Raising governmental powers to the supra-national level would amount to creating a stronger bargaining partner which could even lend its ear to companies adherring to different concepts of control. Companies working in a regime of industrial democracy, on the other hand, would operate less from a position of strength and would rather fear to be confronted with an even more formidable bargaining partner.

Firms operating with a flexible specialization or macro-Fordist concept of control would be less likely to stress the issue of subsidiarity. A macro-Fordist firm would be prepared to extend its coalition pattern at a higher governmental level and establish an international division of labour within one world trade bloc (a *regional division of labour*). This strategy has been followed by a number of European firms over the 1980s and 1990s, such as Philips, Renault and Siemens. A flexible specialization type of firm would have limited bargaining power anyway and as such would not feel threatened by supranational government.

Finally, *policy objectives* differ widely among the five concepts of control. Core firms conforming to the principles of either industrial democracy, macro-Fordism or Toyotism tend to see a legitimate role for national governments to play in promoting competitiveness – although they disagree as to what governments should actually do. Companies operating in the concepts of flexible specialization and micro-Fordism both would want to keep the government's role limited, and orientate it towards generic and particularly anti-trust and intellectual property rights enforcement.

THE MANAGEMENT OF DEPENDENCIES IN INDUSTRIAL SYSTEMS: SHIFTING COHESION, SHIFTING CONCEPTS OF CONTROL

In a closed bargaining arena characterized by high levels of cohesion, i.e. in which all major core firms and their bargaining partners orientate themselves to the same concept of control, none of the three issues discussed here poses a problem. Tensions emerge only if rival concepts of control are vying for dominance, either because an industrial system becomes penetrated by strong companies adherring to another concept of control, or because formerly independent industrial systems with different concepts of control are brought together into a larger legal system – such as the EU.

Over the 1980s and 1990s, the international restructuring race triggered major changes in most national bargaining arenas. These changes were associated with the internationalization of domestic and foreign firms and thus represented the 'clash' of rival concepts of control on an international scale. Table 5.4 (see pp. 96–7) appraises the shifting concepts of control and levels of cohesion in eight industrial systems. (For the sake of comparison, we have also included the US and Japan, but these will not be discussed here.)

In spite of considerable pressure over the 1980s and 1990s, *French* bargaining institutions have shown remarkable adaptability to the international restructuring race. The French industrial system has long protected itself from inroads of industrial complexes representing alternative concepts of control, while those foreign core firms that did establish themselves in France have been forced to *adapt* to French bargaining institutions. The spirit of Colbert has lived on in France: in particular industries with a high public procurement content (defence, aerospace, public utilities, banking and telecommunications) have been able – in close consultation with state agencies – to restructure and remain among Europe's most competitive industries. In the car and computer industries, however, it has proved difficult to complement a weak supply base by big national investment projects, aimed at creating a *filière* (chain) of supply activities. Another French government strategy to defend macro-Fordism has been to strengthen bilateral bonds with Germany (home of the renowned

Mittelstand of small and medium-sized enterprises). At the same time, it has taken a more active (although still ambivalent) approach to the promotion of European integration: over the 1980s, French government and industry bureaucrats have flooded the European bureaucracy.

The cohesion of the *German* industrial system over the 1960s and 1970s was extremely high. The economic success and international competitiveness of its most important core players retained most investments in its national system, fostering the stability of the corporatist bargaining institutions (cf. Grabher 1993). Cohesion has started to slip since the late 1970s. Inroads by foreign core firms only played a minor role in this. More important was that the German institutional setting proved ill-adapted to the challenges of the microelectronics revolution. Furthermore, over the 1970s and 1980s many German firms began to search for a *regional* division of labour within Europe in a modest effort to profit from regional scale economies and in an equally modest effort to escape from domestic bargaining arrangements. After reunification, German firms suddenly faced a potential market of almost 80 million people, representing a growth of potential domestic purchasing power of around 30 per cent (see also Chapter 6 of this volume). The importance of this new market can hardly be overstated: it could absorb the bulk of German exports, and it could refocus attention on domestic expansion and bargaining. The German federal government funnelled hundreds of billions of Deutschmarks to the East, while German core and medium-sized players set up large scale investment programmes, often aimed at creating a division of labour within Germany itself instead of within the European region. Consequently, German's international trade dependence is likely to come more in line with the US and Japanese industrial systems (both dedicated around 8 per cent of their GDP to trade in 1993) (*The Economist*, 1994: 28). Thus there appear to be reasonable chances for a renewed macro-Fordist growth regime within Germany.

Over the 1980s and 1990s, *Dutch* companies and financiers have been among the leading sources of foreign direct investment in the United States – even outpacing Japanese investors. This enormous investment 'leakage' contributed to a gradual de-industrialization, to lower cohesion and to a downward pressure on wages and purchasing power. Moreover, a rapid decline of trade union membership (from 35 per cent in 1980 to around 20 per cent in 1994) undermined the traditional tripartite corporatist bargaining practice. The Dutch government also actively stimulated inward-orientated FDI, and the Dutch economy became a major target of Japanese distribution centres, accelerating the demise of macro-Fordism and creating a gradual shift towards Toyotism.

Over the 1980s, *Sweden* faced only limited inflows of foreign direct investment (below 5 per cent). However, Swedish cohesion was undermined by the internationalization of Swedish multinationals to the European continent, stimulated by the industrial banks. To some extent, this 'hollowed out'

Table 5.4 Diverging bargaining arenas and shifting concepts of control in Europe, the USA and Japan

National industrial system	■ *dominant concept of control (±1980)*[a] ■ *cohesion (indic.)*	*Trends in domestic bargaining arena (1990s)*	*Government's bargaining position (re: industrial/trade policies)*
Germany	■ macro-Fordism ■ strong cohesion	cohesion still considerable; E-Germany offers new chances: towards renewed macro-Fordism?	sustained, partly due to need for coordination in E-Germany
France	■ macro-Fordism (sometimes leaning towards ind.democr.) ■ strong cohesion	gradual opening-up to foreign competition may undermine cohesion (e.g. increasingly weak supply base)	de-nationalizations reflect gradual decline of gvt power; gvt may opt for further concentration (e.g. in cars)
UK	■ micro-Fordism ■ weak cohesion	independence of major core firms lost, increasingly becoming extension of Toyotist core firms	increasingly operating in line with Japanese and/or Toyotist interests
Italy	■ flexible specialization/ macro-Fordism ■ strong regional cohesion	gradual opening-up to foreign competition will undermine cohesion	business response is to seize even more control over gvt
Sweden	■ industrial democracy (leaning towards macro-Fordism) ■ strong cohesion	slipping domestic cohesion; independence of core firms under siege (cf. Volvo, Saab), may end up as extension of foreign micro-/macro-Fordist firms	gvt faced with inability of banks to play traditional role as financiers; gvt power also negatively affected by declining bargaining power of labour

Table 5.4 Continued

National industrial system	■ *dominant concept of control (±1980)*[a] ■ *cohesion (indic.)*	*Trends in domestic bargaining arena (1990s)*	*Government's bargaining position (re: industrial/trade policies)*
Netherlands	■ macro-Fordism ■ medium cohesion	dominance of distribution interests undermines position core firms; Toyotism on the rise	relatively weak gvt will further undermine manufacturing base and thus promote Toyotism
USA	■ micro-Fordism ■ medium cohesion	slipping cohesion due to runaway US firms (1960s to 1990s) escaping from domestic bargaining arena; cohesion further undermined by massive inroads of Toyotist producers	caught between free-market ideology and declining cohesion/competitiveness: relaxes anti-trust regulations, champions 'fair trade'; perhaps rehabilitation of defence policy as disguise for industrial policy
Japan	■ Toyotism ■ strong cohesion	cohesion relatively high yet under stress from 'bubble' economy, temporary increase in workers' bargaining power (due to labour shortage) and internationalization; current restructuring aimed at reviving Toyotism appears successful	national gvt supports core firms' restructuring agenda: to facilitate restructuring of banking system; maintains pressure to save (also to discipline workers) and to reduce pace of internationalization

[a] The dominant concept of control in this table serves as a point of orientation at the state level. However, a dominant concept of control may not be accomplished by all or even by the majority of core firms in a given industrial system.

the corporatist bargaining institutions and stimulated the Swedish government to apply for full membership of the European Union. However, while trade union membership declined in all other major industrial systems, membership *increased* in Sweden from 80 per cent in 1980 to 85.3 per cent in 1985 (OECD 1993: 49). This created a counter-movement from trade unions and large parts of the Swedish population. In this respect, the Swedish 1993 application for membership of the European Union reflected a declining domestic cohesion and posed a testcase of the relative bargaining strength of the Swedish trade unions.

By 1980, the *Italian* industrial system was based on a mixture of flexible specialization and macro-Fordist institutions. These institutions had materialized in a sub-national, i.e. regional, context complemented by weak central state regulation. Over the 1970s, this setting had spurred economic growth, but it also created an extremely closed system in which two *rival* concepts of control co-existed. This unstable balance of power was undermined by two forces. First, the continued rivalry between regions and related concepts of control could not be resolved for lack of a strong central government. Second, the Single European Act forced the Italian government gradually to open up the Italian economy. On the one hand, traditional core firms such as Fiat, Olivetti, IRI, Feruzzi and ENI became confronted with increasing international competition. On the other hand, new business moguls such as Carlo de Benedetti, Silvio Berlusconi and the Benetton family skilfully profited from the (chaotic) remains of the regionally organized clientist system. With a moderate capital involvement, these family-owned holding companies seized control over a considerable part of the Italian industrial and service economy. In the case of Benetton, the family holding company gradually transformed networks of flexible specialization into Toyotist networks of informal hierarchical control. Thus a third concept of control joined the battle for dominance in Italy. The brief ascendance of Berlusconi, a prime minister coming from a non-core part of the industrial system (the media), suggests that the battle for control over the state is likely to continue.

At the beginning of the 1980s, the *United Kingdom* was the only industrial system facing a weak cohesion. Bargaining relations between core firms on the one hand, workers and bankers on the other, had created a disturbed domestic setting. Furthermore, the UK had a high number of foreign investors in the national economy. By 1988, the relative importance of foreign direct investment stock in the UK economy was between 15 and 20 per cent (UNCTAD 1992: 63), a figure only surpassed by the Dutch economy. Although American firms had been the prime investors in the UK economy, and although these shared a micro-Fordist concept of control, US firms regarded their UK activities as an extension of their US home base, and the centre of decision-making processes remained firmly in the United States.

Since the late 1980s, UK cohesion has been further undermined by inward Japanese investment, particularly in manufacturing. In fact, Toyotism may have become the concept of control to which British companies aspire, even if they cannot implement it. On many occasions, the UK government has blocked or frustrated European decision-making, often supporting the interests of Toyotist core firms.[6] Furthermore, it bargained for three provisos in important parts of the 1991 Maastricht Treaty: an exemption from the Social Charter on workers' rights, a clause preventing more power to be given to the European Commission, and an opt-out provision on the membership of the Monetary Union (Milner 1994: 29). The bargaining institution of European Company Councils, for instance, required by the European Commission in companies with more one thousand employees, was agreed upon in September 1994 after twenty years of negotiations, yet will not apply formally to the UK.

THE EUROPEAN UNION AS THE BATTLEGROUND OF FOUR RIVAL CONCEPTS OF CONTROL

We began this chapter by asking why it has proved so difficult to formulate a common EU industrial strategy. We can now conclude that the rivalry between various concepts of control has greatly contributed to this deadlock.

The six European industrial systems which stood at the cradle of the European Community in 1957 (France, Italy, Germany, Belgium, the Netherlands and Luxembourg) each shared and developed a *macro-Fordist* environment. In none of the six additional members entering the EEC in 1973 (Britain, Ireland, Denmark, Spain, Portugal and Greece) did macro-Fordism represent the dominant concept of control. The late 1970s and early 1980s became the period of 'Eurosclerosis', manifested by declining cohesion. Problems were reinforced by Toyotist competition in two carriers of European macro-Fordism, i.e. the electronics and the car industries. Next to coal and steel, the electronics and car industries had been well represented in the six original member states of the European Community, but they had been either non-existent, poorly developed or had virtually disappeared in the new member states. Thus, while political consensus on steel could still be achieved, the car and electronics industries faced a scattered bargaining arena at the European Community level.

In response to the declining cohesion of their complexes and to Eurosclerosis, some major core firms over the 1980s took initiatives to increase integration and competitiveness, leading to acronyms such as ESPRIT, RACE, AMICE, START and BRITE. The year 1983 also saw the birth of the European Roundtable of Industrialists (ERT), providing European core companies with a European discussion forum as well as a sounding board for the European Commission. Due to these combined initiatives, European integration got a new impetus, inevitably shifting some bargaining power towards the European Commission. However, the principle of subsidiarity agreed in the Maastricht Treaty implied that the EU institutional setting remains weak and that the impact of European industrial policies will remain limited.

Thus it can be observed that the *shape* of major European bargaining institutions has tended to reflect those of the strongest and most cohesive industrial systems, i.e. the German and to a lesser extent the French ones. Examples include the areas of competition policy and the creation of a relatively independent European Central Bank. At the same time, however, EU institutions have been *unable* on fundamental issues to force individual industrial complexes to follow the agreed bargaining rules. The European Union has become the *battleground of at least four rival concepts of control*: flexible specialization, macro-Fordism, micro-Fordism and Toyotism. This means that it is very difficult to reach consensus on fundamental issues of competitiveness and industrial policy. The European Union's main competitors do not suffer from this weakness: the United States and Japan only have one or at most two concepts of control in their industrial systems competing for dominance.

The major challenge facing the European Commission and the core EU members today is to represent their gradually disintegrating macro-Fordist concept of control more vigorously and to pressure in particular the UK government to accept these bargaining rules. The discussion on a 'multi-speed Europe' (the core industrial systems of Germany, France, the Netherlands, Belgium and Luxembourg proceeding more rapidly with monetary and political integration than the other member states) may be seen as a desperate attempt to sustain the cohesion of the traditional macro-Fordist European industrial systems, and to limit potentially disruptive competition from other concepts of control.

NOTES

1 This chapter borrows much of its argumentation from a broader study titled *The Logic of International Restructuring: The Management of Dependencies in Rival Industrial Complexes* (Ruigrok and Van Tulder 1995). A follow-up study (Routledge 1996) is to apply the framework presented here to the world car industry.

2 In principle, the term 'industrial complex' also pertains to 'service industries'. Over the 1980s, services contributed a growing share to developed economies' GNP, particularly in the US, leading to claims of 'servitization' as the new key to creating competitive advantage (cf. Vandermerwe and Rada 1988). In reality, the distinction between industry and services (as between agriculture and industry) is becoming increasingly blurred (cf. Cohen and Zysman 1987). For instance, due to outsourcing, services such as bookkeeping or catering that were previously defined as 'industrial jobs' have been *redefined* as 'service jobs', without a change in the content of the work (even if the context, i.e. the dependency *vis-à-vis* the core firm, may have changed substantially). Core firms will often be manufacturing firms but may also be independent service providers (e.g. IBM).

3 The term 'concept of control' has been borrowed from authors of the so-called 'Amsterdam School' of international relations (Bode 1979; Van der Pijl 1984;

Overbeek 1990), who defined a concept of control as 'a coherent set of strategies in the area of labour relations, socio-economic policies and foreign policies' (Overbeek 1990: 26) that presents a specific interest in terms of the 'general interest'. For a discussion of their definition of a concept of control and our critique, see Ruigrok and Van Tulder (1995).

4 As a 'side-effect', this bargaining game has led financiers to become regarded more as long-term 'facilitators' than as 'owners' entitled to immediate dividends on their investments.

5 Divergence over the quest for competitiveness has recently become the object of a heated debate in Flanders (Belgium), France and Portugal, as a result of a publication of the so-called *Lisbon group* (Petrella 1994). This publication argues in favour of a *global social contract* to stem what is perceived as the vicious cycle of seeking to enhance competitiveness by reducing employment levels and by exploiting the environment. An English edition of the *Grenzen aan de Concurrentie* ('Limits to Competition') book will be published by MIT Press (Boston), Spring 1995.

6 Representing the interests of Honda, Nissan and Toyota, the UK government prevented Japanese transplants from being included in the EC-Japan car trade agreement (1991) (cf. Ruigrok and Van Tulder 1991: 197ff). On behalf of ICL (taken over by Fujitsu), it successfully bargained for ICL's admission to EU collaboration programmes and pressured the European Commission to open up EU collaborative programmes to companies from non-EU member states. (In the United States, by comparison, participation in pre-competitive R&D programmes is restricted to companies that are at least 51 per cent American-owned, while *de facto* restrictions in Japan are even more prohibitive). On behalf of Japanese television makers with UK facilities such as Sony, Matsushita and Sharp, the UK government frustrated the adoption of a European High Definition TV standard.

REFERENCES

Andersen, E.S. and Lundvall B.Å. (1988) 'Small National Systems of Innovation Facing Technological Revolutions: An Analytical Framework' in C. Freeman and B. Ake-Lundvall (eds), *Small Countries Facing the Technological Revolution*, London/New York: Pinter Publishers.

Bachrach, P. and Baratz, M. (1969) 'Decisions and Non-Decisions: An Analytical Framework', in R. Bell (eds), *Political Power: A Reader in Theory and Research*, New York: Free Press.

Bode, R. (1979) 'De Nederlandse Bourgeoisie tussen de Twee Wereldoorlogen', *Cahiers voor de Politieke en Sociale Wetenschappen*, 2, 4: 9–50.

Braverman, H. (1974) *Labor and Monopoly Capital*, New York: Monthly Review Press.

Burawoy, M. (1985) *The Politics of Production*, London: Verso.

Cohen, R. and Zysman, J. (1987) *Manufacturing Matters: The Myth of the Post-Industrial Economy*, New York: Basic Books.

Dahl, R. (1957) 'The Concept of Power', *Behavioral Science*, 2: 201–5.

De Banville, E. and Chanaron J-J. (1991) *Vers un Systèm Automobile Européen*, Paris: CPE-Economica.

Dohse, K., Jürgens, U and Malsch T. (1984), 'Vom "Fordismus" zum "Toyotismus"? Die Organisation der industriellen Arbeit in der japanischen Automobilindustrie', *Leviathan*, 12, 4 (published in English in *Politics and Society*, 14, 2, 1985: 115–46).

Economist (1994) *Pocket World in Figures*, London: Penguin and Economist Books.

Galtung, J. (1971) 'A Structural Theory of Imperialism', *Journal of Peace Research*, 8, 2: 437–82.

Grabher, G. (ed.) (1993) *The Embedded Firm*, London: Routledge.

Gramsci, A. (1980), *Selections from the Prison Notebooks*, edited by Q. Hoare and G. Nowell Smith, New York/London: Lawrence and Wishart.

Jacot, H. (ed.) (1990) *Du Fordisme au Toyotisme? Les Voies de la Modernisation du Système Automobile en France et au Japon*, Paris (La Documentation Française): Commisariat General du Plan, février.

Junne, G. (1987) 'Automation in the North: Consequences for Developing Countries' Exports', in J. Caporaso (ed.) *A Changing International Division of Labour*, London: Pinter.

Kenney, M. and Florida, R. (1988) 'Beyond Mass Production: Production and the Labor Process in Japan' *Politics and Society*, 1,6 (1): 121–58.

Lundvall, B. Å. (1988) 'Innovation as an Interactive Process: from User-Producer Interaction to the National System of Innovation' in G. Dosi, C. Freeman, R. Nelson, G. Silverberg and L. Soete (eds) *Technical Change and Economic Theory*, London: Pinter.

—— *National Systems of Innovation: Towards a Theory of Innovation and Interactive Learning*, London: Pinter.

Mathews, J. (1989) *Age of Democracy: The Politics of Post-Fordism*, Melbourne: Oxford University Press, 278 pp.

Milner, H. (1994) *The Domestic Political Economy of International Economic Cooperation: A Comparison of the NAFTA Accord and the Maastricht Treaty*, Paper prepared for the 22nd annual ECPR Conference, April 18–22, Madrid, Spain.

Mjøset, L. (1987) 'Nordic Economies in the 1970s and 1980s', *International Organization*, 41, 3, Summer: 403–56.

Nelson, R. (1993) *National Innovation Systems: A Comparative Analysis*, Oxford: Oxford University Press.

OECD (1993) *Obstacles to Trade and Competition*, Paris: OECD.

Oliver, N. and Wilkinson, B. (1988) *The Japanization of British Industry*, London: Basil Blackwell.

Overbeek, H. (1990) *Global Capitalism and National Decline: The Thatcher Decade in Perspective*, London/New York: Unwin Hyman.

Parsons, T. (1957) 'The Distribution of Power in American Society', *World Politics*, 10, October: 123–43.

Pateman, C. (1979) *Participation and Democratic Theory*, Cambridge: Cambridge University Press.

Petrella, R. (1989) 'La Mondialisation de la Technologie et de l'Économie', *Futuribles*, Septembre 3–25.

—— (1994) *Grenzen aan de Concurrentie*, Brussel: VUB Press.

Pettigrew, A. (1973) *The Politics of Organisational Decision-Making*, London: Tavistock.

—— (1992) 'On Studying Managerial Elites', *Strategic Management Journal*, 13, Winter Special Edition, 163–82.

Pfeffer, J. (1992) *Managing with Power: Politics and Influence in Organisations*, Boston: Harvard Business School Press.

Rothschild, K. (ed.) (1971) *Power in Economics: Selected Readings*, Harmondsworth: Penguin.

Ruigrok, W. and van Tulder, R., with the assistance of Geert Baven (1991) *Cars and Complexes: Globalisation versus Global Localisation Strategies in the World Car Industry*, Brussels: Commission of the European Communities/Monitor-FAST, FOP 285.

Ruigrok, W. and van Tulder, R. (1995) *The Logic of International Restructuring: The Management of Dependencies in Rival Industrial Complexes*, London: Routledge.
UNCTAD (1992) *Handbook on International Trade and Development Statistics*, New York: United Nations Conference on Trade and Development.
Van der Pijl, K. (1984) *The Making of an Atlantic Ruling Class*, London: Verso, 1984.
Vandermerwe, S. and Rada, J. (1988) 'Servitization of Business: Adding Value by Adding Services', *European Management Journal*, 6, Autumn: 314–24.
Van Tulder, R. and Junne, G. (1988) *European Multinationals and Core Technologies*, Chichester/London: Wiley & Sons.
Wallensteen, P. (1973) 'Structure and War: On International Relations 1920–1968', *Political Sciences Association in Uppsala*, 64.
Williamson, O. (1990) 'The Firm as a Nexus of Treaties: An Introduction', in M. Aoki, B. Gustafsson and O. Williamson, *The Firm as a Nexus of Treaties*, London: Sage.
Williamson, O. and Ouchi, W. (1983) 'The Markets and Hierarchies Perspective: Origins, Implications, Prospects', in Francis, Turk and Willman (eds) *Power, Efficiency and Institutions: A Critical Appraisal of the 'Markets and Hierarchies Paradigm'*, London: Heinemann.

6

EUROPEAN ENLARGEMENT, COMPETITIVENESS AND INTEGRATION

Kirsty Hughes

INTRODUCTION

This chapter considers the implications for European integration and European competitiveness of the changes in the economic relations of East and West Europe since 1989. It focuses on the *de facto* enlargement of the EU economy, which is already occurring due to the transition processes in Central and Eastern Europe (CEE), rather than on the specific arguments concerning admission of the CEE countries to the EU. The nature of the latter debate – about EU enlargement – requires first a clearer understanding of the political and economic changes that are occurring irrespective of future EU institutional changes.

The CEE economies are, to differing degrees, becoming integrated into the international economic system, through trade, investment and institutional developments. The CEE economies are developing particularly strong economic relations with Germany. This has important implications for those economies themselves, for the German economy, and for the other West European economies. This chapter argues that this enlargement of the European economy will not *per se* promote or reflect increased European integration but rather represents a process of readjustment of economic relations and interests. This implies a process of structural change that will be likely to reinforce differences in competitiveness rather than encourage convergence.

The chapter first looks at some of the available statistical evidence and then discusses the implications for competitiveness and integration.

FOREIGN DIRECT INVESTMENT AND INTERNATIONAL TRADE

Both foreign direct investment and international trade flows between western and eastern Europe have increased substantially since 1989. This section looks at some of the available statistical evidence, focusing on the Czech Republic,

Hungary and Poland, which through to 1994 have accounted for the bulk of foreign investment into Central and Eastern Europe. Germany is the largest trading partner of these three counties, but in terms of foreign direct investment flows into Central and Eastern Europe, the US is currently in first position and Germany is in second position, ahead of any of the other EU countries. We consider first the foreign direct investment evidence and then the trade statistics. It should be stressed that the data in this area are not robust and that data from different national and different international sources frequently give different outcomes. Nevertheless it is possible to obtain an overall picture of trends.

Foreign direct investment

Table 6.1 sets out the main host countries for foreign direct investment in the transition economies. As can be seen, Hungary accounts for over one third of the total investment flows to date. The Czech Republic, Hungary and Poland account for about three-quarters of inward FDI. Table 6.2 sets outs the ranking of source countries investing into these three countries as a group. The data in this table should be treated as approximate but they do give a clear overview of the ranking across western investors. The US is the largest investor, followed by Germany, and these two countries account for almost half of the investment. Austria and France account for about 8 per cent each of FDI while Italy and the UK along with other smaller countries account for 4–5 per cent each.

This pattern of US and German dominance is repeated across the three countries individually as shown in Tables 6.3 to 6.5. Table 6.3 sets out the largest source countries for foreign direct investment in Hungary excluding greenfield investment. Germany was the largest investor followed by the US and then Austria. Austria, relative to its size, has been responsible for a very large level of foreign investment into Central and Eastern Europe. It is also particularly characteristic of German and Austrian investments that many thousands of small and medium-sized enterprises have been making foreign investments and not only large firms. In the case of the US, there have been mostly large investments by large firms, though there are some indications that small and medium-sized American firms are also showing or have already shown some interest in the area. The UK and France both account for about 7 per cent of FDI in Hungary and the UK presence is stronger in Hungary than in other countries.

Table 6.4 shows cumulative foreign direct investment in the Czech Republic according to main source country from 1991 through to September 1994. Germany is the largest cumulative investor followed by the US and – at a lower level – Austria. The UK appears in this table as part of the 'others' classification, as its investment has been relatively very low. However, for the first nine months of 1994, UK investments were responsible for 7.5 per cent

Table 6.1 Main host countries for foreign direct investment in the transition economies (US $m cumulative 1990–3)

	$M	*%*
Czechoslovakia	2,600	17.2
Hungary	5,441	36.0
Poland[a]	3,522	23.3
Russia	2,000	13.2
Total	15,100	100.00

Note: [a]Polish data to March 1994.

Source: EBRD Transition Report, 1994, except for Polish data – Polish State Foreign Investment Agency (PAIZ)

Table 6.2 Total foreign direct investment in Central and Eastern Europe – Czech Republic, Hungary[a] and Poland (cumulative 1990–September 1994)

Source country	*$M*	*% Share*
USA	2,866	27.0
Germany	2,217	20.9
Austria	890	8.4
France	888	8.4
Italy	535	5.0
UK[b]	487	4.6
Netherlands[b]	472	4.5
Switzerland	430	4.1
Belgium	424	4.0
Sweden[b]	311	2.9
Other	1,084	10.2
Total	10,604	100.0

Notes: [a]Excluding Hungarian greenfield
[b]Approximate estimates made for Czech FDI

Source: Czech National Bank, PAIZ, PRIVINFO

Table 6.3 Foreign direct investment in Hungary[a] (cumulative to September 1994)

Country (ranked by value of investment)	*HUF billion*	*% share*	*Number of companies*
Germany	78.26	27.2	78
USA	62.02	21.5	27
Austria	39.91	13.9	103
UK	20.78	7.2	30
France	21.03	7.3	35
Netherlands	13.86	4.8	12
Other	52.12	18.1	98
Total	287.98	100.0	383

Note: [a]Excluding greenfield investments.

Table 6.4 Foreign direct investment in the Czech Republic by source country (US $m cumulative)

Source country	*1991*	*1992*	*1993*	*To 30/9 1994*
Germany	443.3	581.9	641.0	790.0
USA	54.6	335.7	572.0	650.9
Austria	37.4	75.7	126.0	200.9
Belgium	33.2	118.0	145.0	187.7
France	15.7	234.4	259.0	339.0
Switzerland	1.6	79.8	90.0	133.5
Italy	1.5	66.2	76.0	82.1
Others	7.8	63.6	144.0	314.6
Total	595.1	1555.3	2053.0	2698.7

Source: Czech National Bank.

Table 6.5 Foreign direct investment in Poland (cummulative[a] September 1994, investments > US $1m: expressed in US $m)

Country	*Investments*	*%*
USA	1385	34.2
Germany	380	9.4
Italy	366	9.0
France	268	6.6
Netherlands	262	6.5
Switzerland	193	4.8
Sweden	162	4.0
UK	159	3.9
Austria	155	3.8
Others	720.9	17.8
Total	4050.9	100.0

Note: [a]Most investments are since 1991, but some are earlier.

Source: Polish State Foreign Investment Agency (PAIZ) and own calculations (the PAIZ category *international firms* have been reallocated to countries according to ownership share, and institutions such as the EBRD, are included in *others*).

of foreign direct investment inflows (Czech National Bank). It is important to be aware that these figures are strongly influenced by large single deals such as the VW-Skoda investment and the Phillip-Morris investment which can affect the ranking of source countries. Table 6.5 sets out foreign direct investment in Poland ranked by source country. The US dominates the investments in Poland being responsible for over 34 per cent of existing investments. Germany is second, followed by Italy. However, the Italian figures are dominated by the Fiat investment and there have only been four Italian investments in Poland over a value of $1 million.

Table 6.6 German foreign direct investment in the transition economies (capital outflows, % distribution)

Countries	*1991*	*1992*	*1993*	*1994 (1st qtr)*	*1990–4 (1st qtr)*
Czechoslovakia	66.2	35.2	(40.6)	(23.7)	(41.0)
Czech Republic	–	–	35.8	22.7	36.8
Slovakia	–	–	4.8	1.0	4.2
Hungary	33.8	52.3	38.2	43.0	43.8
Poland	5.2	10.3	17.6	12.4	11.5
Other	–5.2	2.1	3.6	20.9	3.7
Total	100.0	100.0	100.0	100.0	100.0

Note: Brackets indicate totals for Czechoslovakia after 1993.
Source: Bundesbank, German Ministry of Economics.

Table 6.7 German net overseas capital transfers (DMm)

	1991	*1992*	*1993*
Czechoslovakia	799	545	—
Czech Republic	—	—	579
Slovakia	—	—	89
Hungary	462	860	707
Poland	62	154	321
(1) Total CEE & CIS	1,481	1,670	1,817
(2) Total world	30,551	24,830	18,041
(1)/(2) %	4.8	6.7	10.1

Source: Bundesbank, German Ministry of Economics.

Table 6.6 sets out German foreign direct investment in Central and Eastern Europe since 1991. It can be seen that its initial focus in 1991 was strongly on the former Czechoslovakia, followed by Hungary, with Poland receiving only just over 5 per cent of the capital flows to the whole of Central and Eastern Europe. However, over the period the relative emphasis on Czechoslovakia declined and more weight was put on both Hungary and Poland so that for the period as a whole, up to the first quarter of 1994, the largest amount of German investment is into Hungary, followed by the Czech Republic, with Poland receiving over 11 per cent. Table 6.7 gives absolute values for German net overseas capital transfers from 1991 to 1993 and totals for German investment into Central and Eastern Europe and the CIS countries. It can be seen from this table that German investment into the transition economies grew over the three-year period from representing under 5 per cent of total German foreign investment to representing over 10 per cent by 1993. The large increase in the proportion of German invest-

Table 6.8 EU exports to, and imports from, Central and Eastern Europe, by country (1993: ECUm)

	EU		*Germany*		*France*		*Italy*		*UK*	
	Exports	*Imports*	*Exports*	*Imports*	*Exports*	*Imports*	*Exports*	*Imports*	*Exports*	*Imports*
Total CEEC	41,899	38,728	22,052	18,349	3,652	3,341	5,808	6,650	2,712	2,613
Russia	11,476	14,778	5,891	5,435	1,205	1,385	1,465	3,313	682	950
Czech Republic	6,050	4,864	3,956	3,315	386	273	537	441	358	314
Hungary	4,945	3,946	2,667	2,324	358	288	852	654	255	196
Poland	9,873	7,566	5,011	4,354	663	1,385	1,282	706	907	543

Source: External Trade Statistics, Eurostat, 1994

Table 6.9 Percentage share of EU exports to Central and Eastern Europe (1989, 1993)

Source country	*1989 (%)*	*1993 (%)*
Germany[a]	49.0	52.6
France	10.9	8.7
Italy	15.3	13.9
UK	7.7	6.5
Other	17.1	18.3
Total	100.0	100.0

Note: [a]Before October 1990, data is for West Germany.

Source: External Trade Statistics, Eurostat, 1994.

Table 6.10 EU exports to Central and Eastern Europe as % of total extra-EU exports (by country, 1993)

	EU	*D*	*F*	*I*	*UK*
Total CEEC	8.7	13.5	5.1	8.6	3.7
Russia	2.4	3.6	1.7	2.2	0.9
Czech Republic	1.3	2.4	0.5	0.8	0.5
Hungary	1.0	1.6	0.5	1.3	0.3
Poland	2.0	3.1	0.9	1.9	1.2

Source: External Trade Statistics, Eurostat, 1994.

ment going to the transition economies can be seen to be in part a result of a decline in total German investment abroad which may be linked to the German recession in 1992 and 1993. Despite this overall decline, the inflows into Central and Eastern Europe increased substantially.

Trade flows

Turning now to look at international trade flows, the role of the German economy in trade flows is much more pronounced than its role in foreign investment in relation to the other western economies. At the same time, a larger proportion of German foreign investment is going to the transition economies than of its total trade. Tables 6.8 and 6.9 set out the absolute and the percentage distribution of exports from the EU and the four largest EU economies to Central and Eastern Europe including the CIS. Germany is responsible – in 1993 – for over half of EU exports to Central and Eastern Europe, and this is true not only for the area as a whole but also with respect to the individual countries shown namely Russia, the Czech Republic, Hungary and Poland. The overall level of German exports is over seven times that of UK exports. As can be seen from Table 6.9, the rankings in 1993 are clearly linked to the rankings in 1989. In other words, the relatively strong prior links of the former West German economy to Central and Eastern Europe represent one important element of an explanation of its current dominant position. However it is also apparent from Table 6.9 that whereas Germany has increased its share of EU exports over the four-year period, France, Italy and the UK have all experienced a relative fall in their share of EU exports.

These differences across the main EU economies are much greater than their overall differences in global trade shares and trade performance. Table 6.10 sets out the share of CEE exports in total extra-EU exports for the main EU economies. It can be seen that the CEE economies represent a much more important market for Germany (13.5 per cent of total exports) than for the EU as a whole and than for France, Italy and the UK, with the UK having the lowest relative participation in terms of exports (3.7 per cent).

Table 6.11 sets out the net trade balances of the EU and the larger EU economies with the transition economies. While Germany has also taken a large share of imports from the transition economies, it has nevertheless maintained a positive trade balance with these economies from 1989 to 1993. This is in contrast to the EU as a whole which had a deficit on trade with the transition economies through to 1992 but which also had a surplus in 1993. This has attracted substantial criticism in terms of the importance for the transition economies of having access to markets to support and sustain their transition (see, for example, Inotai 1994). The Europe Agreements between the EU and the individual CEE economies should eventually result in free trade in manufactures (Winters 1995). However, they have been criticized as being somewhat disappointing (Winters 1992). A more recent assessment by a number of authors suggests they offer substantial benefits but that moves to free trade could be impeded by too many special exemptions and that the development of appropriate institutions in the CEE economies is also critical (Winters 1995).

Barriers to trade arise not only from direct tariff barriers. Domestic barriers in CEE such as underdeveloped infrastructure and information gaps can be as or more important, together with barriers to selling in western markets such as meeting marking and packing requirements (OECD 1994).

In comparison to its foreign direct investment role, the US is playing a much smaller role with respect to international trade. Table 6.12 sets out US exports and imports to and from Central and Eastern Europe in 1992 and 1993. The US also has a large trade surplus with these economies. Its overall level of exports to these economies is only about one quarter of that of the German level. The bulk of its trade is with the former Soviet Union.

Tables 6.13, 6.14 and 6.15 set out the main trading partners in terms of exports and imports for Hungary, Poland and the Czech Republic. Germany is the largest trading partner for all these countries. It is a key export market

Table 6.11 Net trade balance, EU (total) and EU member states with Central and Eastern Europe (ECUm)

Country	*1989*	*1990*	*1991*	*1992*	*1993*
EU	–3142	–5877	–2809	–1376	3171
D	2761	1052	2544	1393	3703
F	–997	–1517	–802	–265	311
I	77	–1378	–1774	–893	–842
UK	–531	–788	–890	–69	99

Source: External Trade Statistics, Eurostat, and own calculations.

Table 6.12 US exports to, and imports from, Central and Eastern Europe (US$m)

	1992		*1993*	
	Exports	*Imports*	*Exports*	*Imports*
Total CEEC	5,497.2	1,981.2	6,103.2	3,530.4
NIS	3,625.2	1,817.2	3,780.0	2,040.0
Former Czechoslovakia	412.8	242.4	300.0	342.0
Hungary	295.2	349.2	434.4	400.8
Poland	637.2	374.4	916.8	453.6
Total CEEC/Total world (%)	1.2	0.4	1.3	0.6

Source: OECD Monthly Trade Statistics, 1994.

Table 6.13 Czech Republic: main trading partners (% of total imports and exports, 1993)

Country	*Exports*	*Imports*
Germany	26.9	25.1
Slovakia	20.0	17.7
Austria	6.2	7.7
Former USSR	6.0	11.5
Italy	5.1	4.7
Others	35.8	33.3

Source: Statistical Bulletin, Prague, 1994/1.

Table 6.14 Hungary: main trading partners (% of total exports and imports, 1993)

Country	*Exports*	*Imports*
Germany	26.6	21.6
Former USSR	15.3	22.2
Austria	10.1	11.6
Italy	8.0	6.0
USA	4.2	3.9
Others	35.8	34.7

Source: Statistical Bulletin, Prague, 1994/1.

Table 6.15 Poland: main trading partners (% of total exports and imports, 1993)

Country	*Exports*	*Imports*
Germany	36.3	28.0
Netherlands	5.9	4.7
Italy	5.2	7.8
Russia	4.6	6.8
UK	4.3	5.8
Others	43.7	46.9

Source: Statistical Bulletin, Prague, 1994/1.

for all the countries, taking over a third of Polish exports and supplying around a quarter of imports to all three countries. Austria can also be seen to be an important trading partner for both the Czech Republic and Hungary. The former USSR is still one of the largest five trading partners of these countries although its importance is very much reduced in Poland and in the Czech Republic, though Hungary has maintained stronger links. Italy has a relatively strong role in trade. The UK does not appear in the list of the largest five traders in the Czech Republic or Hungary though it is the fifth largest with respect to Poland. France does not appear as one of the largest traders for any of these three countries. What these data show is that Germany is developing much stronger economic links with the CEE countries than any of the other major West European economies. Taking trade and foreign investment together, Germany is the most important economy overall for these economies rather than the US.

COMPETITIVENESS, CONVERGENCE AND INTEGRATION

This section considers the potential implications of the different economic relationships of the major western economies to Central and Eastern Europe. It first considers the key motivations for investment and trade in CEE and why they may differ across western economies. It then analyses the effect on German competitiveness of its greater involvement in CEE, and assesses the implications for the CEE economies themselves and for the other EU economies.

One key determinant of investment and trade is access to markets. Both foreign direct investment and exports may be used by firms as means of establishing initial market positions, and building current and potential future market share in these new markets which have medium and long-run potential for substantial growth. A second motivation for foreign investment may be the low labour costs in these economies combined with the relatively high skill of the labour. This will also influence trade, in sectors where exports from these countries are competitive. Western firms may be establishing subcontracting relationships with CEE firms, but it is not possible to identify the extent of this. In addition, there are particular influences on foreign investment into the transition economies due to the privatization processes that are occurring and the scope for acquisition of properties and assets and joint ventures. In oligopolistic markets, there are also strong strategic motivations influencing export and foreign investment behaviour. (Motivations for, and implications of, foreign investment are considered in greater detail in Estrin and Hughes 1995.) Existing survey evidence on motivation for investment in the transition economies is relatively patchy, but it suggests that markets are the dominant motivation and costs are a secondary motivation that may be important but not as important as markets.

The role of Germany

A number of reasons for higher German involvement in CEE can be distinguished. Geographical proximity is clearly one important determinant of the levels of German foreign investment activity, in particular taken together both with prior economic links, cultural and historical links, and with the costs issue. Geographical proximity lowers transport and communication costs and, in many sectors, may have an important influence on the cost advantages of both investment and trade. Pre-existing links with these countries are also potentially important. Economic relations with the CEE economies are inevitably risky due to the unexpected nature of the transition. A higher level of knowledge and information concerning these economies including economic, political, social and institutional information represents an important advantage, especially in the early stages of the transition. To the extent that there are first-mover advantages, these early information benefits will influence the relative position of western economies in CEE in the future, even once information levels rise and risk falls.

The high wage levels of German industry mean that German firms are faced with a much greater cost differential when evaluating the benefits of producing in, and importing from, CEE, depending on productivity differences. A Dresdner Bank report commented that the CEE countries offer cost structures otherwise only seen in the Far East (DOWC 1994). Labour costs in the Czech Republic are about one tenth of those in Germany and this cost differential is therefore much wider for German firms than for instance for UK firms who have substantially lower labour costs than German firms. The combination of this wider cost differential and geographical proximity may explain a substantial part of the difference in investment levels between Germany and France and the UK.

After the unification boom, German industry experienced its most severe post-war recession. This led to a substantial discussion about German competitiveness and the role of high German costs in impeding German competitiveness (see, for example, Federal Government 1993). The proximity of the Central and East European countries to Germany – offering a low cost means of overcoming the perceived problems in German competitiveness – may have proved strongly attractive to many German firms both large and small. This has led to discussions of Germany as moving towards a new division of labour across Central Europe. It is possible that the German position with respect to Central Europe could become comparable to that of Japan and South-East Asia or of the United States with Mexico. Geographical proximity, subject to the nature of customs and border clearance, can allow a new division of labour and new user–supplier and subcontracting relationships across Central Europe, that more distant countries cannot participate in, or not to the same extent.

If Germany does benefit relatively strongly from its deeper economic relationship with CEE, this could have a positive impact on its competitiveness. Many discussions of EU competitiveness have stressed the need for developed countries to compete in terms of knowledge, skills and infrastructure (Hughes 1993) and the inability of western countries to compete on the basis of a low-wage economy. What may occur in the German case is that its competitiveness will be boosted by the low wage economies of neighbouring countries.

If there are important competitiveness effects, this may imply, in the short to medium run, substantial structural change in German industry as some activities relocate and expand in the former planned economies and German industry refocuses on the higher value-added activities. While such structural change may in the short run result in some unemployment in Germany, in the medium run it may sufficiently increase German competitiveness to provide an overall stimulus to employment. In this scenario, German competitiveness receives a substantial boost not, as was foreseen by some in 1989, from unification, but from its wider links to the transition economies of Central and Eastern Europe.

Implications for the transition economies

The implications for the Central and Eastern European economies are mixed. They may benefit in various ways from western capital and from internationalization, but they may benefit in particular from German involvement given the high overall competitiveness level of German firms. Benefits may include: transfer of managerial know-how across a wide range of functions; technology transfer; access to capital; and access to markets (Hughes 1994).

Overall, the CEE countries have a comparative advantage that may broadly be described as based on a combination of low wages and skilled labour. Exchange rate policy in some countries, notably the Czech Republic, has been chosen to reinforce the low cost advantage. Inflows of technology and capital from the West may contribute in the medium run to the CEE economies catching up on western productivity levels and developing similar patterns of comparative advantage. Thus, a key issue in their development will be the pattern of industrial specialization that emerges and whether this becomes similar to that of the advanced industrial economies or whether it is biased more towards low-cost and low value-added activities. This will depend in part on access to markets (especially EU markets) and to capital, it will also depend on the role of multinational enterprises both in producing in CEE economies and in subcontracting production there. If the current trend towards an emergent German division of labour in Central Europe continues, the question for the transitional economies will be what the medium-run effects are. If they are part of this division of labour due in particular to their low labour costs, they may develop economic and industrial structures that reinforce this, rather than ones that allow them to move up-market into higher value added activities. Alternatively, they may benefit strongly from the transfer of know-how and capital.

There is, in addition, a question of what alternatives are or were available. Inflows of foreign capital in CEE are, in general, perceived to be fairly low relative to both needs and expectations, and relative to investment flows into some developing countries. Given the differences in levels of FDI across CEE countries, it should be possible over time to assess the impact of FDI. There may be an argument that these countries would have benefited from a Japanese-style industrial policy aimed at guiding their industrial specialization and development (see, for example, Radice 1994). Though, this would have been problematic, both politically and financially.

However, there are also political as well as economic issues involved in dependence on any one particular country and on foreign countries in general. In the Czech Republic, Hungary and Poland there are currently mixed views among government spokespeople and more generally about the benefits and role of foreign investment in general, and on the question of being dependent on Germany in particular (Handl 1993). There are concerns on the one hand to diversify the pattern of foreign involvement (Inotai 1992) and on the other hand to strengthen domestic industry. There is a danger, however, that some politicians may find it advantageous to encourage xenophobic reactions to foreign investment.

Implications for western Europe

The development of the CEE economies will inevitably imply a certain amount of structural change throughout western Europe. There are various forces at work here influencing both structural change and competitiveness. In sectors and/or sub-sectors where the CEE economies are more competitive then there will be pressures for structural change in western European industry in particular. At the same time, parts of western Europe may benefit in terms of competitiveness from the supply of cheaper inputs from CEE. Finally, the CEE market offers a major opportunity for firms to expand and to use the profits from that expansion for the development of their global competitiveness. If these market opportunities stimulate a period of high growth this will facilitate structural change.

The involvement of German firms in Central Europe may mean that the German economy experiences these pressures for structural change first; it may also benefit the most. It will undergo structural change potentially earlier than its western European competitors and possibly with less pain if it benefits in terms of competitiveness from its new division of labour and from its greater share of CEE markets. In comparison, the French and British economies appear on current trends less likely to benefit from the developments in the CEE economies and so there may be an increase in the divergence of competitiveness between the German economy and the French and British economies that was already apparent in the 1980s (Hughes 1992). The enlargement of the European economy and the changes in economic relationships, together with structural change and changes in competitiveness, imply major changes in the balance of economic interests over the coming years. These different economic interests will also map quite closely into different foreign policy interests given the role of geographical location.

For the less favoured regions of the EU these changes in economic relations may also prove problematic. The labour costs of the less favoured regions do not compete with the current labour costs of the transition economies. They may therefore experience lower FDI inflows if there are substitution effects to CEE. They may also experience particularly strong pressures for structural change which will precisely require access to technology and capital if they are to respond successfully to these pressures. At the same time, they may benefit least from the new market opportunities in CEE. This will vary across the less favoured regions and Greece, in particular, may be in a position to benefit more from existing trade links to CEE and its closer location (see also Chapter 9 of this volume). Thus, the economic integration of western Europe and CEE brings to the fore questions of divergent economic performance, and the role of policy within the EU in dealing with these divergences.

Convergence, divergence and enlargement

The Single European Market does not of itself encourage or cause convergence across the EU economies, rather, in a more integrated economy different growth poles and areas of decline exist with associated processes of structural change (Oughton 1993). This has to some extent been recognized in the existence and increase in the level of the structural funds. While much attention has been placed on the need to reform the CAP if there is to be eastward enlargement of the EU, there are also major implications of enlargement for the level and role of the structural funds. New members from Central and Eastern Europe would on current rules result in a large increase in structural funds, and the transition economies would be eligible for relatively large sums. Enlargement therefore raises or reinforces questions that need to be asked anyway about the determinants of convergence or divergence within the EU and what the appropriate policies are to deal with convergence and divergence (Michalski and Wallace 1992, Kramer 1993; see also João Confraria's contribution to this volume).

If EU structural funds cannot be raised to levels sufficient to tackle the differences in economic wealth, income and performance then there would be a strong argument for allowing individual countries and regions to fund their own development programmes. This of course currently happens but at the same time EU rules attempt to limit the nature and range of industrial policy intervention in its member states in order to sustain the level playing field. Acknowledgement that, within a wider EU of 20 or more members with varying economic performance, convergence is very unlikely even in the medium run means that the whole debate about what constitutes acceptable local, regional and national industrial and development policies within the EU may need to be reopened and reconsidered.

Current discussions of EU enlargement (see for example, Nuti 1994; CDU/CSU 1994; Wijkman 1994) tend to focus on a multi-tier EU as a means of coping with wide differences in income and performance. This is a means of dealing with diversity not of encouraging convergence (other than through reliance on market mechanisms). It is also an implicit, if not always explicit, acknowledgement that widening and deepening cannot occur together if all member states are to participate in deepening to the same extent. The problem with this approach to the discussion is that the main focus of the 'deepening' discussion is then on the so-called hard-core countries, rather than on what the nature of an equal, single-tier EU should be, with 20 or more members. Discussions of questions of convergence, the location of economic activity and the role of regional and industrial policy may, thereby, be ignored.

Furthermore, whether there is both deepening of the core together with enlargement will depend, in particular, on whether France and Germany decide it is in their interests to precommit to deeper integration before the growing diversity of economic and political interests within the EU, including between France and Germany, make further integration difficult. However, the differing relationships with the CEE countries of the four largest EU economies may make the pursuit of enlargement and integration – whether separately or together – deeply problematic. The challenge is to develop structures that allow and reflect diversity but retain sufficient common purpose and interests to prevent weakening or splintering.

CONCLUSIONS

This chapter has considered the changing pattern of economic relationships between eastern and western Europe subsequent to 1989. The pattern of internationalization associated with changing inter-country economic relationships since then does not imply that the European economy as a whole will simply become a larger and more integrated entity. Rather, we are observing a readjustment of different countries' economic interests and relationships which will have important implications for the future development both of the wider European economy and of the EU itself and which may promote diversity rather than increased integration. On current trends, the dominant economic position of Germany in Central and Eastern Europe – in both trade and investment – and the emerging division of labour associated with this may result in a boost to German competitiveness that will lead to a further divergence between its performance and that of its main western competitors. There are also important issues concerning the future development of the transition economies and their integration into the international economy. The higher level of involvement of Germany in Central and Eastern Europe relative to other West European countries will lead to diversity not only in performance, but also in economic and foreign policy interests within the EU. A larger European economy, and a potentially larger EU, thus raise important questions about differences in economic performance across countries, likely trends in convergence and divergence, and the appropriate policy response. The potential for splintering of European and EU interests does not depend simply on how the EU is enlarged and/or deepened in the next decade, but on the development of current economic trends and relationships in Europe and current policy responses.

ACKNOWLEDGEMENTS

This paper draws in part on a current ESRC project (No. R000235357) being co-directed by the author and Saul Estrin. I am grateful to participants in the *Bologna Workshop on Industrial Strategy and Integration* for their comments. Views expressed are the author's alone.

REFERENCES

CDU/CSU (1994) 'Reflections on European Policy', CDU/CSU-Fraktion des Deutschen Bundestages, September, Bonn.

DOWC (1994) 'Investieren in Osteuropa', DOWC Ost-West Consult, Dresdner Bank AG, Frankfurt am Main.

Estrin, S. and Hughes, K. (1995) 'The Determinants and Effects of Foreign Direct Investment in Central and Eastern Europe', mimeo, London Business School.

Federal Government (1993) 'Report of the federal government on the safeguarding of Germany's future as an industrial location', Bonn.

Handl, V. (1993) 'Germany and Central Europe: "Mitteleuropa" Restored?', *Perspectives: Review of Central European Affairs*, 1.

Hughes, K. (1992) 'Technology and International Competitiveness', *International Review of Applied Economics*, 6, 2.

—— (ed.) (1993) *European Competitiveness*, Cambridge: CUP.

—— (1994) 'Manufacturing Industry in Hungary and Czechoslovakia', *Policy Studies*, 14, 4.

Inotai, A. (1992) 'Economic Implications of German Unification for Central and Eastern Europe', in P. Stares (ed.) *The New Germany and the New Europe*, Washington, DC: Brookings Institute.

—— (1994) 'Central and Eastern Europe', in C.R. Henning, E. Hochreiter and G. Hufbauer (eds) *Reviving the European Union*, Washington, DC: Institute for International Economics.

Kramer, H. (1993) 'The European Community's Response to the "New Eastern Europe" ', *Journal of Common Market Studies*, 31, 2.

Michalski, A. and Wallace, H. (1992) *The European Community: The Challenge of Enlargement*, London: RIIA.

Nuti, M. (1994) 'The Impact of Systemic Transition on the European Community', in S. Martin (ed.) *The Construction of Europe: A Festschrift in honour of Emile Noel*, Dortrecht: Kluwer Academic.

OECD (1994) *Barriers to Trade with the Economies in Transition*, Paris: Centre for Co-operation with the Economies in Transition, OECD.

Oughton, C. (1993) 'Growth, Structural Changes and Real Convergence in the EC', in K. Hughes (ed.) *European Competitiveness*, Cambridge: CUP.

Radice, H. (1994) 'The Role of Foreign Direct Investment in the Transformation of Eastern Europe', in H.-J. Chang, A. Hughes, and P. Nolan (eds) *Economic Reform in the Centrally Planned Economies: An Alternative Perspective*, London: Macmillan.

Wijkman, P.-M. (1994) 'EFTA Countries', in C.R. Henning, E. Hochreiter and G. Hufbauer (eds) *Reviving the European Union*, Washington, DC: Institute for International Economics.

Winters, L.A. (1992) 'The Europe Agreements: With a Little Help from Our Friends', in CEPR (ed.) *The Association Process: Making it Work: Central Europe and the European Community*, London: CEPR.

—— (1995) 'Trade Policy Institutions in Central and Eastern Europe: Objectives and Outcomes', in L.A. Winters (ed.) *Foundations of an Open Economy*, London: CEPR.

7

CREATING A DYNAMICALLY COMPETITIVE ECONOMY

Defining the competitiveness of a nation and a case study of the post-war economic policy which made Austria competitive

Karl Aiginger

AIM AND STRUCTURE OF THE CHAPTER

This chapter investigates the concept 'the competitiveness of a nation'. This term is often used in politics, as well as in popular and even scientific research. However, economists are far from being able to supply a unified and commonly accepted definition. Here we propose a definition, which explicitly relates competitiveness to performance and to the democratically defined aspiration level of an economy. We compare the proposed definition to other concepts. We describe the case study of Austria's post-war development, as an economy which gradually recaptured competitiveness, following a period of hopeless uncompetitiveness during the post-war years. And finally, we apply the proposed concept in the assessment of competitiveness in the USA, Japan, the EU and Switzerland. This evaluation can be neither a thorough nor a comprehensive evaluation, but should demonstrate the usefulness of the specific concept.

THE COMPETITIVENESS OF NATIONS

The timing of the issue

The competitiveness of nations is a highly sensitive political topic. It is usually raised if a nation (a region) fears it could loose its competitiveness. Sometimes the discussion begins when a region which has a competitive edge (a lead) fears to lose its prime position. This is the first hint that competitiveness will not be definable according to mere technical indicators or through the comparison of a country's performance with the average. What does prove important is the definition of competitiveness in relation to some goal, relative to a past or future level of aspiration.

Following the Second World War, Europe felt it had lost its position as economic leader, lagging behind the United States in productivity and progressiveness. Jacques Servan Schriver's call for European co-operation and the creation of large, state-backed firms is a classical document of Europe's feeling of inferiority. The creation of the European Economic Community can be partly seen as a strategy designed to counter the loss of competitiveness to the United States (the second intention was to prevent future wars).

During the 1970s the industrial countries felt they were loosing 'competitiveness' *vis-à-vis* oil-producing and other resource-abundant countries. The Club of Rome forecasted general shortages of natural resources thus creating unsubstantiated prospects of unfavourable terms of trade for the USA, Japan and Europe *vis-à-vis* developing countries possessing natural resources.

The next country afraid of losing its competitive edge was the USA, during the period of slow growth in the 1970s. Substantial literature on the phenomenon of 'productivity slowdown' emerged at the time which a few years later was assessed as a period of rapid, unprecedented development in computer technology.

After the recovery of US growth in the 1980s – achieved through a mixture of cost reduction, decreased corporate taxation and a Keynesian-type budget explosion, helping the US to win the last stage of the Cold War – it was Europe's turn to suffer from 'Eurosclerosis'. Closer co-operation between the nation-states, the transformation of the EU via 'Binnenmarkt' into 'Maastricht-Europe' was the reaction to this fear of losing competitiveness.

The large US trade deficit *vis-à-vis* Japan, as well as the increase of Japan's market shares in high-technology areas (admittedly starting with very small market shares) raised the question as to whether the USA had lost its competitive edge against Japan. Europe, as well as the USA, was envious of the high growth rates in East Asia (Japan, the 'tigers', and even China). See Lester Thurow's latest book for a balanced view on the competitive race in the triad.

At the same time Europe has been struggling with the political and economic consequences resulting from the transformation of socialist countries into market economies. The on-going structural change in western European countries accelerated with the pressure of increasing imports. Ex ante, many countries felt they had lost, or, in the near future they would lose, their 'competitiveness' in industrial production, the reason being that wages were much lower (ratios of approximately 1:10 are the rule) in the transition countries. Real data revealed, however, that exports from western Countries grew faster than imports, opening a large export surplus for western industrialized countries *vis-à-vis* the transformation economies. (See also the chapter by Kirsty Hughes.) But since fears are deeply rooted, it is still argued that ultimately the West will come out at the bad end of the deal. The debate focuses on the competitiveness of locations ('*Standortdebatte*'), but essentially this is only a new form of the old fear of losing competitiveness.

The concept at the firm level

Initially we would assume that competitiveness is easy to define at the firm level, 'Firms are competitive if they can sell their products' would be a tentative first definition (see also Johan Willner's chapter in this volume).

But competitive at which profits? *Zero profits*, of course, provide a *lower bound* in the definition of viable firms.[1] Most firms in the real world enjoy positive profits or some market power; they are able to set prices above marginal costs. But do we not then have to say that firms enjoying some monopoly power – due to technological innovation or to successful product differentiation – are 'more' competitive than those which do not?

In the world of the Cournot oligopoly[2] we find that firms of different efficiency can co-exist (differences in unit costs yield smaller and larger market shares). In Stackelberg's world and in the dominant firms/fringe models,[3] we have some firms with large, and some firms with small profits in the same market.

Are the innovative firms which achieve product differentiation and early starter advantages 'more' competitive than marginal firms? This is a matter of taste, if we want to define competitiveness at the firm level.[4] *On the macro level an open economy hosting a large proportion of firms with market power on the world market is clearly better off.* An industry which can set prices is less vulnerable if wages rise or currency appreciates. Politicians and economists discussing the competitiveness of a country usually do not refer to marginal firms and to domestic markets.

The concept at the national level

Many books have been written on the competitiveness of nations, few of them provide a definition of competitiveness, and none of them offers a concept which I can accept as comprehensive and satisfactory.

An extreme position would be to deny that the competitiveness of nations is an important concept. The neo-classical point of view is that the exchange rate will adjust according to market conditions, to the extent that imports and exports are equalized. However, the consequence of this process, when it works, is that the purchasing power of incomes also adjusts. Most economists would say that an economy that constantly relies on devaluation to close trade gaps has a deeply rooted problem with competitiveness.

Some applied researchers deny the importance of the concept 'competitiveness' for a different reason. It cannot be, they claim, that a country is 'competitive in all industries'. Porter (1990: 6ff) comes very close to this position. The denial is right, wrong and misleading all at the same time. It is *wrong* in so far as a country can in principle be the technological leader in most industries. The USA held such a position following the Second World War. This is, of course, no longer the case in today's closer race among the triad countries. The denial is right, in so far as the international leader in productivity will also have a parallel lead in average wage levels. Cost advantages result from larger leads in technology, compared to a country's lead in terms of wages. Lower 'unit costs' will not be seen in all industries. In the third place Porter's position is *misleading* on the macro level. What researchers and politicians addressing the issue 'competitiveness' want to know, is whether the majority of industries in a country are winning or losing the technology and price races. Therefore, from the macro point of view, competitiveness 'on average' is what matters.

Porter proposes abandoning the '*notion of a "competitive nation"*' and concentrating on the productivity concept.[5] Apart from the question of costs just addressed, a productivity concept on the macro level is a twin concept to the attempt just comparing GDP per capita (or worker). This is often done,[6] but in my opinion the competitiveness issue goes deeper.

The EU (1994) defines competitiveness as the ability to *combine growth with balanced trade*. This short definition suggests maximum achievement. The term 'growth' implies that balanced trade should not depend on devaluation and decreasing wages. On the other hand, this definition implies that when a lagging country is growing faster than other countries without creating trade imbalances (e.g. Japan in the 1950s, maybe China today), it is just as competitive as a front-runner. Furthermore, socio-economic conditions (social net, environmental degradation, unemployment) are not included in the definition.

Several authors stress the dynamic forces important to future competitiveness. Orlowski (1982: 70) combines non-price elements under the heading '*the ability to sell*'; the German Sachverständigenrat (1981: 59) defines competitiveness as the *ability to develop speciality products and technical solutions* which generate income growth under full employment, despite the emerging competition of newly industrialized countries. Url (1971) finally defines competitiveness as the *ability to create the preconditions for high wages*.

The World Economic Forum in Geneva issues an annual report on the competitiveness of nations, using a very broad indicator approach. For a couple of years this report refrained from defining competitiveness, providing only a list of 'factors of competitiveness'.[7] These include data on the absolute size of an economy, per capita figures, output levels and growth rates. Furthermore, this report implicitly entwined the notion of 'cheap production' with elements of 'economic performance'. 'Cheap production' means an environment favourable from the perspective of firms (opportunities for profit-making), 'performance' relates to quality and competitiveness in the most sophisticated market segment, paying high wages, and having high social and environmental standards.

The legally demanded hours of work, energy prices, environmental standards, compulsory health care, social security, etc. are all good from one perspective and bad from the other. In the Forum assessment some indicators were included in different indicator groups with a different sign. In 1993, the Forum felt the urge to publish a 'formula for competitiveness'. It reads '*competitive assets x competitive processes [plus internationalization] gives competitive results*'. And finally, in 1994 the Forum tried a direct definition: '*World competitiveness is the ability of a country or a company to, proportionally, generate more wealth than its competitors in the world markets*'.

Formalizing this notion boils it down to some sort of market-share concept. The market share of a country should be larger than its share of GDP.[8] The 'relevant market' in which a country or a company should have an over-proportionate share seems to be the *stock of wealth*. Maybe it is that part of wealth which is created by exports. The term 'wealth' implies that money and market prices may be too narrow a concept, consumer valuation, surplus and political valuations should be included.

It is a pity that no better explanation is provided in this broad study. It is certainly not helpful that this definition was formulated following the implementation of a basically unchanged set of indicators (though the number of indicators did rise each year) for more than a decade. We do not know whether larger exports at the expense of austerity at home are good or bad for this concept, and we do not know whether countries have different or equal aspiration levels (regarding wages, social security, health and environment). What we do know is that not all countries can be competitive, since the larger shares of some countries have to be compensated by the smaller shares of others.

A tentative definition and its application

We propose a definition which explicitly states that the 'competitiveness of a country' depends on its aspiration level and on its preferences among economic and social goals.

A country is said to be competitive if it sells:

- *enough* products and services
- at factor incomes *in line with the countries' (current and constantly changing)* aspiration level
- at macro-conditions (of the economic and social system) seen as satisfactory by the people

---

For use in a definition, the subjective content of the words 'enough', 'aspired', and 'satisfactory' seems to be counter-productive. We, however, maintain that they are absolutely necessary: an assessment of the competitiveness of a nation can be made only after filling these subjective notions with some content, the content, however, depends on past achievements and current aspirations. And ultimately, an assessment can only be made in relation to these aspirations. They vary from country to country, as used to be the case with aspiration levels.[9] Sometimes an outsider can detect them without difficulty, or substitute them with some objective indicator; sometimes they are deeply hidden in the political, cultural and economic system of a country.

'Enough' exports

Let us start with the notion 'enough exports'. Usually *equilibrium in the current balance* is seen as a good yardstick for today's competitiveness of a nation. But some countries seem comfortable only with a surplus (Japan, Switzerland); some want to include capital imports into their ultimate yardstick; some are unhappy if a negative trade balance is equalized by incomes from a potentially mature service industry (Alpine tourism in Austria).

'Enough' exports could also be measured by some concept of market shares. But then we have to choose the indicator (exports, imports), the regional market (Europe, the world, the US) and the aspiration level (constant, increasing, parallel development between imports and exports, total market or sophisticated markets). It is better explicitly to define the goal and then to determine whether or not this benchmark of competitiveness has or can be reached.

'Aspired' factor incomes

The problem of factor incomes goes deeper. Any current balance can be attained (at least theoretically) if we lower wages, if firms are content with low profits, if the currency is devalued. Since, however, these 'cheap costs strategies' lead away from the final means of the economic process – namely higher income or higher utility – these strategies are in this respect counterproductive. And any 'market test of competitiveness' (as balanced trade, or a rising market share) is directly influenced by factor incomes. A country feeling fine with its position in the hierarchy of wages will tend to assess its economy as 'competitive', while a country facing repeated pressure to keep wages and profits down feels uncomfortable with its performance.[10]

'Satisfactory' macro condition

Competitiveness despite high pensions, high unemployment benefits, low unemployment, low inflation and high environmental standards is more difficult to achieve than the same trade balance at lower levels of social security, employment and environmental preservation.

Different countries have different levels of aspiration with respect to economic goals. In the USA, job security in established firms and a comprehensive health system apparently have low priority. In Japan, large flats, leisure, long holidays and a short working week are not considered as all-important. In Switzerland, reducing the transit traffic has high priority.

Important to the assessment of the competitiveness of the nations are those macro-economic and social conditions, *which are of actual importance*. These are the conditions which are increasing actual costs. A macro goal which is potentially expensive, but not actually targeted, is irrelevant for current and (near) future competitiveness. A macro goal which has high priority, involves costs now or in the near future. If Japanese people press hard to reduce the working week to the European level, the nation will lose its competitive edge (for some time). If European nations press hard for a Swiss-style transit policy, there will be a large financial burden (today). If the US presses hard for comprehensive health coverage, it will face greater difficulties in regaining competitiveness with Japan.

A normative or a positive concept?

The proposed definition delegates the question as to the ultimate ends of a political and economic system to the respective nations. Each country has its own mixture of goals; some have a stronger preference for income, others for leisure or equality. Countries do not have to agree on the degree of public intervention or on the centralization versus decentralization issue. Some countries define their aspiration level without reference to other countries, others with explicit reference. This diversity is explicitly included in the proposed concept.

The alternative would be to define a set of goals, to rank the goals, and then to locate where each country is positioned on this 'objective ladder of competitiveness'. For example, we could use GDP/capita, unemployment, and price stability as the main economic goals, and eventually add a basket of socio-political goals ('social indicators') such as life expectancy, enrolment rates (in secondary schools), crime figures, medical services, ecological preservation, etc. The advantage of this approach is that it appears to be more objective. Once the set of goals, its weights, the indicators with which they are measured, are defined, the approach is indeed objective. But in the first place all nations are coerced into a preference scheme, and second, it assumes that all countries have the same aspiration level.

Our approach, on the other hand, permits various mixtures and bundles of goals. Environment, equality and comprehensive health care do indeed have different priorities in different countries – even for those in similar income positions. Second, it incorporates the aspiration level, in so far as two countries with the same level of income can be content with their position or stride towards rapid change. For example, let us examine the Czech Republic and the former East Germany. Although the level of income was much lower than that of the western neighbours in both countries, the Czech Republic accepted to climb up slowly at a slow and steady pace, while former East Germany wanted to reach western standards in one step. The competitiveness of the industrial base was lost in the latter, while it improved under the shelter of low wages and an undervalued currency in the former.

So, it is our proposition that the subjective assessment of the goals is an indispensable part of a definition. We return to this premise in the last section, where we tentatively apply the concept to some countries.

CASE STUDY: THE POST-WAR DEVELOPMENT OF AUSTRIA

Austria exemplifies a country which entered the competitiveness race at the end of the Second World War very poorly positioned. In a gradual approach Austria reduced the gap between itself and the leading industrialized nations. Today, Austria is among the countries enjoying a good overall performance – whether measured in GDP/capita, social, or environmental standards. The aspiration level for all these goals was raised step by step, reducing the income gap came first, achieving the European average second, and finally catching up with the leading industrialized countries. The aspiration level was not narrowly defined according to income, but included such goals as stability of employment and prices, as well as social and environmental goals. At no time did Austria have to revert to a low-cost strategy in facing a severe problem of competitiveness. However, for a long time wages fell intentionally short of productivity (providing opportunity for high investment and good training) and until 1970, Austria's currency was deliberately kept somewhat undervalued.

Economic preconditions and development

At the end of the Second World War, industrial production in Austria collapsed to about one third of the pre-war level, due in part to physical destruction and to the lack of energy and raw material. Demand from the military-industrial complex in Germany broke down: questions of ownership, property rights and management hampered production.

The war regime could be described as a planned economy with decentralized production. Prices and output goals were fixed, but firms had some leverage in fulfilling the goals. Investment was centrally planned, Nazi Germany did explicity build up a few large firms for steel production, aluminium and basic chemicals to exploit Austria's natural resources, as well as to diversify the locations of the basic goods needed for the war machine. In comparison with the final period of the socialist era in eastern European countries, the efficiency of the bureaucratic planner as well as of the management, was definitely superior. Political and military obsession on the side of the planners, and fear and repression from the workers' point of view were substitutes for direct financial incentives.

A gradual approach to price liberalization

In today's terminology we would say that Austria chose the gradual approach. In the first years after the war Austria enforced a quantity and price control for important products (food, clothing, lodging). Quantity controls (for industrial products) and rationing schemes for consumer goods were gradually removed over the years 1946–9, food stamps finally disappeared in 1950 (Meihsi 1969). Prices were first directly set by government, afterwards upper ceilings were determined for the absolute price. In the 1950s, price control shifted from the government to the social partners.[11] Starting in 1958, a voluntary price commission (see 'Preis- und Lohnkommission', Social Partnership) fixed 'maximal rates of price increase' for important manufacturing products and for consumer goods. The Association of Employers guaranteed the compliance of the firms with the agreed price increases, while the trade union monitored wage discipline. Both associations were organized centrally, giving more power to the top than to the sectoral branches.

The approach was pragmatic and comprehensive. In judging which prices should be fixed and which could be determined by market forces, demand and supply conditions were considered. Eventually import competition reduced the importance of price monitoring. In some industries the (threat of) trade liberalization was used as an instrument to dampen prices in industries which were suspected of pushing prices upward.

A late revival of price negotiation came during the 1970s in the wake of the oil shock. At the beginning of the 1990s the system was phased out, although some price monitoring remained. A department in the Ministry of Economics, for example, observes the parallel increment of oil prices on the world market and of petrol prices in Austria (and when prices differed too much the Ministry was permitted to set maximum prices).

Patience threatens to run out: the crisis of 1950 and new credibility

There was no smooth economic development in post-war Austria. The wage aspirations of workers had to be limited, so that business would have an opportunity to accumulate internal cash (self-financing) for the new investment. Five tripartite wage price agreements ('Preis- und Lohnabkommen') tried to combine moderate wage increases with sensible price reforms. Fixing a direct link between wages and productivity promoted the correct signals and incentives – as we would say in today's terminology – to workers. The negotiators from employers and employees exhibited a high degree of general responsibility in these negotiations and the direct involvement of the Austrian

Institute of Economic Research provided not only the statistical facts but also the economic expertise necessary for the difficult compromises.

Nevertheless, the efficiency of the agreements decreased from one phase to the next, as firms learned to 'play against the agreements',[12] and prices increased before and after the agreements. Workers' disappointment with slowly improving living standards rose; the necessity of restricting aspirations today to achieve a better outcome tomorrow was no longer accepted. The climax was reached in October 1950, with demonstrations and an attempt to call for a general strike. The prestige and the political sensitivity of the trade union leaders were at that time high enough to cope successfully with the problem (more information was provided to members, communists were scapegoated). The other side of the social partnership helped by announcing a voluntary absolute price decrease ('breaking inflationary expectations'). The government announced a strict budgetary and monetary policy and reinforced 'credibility' by putting a liberal hard-liner into the Ministry of Finance and by committing itself under stricter liberalization rules (OECD). Austria had by that time fortunately attained price competitiveness in its manufacturing sector, although at low wages and with an undervalued currency.

Increasing the relevance of the future

Time inconsistency means that the government's discount rate is too high and that short term goals are overvalued at the expense of long-term success. Among the multiple equilibria an economy can reach, an economy attains some 'bad equilibrium' instead of a better one (see Calvo, Frenkel in Winckler 1992: 114).

The Austrian government, in a joint effort with the social partners (organizations of employers and trade unions), implemented a long-term horizon into its economic policy and implicitly reduced the time discount of policymakers. Making economic policy predictable, stabilizing demand, prices, and profit shares is an important strategy for reducing risks. Keeping interest rates down, and shortening pay-off periods were important means.

Accelerated depreciation was an instrument specifically important and successful in increasing the relevance of future earnings at the expense of current profits or consumption. For investment goods (especially machines), an extra proportion of the purchasing value (up to 80 per cent) could be deducted from profits in the first year. This greatly reduced the pay-off period and therefore the investment risk. This instrument also decreased ex-post profit tax rates in the case of investment chains (if one investment followed the next). Continuously rising investment was the rule rather than the exception in high growth period.

Accelerated depreciation is an unbureaucratic instrument for discrimination between firms which use profits for consumption and firms which apply them to reinvestment. Second, it is a means of favouring successful firms (since the subsidy effect is conditioned on profitability). Third, it is an instrument which promotes manufacturing at the cost of distribution. It can additionally be used to discriminate between machinery and building (this was done) or between domestic and exporting industry (this was not done, and may now be incompatible with international trading rules).[13]

Discriminating between sectors

Besides the general tax credits, there is an extended system of inexpensive cheap loans and subsidies. The system was founded as part of the European Recovery Programme. The amount of subsidies increased over time, peaking in the late 1970s. Its net value is estimated at 2 per cent of value added in manufacturing, neither larger nor smaller than in other West European economies.

Direct subsidies in general seek to discriminate between firms (otherwise cheaper instruments such as lower tax rates are available). Whether they seek to discriminate according to sectors, size, regions or performance differs. Whether the discrimination is made *explicit* or implicit is *crucial*.

It is not easy to find out ex-post which firms were targeted by the ERP credits. To the best of my knowledge, specific goals were never made explicit. The programme intended to enforce reconstruction, technical progress and the competitiveness of Europe in the growing world economy. The participating countries were obliged to submit a plan for short-term and medium-term investments. In Austria, a special department of the Ministry of Economics (up to 1949 in the Department for Planning and Reconstruction), together with experts from the Austrian Institute of Economic Research, combined investment plans proposed by firms with some industry specific information, designing the so-called 'annual programmes'. These annual programmes can be loosely understood as 'soft sectoral plans'. The proportions of credits alloted to the sectors did not deviate significantly from the investment structure of the large enterprises. Looking at plans and statistics does not reveal much distortion, nor does the sectoral structure differ between submitted and approved credits. It can be seen that the nationalized sector received a larger proportion of the funding than its output share. The veil over the actual decision process may sometimes be lifted by historical research; casual evidence and discussions with agents who participated in the process did not reveal any consistent method of discrimination.[14] Nevertheless only one third of manufacturing investment was financed by this scheme. In hindsight the programme appears to have been a source of cheap finance, disciplining firms to make articulate plans and forecasts. The international source of the money ensured that the projects would prove sensible (this is called the 'credibility issue', the ERP agency served as the outside agent, which guaranteed credibility and solved the domestic prisoners' dilemma).

Later on, subsidies increased in Austria along different lines and in different agencies. Some schemes discriminated between sectors, usually favouring mature and declining industries (textiles, apparel, paper and pulp). Written intentions indicate that most schemes focused on productivity increase or export promotion (environmental preservation and energy consumption were added in the 1970s). The volume of subsidies reached its maximum during the 1970s, when it was used to combat recession, stabilize employment and counteract a rising market interest rate.

Although usually no *ex ante sectoral discrimination* was planned, ex-post analyses showed that the schemes in general favoured capital-intensive, basic goods industries and other mature sectors. The system discriminated in favour of large enterprises, and slow-growing firms.

A market-based instrument to boost competitiveness: 'Topinvestitionen'

Schemes that propagate rather general and partly conflicting goals ('productivity increase', 'employment stabilization', 'export promotion' or 'import substitution'), discriminate ex-post in favour of branches in which large firms exist and vested interests are well organized.

This analysis applied a specific market-based instrument designed to increase the competitiveness of Austrian manufacturing. Specific credits were granted to innovative firms in the most sophisticated market segments (called 'Topinvestitionen').

The idea of Topinvestitionen is that, while government does not know which industrial sectors will be the most important and profitable ones in future, *there is a consensus on the characteristics of firms which want to be competitive in the most sophisticated market segments*. Firms could qualify for inexpensive credit if their past performance and their planned innovations received a high score, according to a specific list of criteria. The criteria referred partly to the *firm*, partly to the *project* and partly to the *market* in which they were engaged. Benchmarks were fixed, transferring firm data into grade points.

Among the criteria were:

- past *performance of the firm*: growth, cash flow, exports;
- *the use of specific inputs*: qualified labour, research personnel, low energy intensity; and
- *project impact*: increase in exports, in unit value of the product, innovative content (own research), market growth in the EU, positive specialization of leading countries in the specific industry (RCA value).

The list included 30 variables, for each of which an expert group had set quantitative limits. A firm qualified for the credit when it accumulated a specific amount of fixed points.

The economic philosophy behind this scheme was the product cycle theory: firms in advanced industrial countries should produce a product mix in the first and second phases of the product cycle. In the case of this process a firm must use sophisticated inputs and specialize in rapidly growing, diversified markets, in which leading countries have a comparative advantage.

The expertise and independence of the rating group was decisive in the implementation of this programme. The final decision was reached by an independent commission, rather than a political decision-making unit. Usually the final decision had been made by a government department following advice from experts or a commission.

From the perspective of a market-orientated philosophy cheap money for excellent firms is justified, since firms investing in new technologies and in new markets have specific costs which cannot be completely recovered by sales. Innovative firms create spillovers for other firms, they invest in human capital as well as in new technologies and markets. On a less philosophical level, two arguments are important. The new scheme replaced an older, heavily distorted scheme that favoured mature industries (with negative externalities). Second, the scheme helped the Austrian economy gain competitiveness in the most sophisticated sectors. And an economy coming from behind and surpassing average wage levels, had to transform its policy from imitating to innovating.

Between 1982 and 1994, some 27 billion (27,000 million) ATS were given to the TOP-FIRMS. Several ex-post analyses (by the author of this paper and his colleagues at the Austrian Institute of Economic Research, WIFO) have shown that the programme was a success in the sense that the structure of the credits were consistent with the programmes goals and that the firms involved performed better than average and improved their performance as a result of their participation.

During the 1980s the amount of credits granted according to this scheme decreased for three reasons. First, the amount of subsidies in general were curtailed. Second, special interest groups complained that credits from this scheme were very difficult to obtain (above all, politicians could not guarantee *ex cathedra* that a specific firm would receive cheap money). And public opinion complained that giving money to the firms in a good financial position made no sense.

Though I was a promotor of this scheme, assisting in its implementation, and monitoring its progress, I feel that its gradual phasing out may not be too bad. The capital market has improved during this decade, so that risky and innovative firms now have a better chance of receiving equity financing. Second, the core of the ideas has spread among firms and institutions. The largest source of subsidies – the ERP fund – is now using similar criteria, though not with the same rigour and not entirely independent of political pressure. The firms have learned to assess their own performance according to some of these criteria.

The rise and fall of the nationalized industries

Some 15 per cent of Austrian industry, especially large firms in the basic goods sector, were nationalized after the Second World War (partly due to lack of owners, partly following a political vision). Among the economic reasons for keeping the firms nationalized in the 1950s, was the belief that a small country needed a core of domestic firms, which could produce cheap and technologically advanced basic goods, permitting the development of processing and refining industries.

The nationalized industry was quite successful in its first phase. Reconstruction was speedy, basic production goods were supplied to Austrian firms at low prices and in a high quality. In the early 1960s there was some political debate as to whether nationalized firms should be allowed to expand into the final goods sector – the outcome of which was positive. Up until the end of the 1970s, sales and exports grew faster than in the private sector.

As product markets became diversified, multinational firms were divisionalized, commodity markets were flooded by excess supply, and the nationalized firms registered losses. Several government bailouts and structural reforms did not help and the story of a nationalized Austrian industry pretty much ends in November 1993. The public majority stake in all viable firms was sold off by the end of 1995.

Rules for foreign capital

Austria had a liberal policy with respect to the investment of foreign capital, the reason being that these firms produced at a higher technological level and helped to increase the competitiveness of the manufacturing sector in Austria. More than one third of the manufacturing industry is owned by foreign firms. They were helpful in promoting technical progress and new organizational techniques. The sector of foreign-owned firms had superior performance according to several economic criteria (productivity per worker, growth of sales, profits). Through the course of decades, the amount of capital inflow was larger than the investment of Austrian firms abroad. The pattern has changed in recent years: Austria's investment abroad now is larger than foreign investment in Austria.

Austria never lost its favourable attitude towards capital inflow, but did gradually change its philosophy after catching up with European productivity and wage levels. Incoming investors are told to anticipate that cheap labour and high subsidies are not the input which Austria will continue to use to maintain a comparative advantage. Investment should draw upon the qualifications of Austrian workers as well as Austria's high level of productivity. Second, there are few multinational firms with headquarters in Austria. This creates a problem for Austria, because multinational firms often concentrate such productive services as research near their headquarters. Austria therefore encourages firms to establish a headquarters or at least a regional or divisional centre in Austria. Austria also tries to persuade existing firms (in the nationalized industry) to retain their headquarters in Austria (sometimes by keeping a majority of the assets in Austria). The main strategy, however, is to make the tax system and economic environment generally favourable for the establishment of headquarters.

Governance structures in market economies

Each Western country has some governance structure for its sector of large industrial firms. The situation is quite different from what is illustrated in textbook economics and varies across Western countries.

- In the USA, anti-trust legislation has had an important impact on the shaping of modern industry. While suspicions are high towards price fixing, concentration rates, price discrimination and pre-emption, and violations have sometimes been drastically punished, anti-trust policy has not prevented the emergence of large and very large enterprises. Import duties and anti-dumping legislation are believed to be justified by the general principles of free trade (and not regarded as instruments misused by special interests). While low wages and low energy prices are considered important to the competitiveness of the domestic economy, much lower wages and even lower pollution standards in Mexico justify special restrictions on imports from this country (see the discussion about and the annex to the NAFTA). Technology policy carried through more indirectly via military demand, but support for an industrial policy which fosters the development of supercomputers and HDTV is growing. The governance structure changes over time, see the increasing importance of the argument of supporting the 'competitiveness' of the USA vs. Japan; witness the decreasing threat to economic welfare seen in mergers, and the vanishing impact of consumer interest organizations and trade unions in recent years.
- In Germany a governance structure emerged with an important role for large banks. Anti-trust policy had been more important than in other European countries, though it is sometimes softened by the strive for competitiveness in the world market. Industrial policy makes use of massive funds for research, regional investment subsidies, subsidies for shipyards and coal industry (and now restructuring in the new Länder). In France industrial policy includes sectoral development strategies, the creation and promotion of large firms (including nationalization to create national champions). Implicit governance follows from the education system, where the 'elite' in government and in large firms passed through the same management schools.
- The role of industrial policy in Japan is well discussed in the literature including the role of MITI, of banks and of *keiretsus*. Policy for

structural change in declining industries as well as promotion of important sectors in the medium term plans (visions) should be kept in mind. Low interest rates, high investment quotas, long working time and lifetime employment are some features which could not be maintained without implicit governance structure. The system is extremely efficient in promoting collusion (in prices, import restriction, technologies), but in contrast to other similar attempts able to promote efficiency and competitiveness and even to enforce disinvestments. Korea, Taiwan, Indonesia and Singapore all have their own systems of industrial policy, each quite far away from textbook market economies and theoretically founded arguments for interventions. Some authors call these systems 'managed market economies' (see Wade 1990; Bayer 1991).

- The European Community explicitly calls for an Industrial Policy (see Hutschenreiter 1993) on the Community level as well as on the national level (see also the chapter by Christine Oughton and Geoff Whittam in this volume). It should help to increase the competitiveness of the countries by the promotion of 'accelerators' and 'multipliers'. The approach should be horizontal (encouraging preconditions of growth not targeting specific sectors). But there exist sectoral programmes for specific mature sectors (steel, textiles, cars) and for generic technologies (biotechnology, electronics, etc.).

The Austrian variant of governance structure is the so-called social partnership. Not unlike the system of corporatism in other small economies, it has specific features. The system is more comprehensive (all kinds of economic decisions are shaped by employers' federations and trade unions), it is more centralized (decisions are top-down, financial strength lies in the headquarters) and it is more successful (measured in hours lost by strikes, or in attaining goals like growth, stability).

Regarding the question of the competitiveness of the Austrian economy, the social partnership had two very profound effects. First, it helped to keep down ambitious (and fast rising) aspiration levels, and second it guaranteed that in phases in which competitiveness was threatened (a current account deficit widened), active measures (investment promotion, retraining) were applied instead of passive measures (wage cuts, layoffs).

Having such an *intermediate layer of institutions* helps to implement more sophisticated macro-economic or industrial strategies. *Social partnership* is such a layer in Austria, *financial non-commercial intermediaries* another, MITI and *kereitsu* are such institutions in Japan, the Deutsche Bank, Treuhand and *Volkswagenstiftung* are some important ones in Germany. *These institutions enforce continuity in periods of political instability, they help to increase the time horizon of politics and firms.* And these institutions help to internalize external economies (Coase institutions). It has to be guaranteed that these institutions remain flexible (immune to Olson's forecast), incorporate market signals and are not captured by special interests. Of course they should not be the old planning boards in a new disguise.

APPLYING THE CONCEPT OF COMPETITIVENESS TO AUSTRIA

Austria's economy is competitive in the 1990s, supported by the following qualifications and in respect to the following aspirations:

Austria sells enough products to balance its current account The trade balance is negative (approximately 5 per cent of GNP), services exported are much greater than services imported, so that the current balance is in some years positive and in some years negative. The currency reserves of the national bank are increasing over time. The market shares of Austrian exports are increasing, remarkably in the European market, more slowly on the world market.

Although there is no fundamental problem, some fears are expressed from time to time. There have been and are periods in which the balance is negative (end of the 1970s, 1994) and then part of the business community expresses fears also as to whether Austria is fundamentally competitive. Another line of argument holds that an industrialized country should not run a deficit in its trade balance, still another that prospects for tourism are not that good and that this service sector will not forever be able to balance the trade deficit. The examples show that what seems to be 'enough exports' for some people, or what is enough for today, may not be enough for others or for tomorrow.

Austria is competitive at its aspired wage level Wages have been lower in Austria for a long time. In the 1970s per capita wages reached the European average; this had been a political goal (to attain 'Europalöhne' was a political demand at the end of the 1960s). But the pressure for higher wages has always been in line with a productivity increase. In fact, today the value added per employee in Austrian manufacturing is as high as in Western Germany and higher than in most other countries, while wages are 10–15 per cent lower than in the highest wage countries. So aspirations have always been in line with the technological potential, although perhaps at the lower end of the technologically feasible 'band'. The Austrian Schilling has constantly appreciated in relation to other currencies, so that purchasing power is rising. GDP per capita at purchasing power is among the highest in the industrialized countries (lying between rank 4 and 10 in different statistics and years).

Austria is competitive at macro conditions and is considered satisfactory by its people GDP is growing at a higher rate than in other economies, inflation is low, unemployment – though higher than in the USA and than in past decades – is low by European standards. The social net is more comprehensive, environmental regulation stricter than in other countries. Out of the criteria of the Maastricht treaty for European convergence all goals exept reducing the budget deficit have been met by Austria (and Austria's position towards this goal is better than in the average of the other EU members).

Austria has no deep fear that its competitiveness will be threatened in the future. Now and then some dissatisfaction is expressed due to the concentration of many industries, as well as due to the low amount of research and development, and Austria's lack of competitiveness in the most advanced sectors as in telecommunications. Wages are still far from Swiss levels, technical excellence is far from US achievements, marketing and globalization are sometimes undervalued, and Austria has few large firms. If very high aspiration levels are set, many deficits arise. But from a historical perspective, and the commonly accepted aspiration level, the performance is seen as remarkable.

ASSESSING THE COMPETITIVENESS OF SWITZERLAND, THE USA, JAPAN AND THE EU

The competitiveness debate in Switzerland

Switzerland sells enough products, its current account balance is positive, and market shares are approximately constant. The economy has a very strong active balance in outward direct investments. *Switzerland enjoys this performance at the highest factor incomes in Europe.* The currency is one of the strongest in the world and enjoys long-run appreciation against most other currencies. Income growth in national currency is below average, but this does not seem to be a problem (it does not fall short of a rise in the aspiration levels).

The macro conditions in Switzerland can, through the perspective of an outsider, only be assessed as very satisfactory: inflation is low, so is unemployment, the economic position is strong. The firms are internationalized, human capital and research are given high priorities, and Switzerland is famous for its clean environment.

Objectively taken, Switzerland is one of the most competitive economies in the world. Nevertheless, there are now and then domestic debates on Switzerland's competitiveness. A reason for this is that Swiss firms are not leaders in technology, at least *not in each and every industry or technological area.* Another fear is that staying outside of European integration could eventually become a problem. Also problematic could be the domestic demand for high ecological standards – inter alia the switch of the transit traffic from road to railway may not be financially viable. Competitiveness could be threatened, should firms have to invest enormous amounts in rerouting traffic.

This discussion proves that an economy believed by many to be the most competitive by objective standards, may not be felt to provide 'enough' by a nation, whose aspiration level exceeds its current performance.

The competitiveness of the USA and Japan

The US economy is not competitive, in so far as it sells too few products. The current account is in the red at about 2 per cent of GDP. The amount may narrow in the mid-1990s, but will remain quite large. US market shares in world imports and in important high tech subsegments are declining. Such a position occurs *when GNP/capita and manufacturing productivity are high.* Median incomes have been stagnating for more than a decade and manufacturing wages are now positioned between Europe and Japanese levels ($16.30/hour; compared to $21.60 and $15.30). Profits are high, some firms have large shares in the world market and are technology leaders. The currency is devaluing over the long run.

Macro performance is mixed. Employment growth is high, unemployment is low, the dispersion in incomes is large and growing. The priority for research remains high, education is the best in the world for the most highly qualified segments, but is very inadequate for lower segments. A comprehensive health system is not available and does not seem to be financiable.

The debate on losing competitiveness, especially in relation to Japan, climaxed in the late 1980s, focusing on deficits in the balance of payments and on the decline in market shares for electronics and cars. In the middle of the 1990s, the mood is more optimistic, the feeling is expressed that the USA has regained leadership in telecommunications, aircraft, networks, electronics and cars. The trade balance deficit is now considered as less severe, and less importance is attributed to declining median incomes and the increasing spread between high and low incomes and vocational standards. The subjective characteristics of moods in society, as well as in the economy, can be well demonstrated by the American position.

The Japanese economy sells enough products, enabling constant production of a highly active current account. The Japanese people would never be content if the Japanese balance were only levelled. Constantly increasing reserves are seen as important substitutes for a lack of natural resources.

The competitiveness rests on low wages, long working days and short holidays. This downgrades 'performance' for an outside evaluator. But it is no problem for competitiveness, since wages and working relations conform to Japanese aspiration levels. *The other pillar of competitiveness is efficiency and technological innovation.* Gross profits are high and stable, firms are strong, the currency is appreciating. Investment shares are large, government and big business exercise a strong influence on personal relations. Japan is often described as a dual economy, since many small firms with low wages and unstable employment also exist.

GDP per head is increasing very quickly, and is now quite high. Since domestic prices are high, this is not true to the same degree for purchasing power. Unemployment is practically non-existent, inflation low. The social net and environmental standards are not seen as unsatisfactory. Outside observers would note that flats are very small for a high-income country and that gender relations are not fair, but since we have to accept the national aspiration level, this is no problem for competitiveness.

The competitiveness of Europe

There are long and sophisticated studies on this topic. The situation differs very much across countries; neither the economies nor the political and social systems are homogeneous. We do not want to address all these issues now, but do want to apply some elements of our proposed definition.

Europe sells enough goods in so far *as its current account is balanced.* The EU's market shares in world imports are declining, and this is true for many technologically intensive product groups.

The wages are higher in Europe than in any other bloc in the triad. This is good news in so far as high wages are the ultimate goal of economics, but it lowers the competitiveness for less sophisticated products. Many countries try to fulfil both aims (high income plus competitiveness) by reducing the wedge between wage cost and net income out of wages. The cost of the non-unification of Europe is high, the concept of '*Binnenmarkt*' tries to reduce this cost component.

Macro performance is mixed. The growth rate is lower than in Japan and in the Pacific Rim, not much below the US level. Unemployment is higher, but incomes are more equal, and the social net and health care systems function relative to other continents. The working weeks are shorter, holidays longer, and retirement earlier.

Aspirations to increase these leisure benefits are now not pressing. Macro economic performance should become more equal among countries, the goals of price stability, interest rates and budget discipline are rather demanding, according to the Maastricht convergence criteria. Reducing the budget deficit of federal and local governments is the goal most difficult to reach. There is no goal set for employment in the criteria.

CONCLUSIONS

This chapter discusses various attempts to define the concept of competitiveness on a national level. After reviewing the concepts for competitiveness of a nation we propose the following definition

A country is said to be competitive if it

- sells *enough* products and services
- at factor incomes in *line with the countries' (current and constantly changing)* aspiration level
- at macroconditions (of the economic and social system) seen as *satisfactory* by the people

In presenting this definition we had to make several choices.

- We chose to maintain the notion of competitiveness of a nation, despite several problems, due to its frequent application in the political and economic debate. Of course the concept does not imply that each and every firm in a country said to be competitive can exhibit superior performance in relation to each and every foreign firm. A macro concept refers to an aggregate or to a majority of broadly defined sectors.
- Between attempts at defining competitiveness by objective standards or by subjective elements, we recognize a need for both possibilities, but particularly emphasize that any assessment implicitly relies on subjective elements. We reject postulating preferences, weighting them, and finally choosing an identical set of indicators for all countries. Rather we allow for different aspiration levels regarding the amount of targeted exports, the aspired factor incomes and the macroconditions.
- When choosing between technical and economic concepts, we lean towards the economic approach. Measuring competitiveness merely against technical indicators excludes important social, organizational and distributional aspects, as well as aspirations. Implicitly, our concept includes the relation between aspired factor incomes and technology. If the technical standard is superior, high aspirations can be achieved without losing the ability to sell (see Switzerland).
- In choosing between a narrow approach, focusing on exports or market shares alone, or a broader concept, we prefer the latter. Exports can be raised and market shares increased, when wages, social and environmental standards are lowered, currency is devalued, and working time is increased. This passive approach leads away from the final economic ends, and people will not have the feeling that they are 'competitive' after such strategies have been applied. The implication is that in choosing between a 'cheap inputs' approach and a 'dear output' approach, we find the latter as more relevant. Competitiveness based on research and human capital, and reflected in good performance in sophisticated markets, is of higher quality than that based on low input prices.
- In choosing between static and dynamic approaches, we choose the dynamic perspective. Since measurement always starts from past figures, this means looking for indicators of future competitiveness. Competitiveness is not a state once reached and then maintained for ever,

> but is a dynamic process in which factor incomes, aspirations, and macro-conditions are constantly changing, as does the competitive output such as exports, market shares and current balances.

The Austrian economy serves as an example. Austria's initial task was to recover competitiveness after the Second World War. A low level of competitiveness was reached in the 1950s, with low wages and an undervalued currency. In the course of the next decades, aspiration levels, wages and incomes caught up first with the European average and then with a group of leading European countries, per capita income is now well above the average of the European Union. Economic policy has kept wage increases and aspiration levels in line, channelling profits into investments, education and infrastructure for future growth, and restraining from the temptation of increasing short-term exports by offering cheap inputs.

The concept is then applied in a description of competitiveness in Switzerland, the USA, Japan and the European Union. The main point is to demonstrate that competitiveness is a complex but useful concept, and that a definition is needed which contains subjective elements and broad perspectives.

NOTES

1 Zero profits imply the rule 'price equals total average costs'. Profits are long-term profits including risk, compensation for the employees, etc. Zero economic profits are the outcome of the competitive model in micro-economics, with many firms and homogenous products.

2 In this model firms set quantities and the price cost margin of a given firm depends on its market share and price elasticity of demand.

3 In the Stackelberg model a dominant firm chooses its quantity first, the other firms maximize profits given the decision of the dominant firm. In the dominant firm/fringe model the first has positive profits, the fringe supplies at zero profits.

4 In a closed economy monopoly power for a given degree of product diversification reduces total surplus. If monopoly power comes from successful product innovation the increase in consumer surplus due to product differentiation has to be valued against the deadweight loss.

5 Porter arrives at this view after dismissing different concepts of competitiveness ('every firm is competitive', 'positive balance of trade', 'market share', 'job creation') and then stresses that the search for a convincing explanation of both national and firm prosperity must begin by asking the right question. We must abandon the whole notion of a 'competitive nation' as a term having much meaning for economic prosperity. The principle goal of a nation is to produce a high and rising standard of living for its citizens. The ability to do so depends not an the amorphous notion of competitiveness but on the productivity with which a nation's resources (labour and capital) are employed.

(Porter (1990: 6)

He continues on the same page, 'The only meaningful concept of competitiveness at the national level is national productivity'.

6 Beck (1990: 11) uses GDP/head in international currency plus the growth rates of the same as a first approximation for the evaluation of competitiveness of the Swiss economy. Later Beck defines competitiveness as the ability to promote structural change thus leading to an efficient use of resources.

7 The factors of competitiveness are

- domestic economic strength
- internationalization
- government
- finance
- infrastructure
- management
- science & technology
- people

8 In economics it pays to be exact. If I understand the formula correctly the following mathematical expression is that which comes nearest to the somewhat vague definition: $(MS_i/MS_w)*GDP_w/GDP_i > 1$ where *MS* are market shares in the wealth market and *GNP* is Gross National Product, *i* is a specific country and *w* denotes world.

9 I am grateful to Pat Devine for telling me at the *Crete Workshop on Competitiveness, Subsidiarity and Objectives* that there is a definition of efficiency by Singh (1977) quite similar to my concept of competitiveness: 'we may define an efficient manufacturing sector as one which (currently as well as potentially) not only satisfies the demands of consumers at home, but is also able to sell enough of its products abroad to pay for the nation's import requirements . . . the sector must be able to achieve these objectives at socially acceptable levels of output, employment and the exchange rate' (Singh 1970: 128). See also Pat Devine's contribution to this volume.

10 In Austria, for example, economic policy in the late 1960s had the goal to attain 'the European wage level', and competitive performance was evaluated with respect to the attainment of this goal. If the Portuguese people feel happy with their wage level they will assess their economy as 'competitive', if they feel a strong pressure for higher wages, they will arrive at a different assessment. The analyst of the competitiveness of nations has to keep this in mind: either he/she postulates a certain level of factor income as a norm (European average, US average) or he/she accepts a political goal. But any verdict has to be made in relation to an explicit or implicit aspiration level.

11 The development was not so smooth if we watch the details. The system of government led price control (including tripartite negotiations which were moulded into government price regulation) ended about 1950 (with exceptions for bread, raw materials and energy prices). In the liberalization policy that followed, price controls seemed to be unnecessary. Later in the 1950s the voluntary system of price and wage negotiations (with maximal rates of price increase) was created.

12 This is a mechanism predicted by rational expectations theory.

13 No instrument works too long. Over time additional schemes came into effect. Tax depreciation as high as 120 per cent of the purchasing value became possible (favouring capital intensive firms with long periods of depreciation), tax free reserves (for firms which did not see urgent investment opportunities), and finally tax credits for unprofitable firms eroded the tax base. Finally the system was

considered to favour capital intensive firms and domestic monopolies while discriminating against investments in research, human capital, young firms and entry. The system was scrapped, the subsidies were cut and the nominal tax rates reduced to compensate the profit squeeze. For the period in which capital markets did not work properly and firms had to rely on self-financing, it was an *important investment resource for profitable firms* in manufacturing. It was an instrument to reduce the time discount and a guarantee to employees that profits would be reinvested.

14 A strict discrimination between manufacturing sectors (neither a planned nor an actual one) is not remembered. Some of the answers were: 'Every sensible programme was approved', 'sometimes there were discussions whether basic industries or consumer industries should be favoured'. One remark which shows that policy considerations existed was the following 'the paper and pulp industry was forced to propose investments by the threat of import liberalization'. And definitely there was a discussion about how large the capacities should be in the firms inherited from Nazi Germany (the Ministry of Planning and Reconstruction worked out four sectoral plans, but they were not directly related to the ERP programme), it was also controversial whether Austria should get a car production facility.

15 This is not the place finally to assess the reasons for the failure of nationalization nor to rank them. The determinants of the late failure include the *industry problem* (too many basic goods), the *organizational problem* (too bureaucratic an organization), the *soft budget problem* (no exit from unprofitable sectors) and the *monitoring problem* (how to judge the performance of firms).

The principles for management or the objectives nationalized firms should pursue have never been defined explicitly. The goals which were actually pursued have varied, the organization and the management structure were changed frequently.

Whether goals of nationalized firms differed from private ones has been controversial. In good times some people (and politicians) expected the nationalized firms to be the spearheads of the technological progress and/or innovators in shop-floor democracy and codetermination. In bad times politicians expected nationalized firms to stabilize employment. But neither of these aims was defined explicitly or written into any law or charter.

The decision process in the nationalized sector and the degree of interference by government changed over time. Sometimes a department of government was responsible directly for the decision of firms (including investment plans), usually some intervening agency (holding company) was responsible. The recruitment process for top management favoured political selection.

REFERENCES

Aiginger, K. (1987) *Production and Decision under Uncertainty*, Oxford: Blackwell.

—— (1993a) 'Determinants of Net Trade Flows between East and West', paper presented at the European Association of Industrial Economics (EARIE), Tel Aviv.

—— (1993b) 'Strategic behaviour of Austrian firms towards Central and Eastern Europe', paper presented at the Austrian Economic Association (Nationalökonomische Gesellschaft), Graz.

——(1993c) 'Collusion, concentration, profits', *Empirica* 20(2).

—— (1993d) 'Chancen und Gefährdungspotentiale der Ostöffnung: Konsequenzen für die österreichieche Wirtschafts', 3 Bände, WIFO Gutachten (jointly with

Geldner, N., Kramer, H., Peneder, M., Schnitzer, Y., Stankovsky, J.) Vienna.

Aiginger, K and Finsinger, J (1994) *Applied Industrial Organization*, Dordecht, London: Kluwer.

Bayer, K (1991) *Strategic Planning for Industrial Restructuring*, Vienna: Austrian Institute of Economic Research.

Beck, B. (1990) *Die internationale Wettbewerbsfähigkeit der schweizerischen Exportindustrie,* Bern, Stuttgart: Paul Haupt Verlag.

Beirat für Wirtschafts- und Sozialforschung (1994) *Wirtschaftsstandort Österreich,* Vienna.

Beirat für Wirtschafts- und Sozialfragen (1991) *Industriepolitik*, Vienna.

Bianchi, P., Cowling, K. and Sugden, R (1994), *Europe's Economic Challenge*, London, New York: Routledge.

Butschek, F. (1993) 'External shocks and long term pattern of economic growth in Central and Eastern Europe' Mimeo, Vienna.

Calvo, G.A and Frenkel, J.A. (1991) 'Credit markets, credibility and economic transformation'. *Journal of Economic Perspectives*. 5(4).

—— (1992) 'Transformation of centrally planned economies: credit markets and sustainable growth'. in G. Winckler (ed.) *Central and Eastern Europe, Roads to Growth*, Washington: IMF.

Europäische Wirtschaft (1994) 'Die Wettbewerbsposition Europas in der Triade'. *Jahreswirtschaftsbericht,* 55.

Fath, J (1992). 'Industrial policies for countries in transition', *WIIW Forschungsberichte* 187.

Geroski, P.A. (1989) 'European industrial policy and industrial policy in Europe'. *Oxford Review of Economic Policy*, 2: 20–36.

Grossman, G.M. (1990) 'Promoting new industrial activities: a survey of recent arguments and evidence', *OECD Economic Studies*: 87–125.

Hahn, F.R. (1993) 'Theoriegrundlagen moderner industriepolitik', *WIFO Working Papers*, 60.

Hilpert, H.G. (1993) 'Japanische Industriepolitik', *IFO Schnelldienst* 17/18: 7–22.

Hummel, M. (1993) 'Industriepolitik – Kontrovers'. *IFO Schnelldienst* 17/18: 3–7.

Hutschenreiter, G. (1993a) 'Industriepolitik der EG: Grundilagen und neue Intiativen', *WIFO–TIP,* Vienna, July.

—— (1993b) 'Neue Ansätze zu einer Industriepolitik der EG', *WIFO Monatsberichte*, 5.

Klodt, H. (1993) 'Europäische Industriepolitik nach Maastricht', *Weltwirtschaftliches Archiv*: 263 ff.

Kursch, D.B. (1993) 'Zur Debatte über die Industriepolitik in den USA,' *IFO Schenelldienet* 17/18: 23–25.

Landesmann, M. (1993) 'Industrial policy and the transition in East-Central Europe', *WIIW Forschungsberichte* 181.

Laski, K. (1992) 'Transition from command to market economies in Central and Eastern Europe', *WIIW Forschungsberichte*, 196.

Leo, H. (1994) 'Technological position and industrial structure of Austria', In B. Böhm and L.F Punzo (eds) *Economic Performance: A look at Austria and Italy*, Berlin: Physica.

Lindbeck, A. (1982) 'Industrial policy as an issue in the economic environment'. The Institute of International Economic Studies, Stockholm.

Meihsi, D. (1969) 'Die Landwirtschaft im Wandel der ökonomischen Faktoren', in W. Weber (ed.) *Osterreichs Wirtschaft-gestern, heute, morgen*, Berlin.

Passeron, H. (1993) 'Die Entwicklung der französischen Industriepolitik, Zur Debatte über die Industriepolitik in den USA', *IFO Schnelldienst,* 17/18: 30–33.

Peneder, M. (1994) *Pattern of Industrial Competitiveness*, Vienna.

Porter, M.E. (1990) The *Competitive Advantage of Nations*, New York: The Free Press.

Singh, A (1977) 'UK industry and the world economy: A case of deindustrialization', *Cambridge Journal of Economics*, 113–136.

Streissler, E. (1972) 'Investment stimulation and the hierarchy of individual plans', in W. Schmitz (ed.) *Convertability, multialteralism and freedom* Vienna.

Urban, W. (1992) 'Economic lessons for the East European countries from two newly industrializing countries in the Far East'. *WIIW Forschungsberichte* 182.

US Report of the President (1984) *Industrial Policy*, Washington.

Wade, R. (1990) *Governing the Market: Economic Theory and the Role of Government in East Asia Industrialization*, Princeton.

Weder, G. (1993) 'Coase institutions', *Weltwirtschaftliches Archiv* 3.

Winckler, G. (1992) *Central and Eastern Europe, Roads to Growth,* Washington: IMF.

Zemplinerova, A. (1993) *The Demonopolization of the Previously Centrally Planned Economies,* Prague: El CERGE.

8

COMPETITIVENESS AND INDUSTRIAL POLICY IN PORTUGAL

João Confraria

INTRODUCTION

Competitiveness, of firms, industries, regions or nations, seems to be an increasingly popular subject in the political debate and even in some academic work. Perhaps as an undesirable consequence of this, there are several ambiguities related to the concept and to its role in policy making. These are addressed in the next section, highlighting the relation of competitiveness to more familiar concepts in industrial organization and suggesting some empirical difficulties in its evaluation. These ideas are used in a third section, to make a comparison about the role of competitiveness in Portuguese industrial policy, in two different historical periods: before 1973, when some protectionist policies prevailed notwithstanding Portuguese participation in the European Free Trade Association; and after membership of the European Economic Community, in 1986. In the fourth section we discuss specific issues arising from the European Union, concerning the evolution of the Portuguese economy and bearing in mind the role of the Community Support Frameworks. First, it is argued that the total amount of external funds available to the Portuguese economy has remained stable – increasing transfers from the European Union have mainly offset the decline in emigrants' remittances. Second, it is suggested that, given the changes in the dynamics of investment that are to be expected from the European Union, it seems useful to define more clearly the objectives of structural funds.

THE 'COMPETITIVENESS' ISSUE

Several widely used definitions of competitiveness of firms, countries or regions, point to the ability to achieve sustainable high levels of income and employment in an 'unprotected' environment. For instance, the OECD (1994b) proposes as a working definition of competitiveness 'the ability of companies, industries, regions, nations or supranational regions to generate, while being and remaining exposed to international competition, relatively high factor income and factor employment levels on a sustainable basis'; America's Competitiveness Policy Council (1992) defined competitiveness as 'the ability to produce goods and services that meet the test of international markets while our citizens earn a standard of living that is both rising and sustainable in the long run'.[1]

At the firm level, these concepts of competitiveness lead to some ambiguities. For instance, what should be said about the competitiveness of a firm that manages to increase factor incomes per unit of factor employed but fails to maintain a high level of employment? And in the opposite case, whenever low factor incomes per unit of production factors used coexist with high levels of employment? Perhaps a less ambiguous concept of competitiveness at the firm level results from Stigler's survival test (1958); anyway, his idea is explicit in every definition of competitiveness based on increasing market shares.

The discussion of competitiveness at the industry and country level raises more complex problems.[2] In a closed economy, the concepts mentioned above are close to the concept of market performance in the structure-conduct-performance paradigm currently used in mainstream industrial organization. Scherer and Ross (1990) suggest a definition of market performance that includes strict efficiency criteria, e.g. production and allocative efficiency at the firm and industry levels, as well as broader economic and social objectives such as technological progress and the contribution of each market to full employment, economic growth, price stability and equity. Obviously, competitiveness at the industry level may be taken as very close to market performance; if the definition is used in every market in the economy it leads to a concept of competitiveness at the economy level. Value judgements about the weights to be given to each of the above mentioned variables are necessary, leading to different and sometimes conflicting views on the evaluation of market performance at the economy level.[3]

International trade and international mobility of capital and labour add several distinctions between these notions of market performance and competitiveness – at least concerning the variables included in the definition that are directly related to international trade.

The point to be stressed is that mobility of goods and/or factors of production imply a change in the geographic definition of markets. Agents from different communities (countries, regions) interact in international markets and it seems safe to suggest that each community is particularly interested in the results (e.g. shares of market sales or of market surpluses) achieved by a subset of the agents involved in the transactions – those that in some sense belong to that community. Different competitiveness concepts are all based on some criteria of 'good' economic 'performance' by the economic agents belonging to those countries or regions, even if different value judgements attached to the selection of the set of variables that define 'good performance' cannot be avoided. Some implications follow from this. (In what follows, for the sake of simplicity, we consider that, for a given community, 'good performance' depends on market surpluses owned by the members of that community.)

First, in open markets competitiveness of regions or countries is not directly related to overall market performance – it depends on the values or the shares of e.g. market surpluses owned by the firms, workers and consumers that belong to those regions or countries. However, market performance, as defined above, is still relevant for this 'community-centred' concept of competitiveness, as long as success in markets where firms are considered to be efficient has not the same consequences as success in markets where inefficiencies prevail.

Second, as international trade implies reallocation of resources, competitiveness at the economy level does not result from competitiveness in every market. In different industries, shares or values of surpluses owned by residents from a given country or region change over time, according to changes in preferences, endowments of resources and technologies.

Finally a concept of competitiveness at the community level focused on the value of total market surpluses owned by members of the community is perhaps more useful than a similar concept focused on the shares of those surpluses. In the latter case, economic relations among communities lead to a zero-sum game and, as a matter of fact, the notion does not seem to be particularly interesting – some communities may be losing in relative terms, even if incomes are increasing everywhere, as is to be expected from international trade.

However, empirical difficulties remain to be solved about the relevant geographic definition of a given market and whenever one has to decide who are the economic agents that belong to a given community – and so are to be included in the community's competitiveness concept.

The problem of agreeing upon a suitable definition of a geographic market is common to several areas of industrial organization (Jacquemin and Slade 1989). Concerning competitiveness, further ambiguities arise if a subset of firms competing in a given international market benefit from strategic trade policies, e.g., subsidies from national or regional governments or protected positions in other geographic markets. If these policies lead to increasing shares of total market surpluses that does not necessarily mean that the country or region is competitive, because in at least some markets firms are not fully exposed to international competition.

On the other hand, if the relevant community is the nation-state, should one include a firm owned by nationals who use the domestic profits to invest abroad and should we exclude a firm owned by foreigners who reinvest the profits in the domestic economy? This discussion relates to the privatization processes happening almost everywhere. Actually, even in the absence of externalities, there may well be a difference between the private and social rates of return if the private investor is a non-resident investor and if it does not make sense to include his profits in the social welfare function of the national government. In this case, under a domestic point of view, enhancement of social welfare may be consistent with some inefficiency at the firm level, providing the market surpluses belong to residents.[4]

These ideas are also relevant for different definitions of the trade balance. Given the current national accounting framework, exports and imports are defined according to geographic criteria and increasing exports from one country or region are often considered part of a process of increasing competitiveness of that country or region. However, it seems also sensible to argue that increasing exports by affiliates of transnational corporations tells more about the ability of the transnational corporation to remain competitive in the international market than about the competitiveness of the country or region.[5] Moreover, the transnational corporations' profits are not part of the social welfare function of the community – unless it seems clear that it has a long-run commitment to the host country, (see also the chapter by Christos Pitelis, Roger Sugden and Lena Tsipouri).

Mobility of labour adds a different type of problem. Full employment is one of the variables often included in concepts of competitiveness of a country or of a region. However, full employment, meaning the 'absence' of unemployment, may be consistent with declining employment as long as people migrate – even if the domestic economy grows at socially acceptable rates, for longer periods, the negative impact of emigration on economic growth may be offset by a positive impact through emigrants' remittances.

Summing up, the concept of competitiveness of a given community is related to the survival and economic prosperity of that community and, in this sense, it seems to be useful for policy-making purposes. In any given country or region, communities and governments do not seem to be particularly worried about overall performance in international markets (meaning, for the sake of simplicity, the total amount of producers' and consumers' surpluses) but only in 'good performance' by a subset of economic agents belonging to the community. Difficulties with the concept come from the definitions of the set of agents, members of the community, and of 'good performance'.

COMPETITIVENESS AND THE OBJECTIVES OF INDUSTRIAL POLICY

The role of competitiveness, as defined above, in Portuguese industrial policy – and, as a matter of fact, in economic policy – has changed over the years. Perhaps the most meaningful comparisons are to be made between industrial policy during the period of industrialization, from the early 1930s to 1973 and industrial policy after membership of the European Economic Community, from 1986 onwards.

Market performance in protected markets

Half a century ago, when industrialization became one of the most important objectives of economic policy,[6] the major objectives of industrial policy were: first, to devise policy instruments, in the framework of markets protected from imports, to improve efficiency at the firm level, modernizing installed technology and increasing the scale of production; second, to develop domestic entrepreneurship and, finally, to implement import substitution policies.

The first objective implies a concept of market performance based on decreasing the average cost of production and not necessarily on increasing the total amount of market surpluses. Some trade-off between static losses and dynamic gains might be present: it was argued that a persistent feature of economic policy up to 1974 was to increase profits in the short run to increase investment and future income (Moura 1969). Actually this was possibly a second best, as it is widely accepted that the Portuguese banking system lacked institutions for financing industrial development (Pintado, 1964; Bessa, 1988). Anecdotal evidence also suggests that some of the biggest firms by 1973 had achieved remarkable rates of growth during the previous decades reinvesting profits obtained in protected dominant positions in the domestic market.[7] However, these groups might be an exception; absence of price and investment competition allowed for 'satisfying' behaviour from many dominant firms and coalitions.[8]

These policies were generally consistent with the objective of fostering the growth of Portuguese-owned firms; under the regulatory framework in place, public agencies had a substantial amount of discretionary power to approve inward foreign direct investment (Matos 1973).

Concerning import substitution, it was argued that the private sector would not be able to develop new industries; most arguments used to support this position were implicitly founded on the assumption of risk averse behaviour by private firms, on the small dimension of the domestic market and on the time needed to master new processes and techniques; actually these arguments were accepted for almost forty years as acceptable foundations for industrial policy-making.[9] However, it was clear that in many industries developing domestic production was not consistent with the two previous objectives. First, in capital and intermediate goods industries, developing domestic production often required higher import protection, increasing the costs of producers in forward stages of production; actually, trade policy has not been focused on infant industries, as from 1958 to 1970 effective protection rates were often higher in the industries with larger shares of employment and value added (Silva 1986). Second, in many industries, the development of domestic production required foreign investment; in this case, it seems clear that the large discretionary powers granted by law to the government were often used to award licences to foreign investors: in the early 1970s foreign-owned firms accounted for a substantial share of exports, namely in non-traditional industries (Rodrigues *et al.* 1977).

A striking feature of industrial policy during this period has been the relatively small role given to export promotion; actually it may be argued that, given the regulatory framework, this was an important failure in industrial policy (Confraria 1995). However, that does not mean lack of interest for surpluses in international markets; as a matter of fact, in the canned fish industries, one of the very few cases where Portuguese producers had meaningful shares of external markets, there were proposals to build a coalition of exporters (Salazar 1931). Probably the government and public agencies were deeply sceptical about the export capabilities of domestic firms – and only some years after membership of the European Free Trade Association, in 1960, this view began to change.[10]

Industrial policy and competitiveness in the European Community

An appraisal of objectives in industrial policy, after membership of the European Community in 1986, to 1993, can be made through the incentive systems in place and grouped under Pedip (*Programa Especifico para o Desenvolvimento da Indústria Portuguesa*).[11] The traditional objectives of improving efficiency at the firm level, remained as one of the most important objectives of industrial policy, but there was renewed emphasis on export growth and on R&D and distribution policies (namely in export markets).

These objectives seem to be fairly consistent with the definitions of competitiveness above discussed, as manufacturing became fully exposed to international competition, with positive effects on consumer surpluses. Moreover, emphasis on R&D and on distribution policies suggest a deliberate attempt to increase the value or the share of domestic producers in international markets surpluses. However, in most cases, firms investments have been concentrated in physical assets (GEP 1994). This may well suggest lack of managerial and entrepreneurial talent necessary to pursue different strategies at the firm level, but it is also consistent with a real technological problem resulting from training and technical education (GEP 1993). If so, for many firms current competitiveness problems are still related to the traditional problems of technological and economic inefficiency – a simple matter of survival and not necessarily of increasing profits per unit of sales in external markets.

As part of the emphasis on export growth, deliberate policies for attracting large foreign projects in non-traditional industries have been pursued, leading to a few large investments in the vehicles and components industries. This approach to foreign investment is similar to the one pursued up to 1973, even if the bargaining position of the government has changed – being part of the European Union is useful for the purpose of attracting investment, but government policies must be consistent with European Union guidelines on competition policy – something governments did not have to care about before 1985. Foreign ownership of assets and market surpluses has rarely been a public policy issue, except whenever doubts arose about the long-run commitment of foreign investors to the country.[12] That is, the government tends to consider foreign owned firms as residents of the country, implicitly accepting their objectives for industrial policy purposes.

COMPETITIVENESS AND CONVERGENCE

From the 1950s to 1973, the Portuguese economy growth rate had been greater than the average growth rate in the European Community, leading to a process of convergence in GDP (Neves 1974; Oughton 1993) – however, accepting, for instance, the OECD definition of competitiveness it is not clear that the Portuguese economy and Portuguese manufacturing were competitive as that economic performance has not been achieved with exposure to international competition. The discussion in the second section adds further qualifications to this, because performance in the labour markets was not as good – real wages doubled between 1964 and 1973, but employment did not increase; unemployment rates remained very low because of emigration and conscription (Confraria, 1994).[13]

After 1986, the economy managed to achieve higher growth rates than the Community's average only until 1990–1 (Neves 1994; see also Piera Magnatti in Chapter 11). Moreover, the average growth rate in GDP per capita from 1986 to 1992 is much below the rates achieved in the 1960s and similar to the rates achieved from 1974 to 1985 – a period when the economy suffered the full impact of two oil shocks (Confraria 1994). This raises some doubts about the competitiveness of the Portuguese economy in the European Union and suggests the need to discuss the full implications for the economy of the current process of European economic and monetary integration.

A single currency area requires either a high degree of factor mobility or the 'possibility' of similar economic disturbances; empirical evidence suggests that, in manufacturing, the countries of the European Union became increasingly dissimilar during the past decade, which is consistent with what should be expected from a pattern of inter-industrial specialization (Confraria 1994). Moreover, it seems possible to argue that a major consequence of the Single European Act and of the Maastricht Treaty will be to reinforce such 'dissimilarities', favouring patterns of regional and national specialization (Krugman 1991). If so, the success of the European Union will depend above all on labour mobility among member countries – which will have enormous political, social and economic implications.

This problem may be related to the role of Community transfers in the European Union economy. The point is to make clear what is the final purpose of these transfers: to implement a redistribution mechanism between rich and poor regions or a redistribution mechanism between losers and

Table 8.1 Subsidies and transfers received from abroad (% GDP)

	1980	*1981*	*1982*	*1983*	*1984*	*1985*	*1986*	*1987*	*1988*	*1989*	*1990*	*1991*	*1992*
Greece													
Subsidies	0	0	2	3	2	3	4	3	3	4	4	4	4
Current transfers	3	3	3	3	3	2	2	3	3	3	3	3	3
Capital transfers	0	0	0	1	1	1	1	1	1	1	1	1	2
Total	3	4	5	6	6	6	7	7	7	7	8	9	9
Ireland													
Subsidies	n.a.	n.a.	n.a.	n.a.	n.a.	n.a.	5	4	4	4	5	5	4
Current transfers	n.a.	n.a.	n.a.	n.a.	n.a.	n.a.	2	2	2	2	2	2	2
Capital transfers[a]	n.a.	n.a.	n.a.	n.a.	n.a.	n.a.	1	1	1	1	1	2	2
Total	n.a.	n.a.	n.a.	n.a.	n.a.	n.a.	7	7	7	6	7	9	8
Italy													
Subsidies	0	0	0	0	0	0	0	0	0	0	0	0	0
Current transfers	1	1	1	1	1	1	1	1	1	1	1	1	1
Capital transfers	0	0	0	0	0	0	0	0	0	0	0	0	0
Total	0	0	0	0	0	1	1	1	1	1	1	1	1
Portugal													
Subsidies	0	0	0	0	0	0	0	1	1	1	1	n.a.	n.a.
Current transfers	12	12	11	10	11	11	10	10	9	9	8	n.a.	n.a.
Capital transfers	0	0	0	0	0	0	1	1	1	1	2	n.a.	n.a.
Total	12	12	11	10	12	11	11	12	12	11	10	n.a.	n.a.
Spain													
Subsidies	n.a	n.a	n.a	n.a	n.a	0	0	0	1	1	1	1	1
Current transfers	n.a	n.a	n.a	n.a	n.a	1	1	1	1	1	1	1	1
Capital transfers	n.a	n.a	n.a	n.a	n.a	0	0	0	0	0	0	1	1
Total	n.a	n.a	n.a	n.a	n.a	1	1	2	2	2	2	3	3

Note: [a]Net of capital transfers to the rest of the world.
Totals for each year are different from sum of parts because of rounding errors.

Source: OECD (1994a).

Table 8.2 Gross fixed capital formation and savings (% GDP)

	1980	*1981*	*1982*	*1983*	*1984*	*1985*	*1986*	*1987*	*1988*	*1989*	*1990*	*1991*	*1992*
Greece													
Gross fixed capital formation	24	22	20	20	18	19	18	17	17	19	20	19	18
Gross savings	29	25	17	17	15	13	15	15	17	15	14	15	16
Ireland													
Gross fixed capital formation	28	29	26	22	21	18	17	15	16	17	18	17	16
Gross savings	15	13	16	16	16	15	15	16	16	16	20	21	19
Italy													
Gross fixed capital formation	24	24	22	21	21	21	20	20	20	20	20	20	19
Gross savings	25	23	22	22	22	22	21	21	21	20	20	19	17
Portugal													
Gross fixed capital formation	29	31	31	29	24	22	22	24	27	26	26	26	26
Gross savings	27	22	21	20	19	21	25	27	25	27	27	25	25
Spain													
Gross fixed capital formation	22	22	22	21	19	19	19	21	23	24	25	24	22
Gross savings	21	19	20	20	21	21	22	22	23	22	22	21	19

Source: OECD (1994a)

winners, given the dynamics of European Integration? For each of these objectives, what is the corresponding 'optimum amount' of funds?

Concerning the Portuguese economy these issues became increasingly important during the 1980s because of the historical 'addiction' of the economy to transfers from abroad. The amount of subsidies and transfers from abroad, as a percentage of GDP, is greater in Portugal than in any other of the less developed countries of the European Union; this happens because of historically high current transfers from abroad, mainly emigrants' remittances (Table 8.1). As a percentage of GDP, current transfers have been declining steadily during the 1980s. This decline has been largely offset by subsidies and transfers from the European Economic Community. Basically, that is, notwithstanding these subsidies and transfers, the total amount of external resources available to the Portuguese economy declined, as a percentage of GDP, from 1980 to 1990.[14] The opposite happened with Greece and, from 1986 to 1992, with Ireland and Spain. Moreover, the remittances of Portuguese emigrants will probably go on declining, because emigration reached a peak in the early 1970s and, after the dramatic fall of 1974 and 1975, has remained at very low levels.

Although emigrants' transfers increase national disposable income and might be used directly for consumption, it seems clear that most of them are saved. From 1980 to 1992, Portugal had consistently the highest rates of savings and of gross fixed capital formation among the five countries considered (Table 8.2). If there is a decline in the savings rate then, given the likely decline of current transfers from abroad, capital transfers from the European Union will have an increasing role in financing investment.

CONCLUDING REMARKS

In a sense, discussions about competitiveness of a region or of a country are part of the age-old debate about the conditions of survival and prosperity of given communities, with regional or national dimensions. However, under different historical conditions, countries or regions may well make a choice of objectives and instruments of economic policy not entirely consistent with the pursuit of competitiveness, as defined at the beginning of the second section; this was the case of Portugal, from 1945 to 1973, but the final result, GDP growth, seems reasonable. Currently, in the framework of the European Union, the pursuit of competitiveness, given free circulation of goods, labour and capital, is possibly an unavoidable objective of economic policy but it seems increasingly difficult to attain it. If this is a result of the dynamics of the current process of European integration, a short-run consequence of the changes in policy at the source of that process or even a consequence of possible mismanagement of domestic economic policies is an open question and, certainly, a most interesting subject for further research.

NOTES

1 Other definitions are generally consistent with these views, even if they focus only on some variables, such as market shares (Hughes 1993), or if they include additional variables, such as R&D and human capital (see Karl Aiginger's contribution to this volume). In the second case the new variables can be understood as conditions for achieving higher incomes and increased 'competitiveness'.

2 The notion has even been dismissed as irrelevant. Porter (1990) stated that 'we must abandon the whole notion of a competitive nation as a term having much meaning for economic prosperity.' Intriguingly, his book is entitled *The competitive advantage of nations*.

3 It may be suggested that at least some of these ambiguities are also present in the OECD and the Competitiveness Council definitions through the use of the word 'sustainable'. Anyway it seems clear that the definitions mentioned above focus on economic growth in a non protected environment – and it is in this context that different economic and social objectives should be evaluated. For instance if a community is happy with current income and chooses to maintain absolute income levels (zero growth) as well as pursuing other social objectives it should not be considered as competitive, according to these definitions – even if those objectives are successfully attained.

4 A particular case of this may happen whenever a firm is closed by a non resident buyer, assuming that resources employed in the firm become unemployed for a long time.

5 See OECD (1994c) for estimates of trade balances according to this 'ownership' criterion.

6 See (Dias 1946).

7 For instance, in a letter addressed to the Minister for the Economy, in the late 1940s, one of the most important Portuguese industrialists, A. Champalimaud, whose firms controlled more than 65 per cent of the cement market opposed an entrant's project stating that there were really high profits in the industry but that he needed them to invest in other industries (quoted in Confraria 1992).

8 There are some problems with the idea that managers' objectives might be to lead a quiet life, but the discussion is often focused on joint stock companies. Discussing the objectives of Portuguese managers in this period, it must be noted that most of the firms and many of the largest were controlled by a single owner or by a single family – and in this case it is easier to allow for firm management according to wider social objectives. It is useful to recall a letter sent to Prime Minister Salazar by a coalition of flat glass producers, defending the coalition: they argued that, as competition was suppressed, they had more time to spend with wives and children and all their family life would be more relaxed, contributing to the wider objective of preserving family values (quoted in Confraria 1992).

9 For instance see the rationale for industrial policy presented by two members of different governments, with the industry portfolio (Dias 1946, 1960; Martins 1970).

10 On industrial policy in the early 1970s see Martins (1970).

11 See MIE (1993).

12 Particularly if foreign investors previously supported by the government decide to close plants, as is currently the case of the French firm Renault.

13 It may also be suggested that part of the increase in GDP did not mean increased competitiveness as long as it was the result of increased inward investment; however this argument depends on the value of profits sent abroad, as income or through transfer pricing – evidence about this is scarce.

14 The decline is slightly greater if transfers from Portugal to the European Union, basically indirect taxes, are taken into account.

REFERENCES

Bessa, D. (1988) *O processo inflacionário português*, Porto: Edições Afrontamento.

Competitiveness Policy Council (1992) *Building a Competitive America*, First Annual Report to the President and Congress, Washington.

Confraria, J. (1992) *O condicionamento industrial*, Lisbon: DGI.

—— (1994) 'Issues in Portuguese economic integration', Lisbon Workshop, Industrial Economic Strategies for Europe.

—— (1995) *Desenvolvimento económico e política industrial*, Lisbon: Edições UC.

Dias, J. (1946) *Linha de Rumo*, Lisbon: Livraria Classica Editora.

—— (1960a) *I inha de Rumo*, Lisbon.

—— (1960b) 'Política Industrial', Conference at Oporto University.

GEP (1993) *O Mercado Único. Análise de um inquérito*, Lisbon: Gabinete de Estudos e Planeamento do Ministério da Indústria.

—— (1994) *O PEDIP e a evolução da indústria portuguesa. Perspectivas de uma avaliação*, Lisbon: Gabinete de Estudos e Planeamento do Ministério da Indústria.

Hughes, K. (ed.) (1992) *European Competitiveness*, Cambridge, Cambridge University Press.

Jacquemin, A. and Slade, M. (1989) 'Cartels, collusion and horizontal merger' in R. Schmalensee and R. Willig (eds) *Handbook of Industrial Organisation*, vol. 1, Amsterdam: Elsevier Science Publishers.

Krugman, P. (1991) *Geography and Trade*, Leuven: Leuven University Press and Cambridge: MIT Press.

Martins (1970) *Caminho de Pais Novo*, Lisbon.

Matos, (1973) *Investimentos estrangeiros em Portugal*, Lisbon: Seara Nova.

MIE (1993) PEDIP. *Colectânea de Legislação*, Lisbon: Ministério da Indústria e Energia.

Moura, F. (1969) *Por onde vai a economia portuguesa?* Lisbon: Dom Quixote.

Neves, J. (1994) *The Portuguese Economy*, Lisbon: UCP.

OECD (1994a) *National Accounts*, Paris.

—— (1994b) 'Framework conditions for industrial competitiveness: the OECD Industry Committee Project', DSTI/JND(94)4.

—— (1994c) *The Performance of Foreign Affiliates in OECD Countries*, Paris.

Oughton, C. (1993) 'Growth, structural change and real convergence in the EEC', in K. Hughes (ed.) *European Competitiveness*, Cambridge: Cambridge University Press.

Pintado, (1964) *Structure and Growth of the Portuguese economy*, EFTA.

Porter, M. (1990) *The Competitive Advantage of Nations*, London: Macmillan.

Rodrigues, F., Ribeiro, J. and Fernandes, G. (1977) *O sector exportador português e a internacionalização da produção*, Lisbon: GEBEI.

Salazar, O. (1931) 'Sobre a indústria das conservas de peixe – relatório de uma visita aos centros conserveiros' in O. Salazar (ed.), *Discursos e notas políticas, 1943–1950*, s/d Coimbra: Coimbra Editora.

Scherer, F. and Ross, D. (1990) *Industrial Market Structure and Economic Performance*, Boston: Houghton Mifflin.

Silva, A. (1986) 'An analysis of the effects of preferential trade policies through the estimation of quantitative models: the case of Portugal', unpublished Ph.D. dissertation, University of Reading.

Stigler, G. (1958) 'The economies of scale', *Journal of Law and Economics*, vol. 1, (October): 54–71.

9

GREEK OUTWARD INVESTMENT, COMPETITIVENESS AND DEVELOPMENT

*Christos Pitelis, Roger Sugden and Lena Tsipouri**

INTRODUCTION

Outward investment has recently been a focus for relatively popular attention in Greece.[1] While for a very long period of time – during the country's rapid industrialization and afterwards (1960–80) – outward investment to Western and developing countries had been marginal, and government policy had only emphasized inward investment, the opportunities arising from new investment in the Balkan countries has recently changed the scene completely.

In many respects there appears to have evolved quite a widespread presumption that direct foreign investment outside Greece is desirable, based in part on economic criteria. Investment in the Balkans was initiated by Greek firms but even more recently the government has taken up the banner in its consideration of policy initiatives, and the issue has snowballed; see, for example, the recent amendments to law 1890/92, regarding support for investment in Albania. Moreover, it also appears that outward investment is a topical issue in other countries, both those with a well-established manufacturing tradition and also latecomers, including other less favoured regions of the European Union. For example, the Portuguese Minister for Industry and Energy recently itemized the internationalizing of Portuguese industry via 'manufacturing and marketing investment in foreign markets' as a policy objective (Amaral 1994).

The extent and nature of Greek outward investment has not been determined and its impact has been largely unexplored in the academic literature, which is hardly surprising as regards the recent upsurge precisely because it is so recent. This is not to say that outward investment has been totally ignored. For example, Giannitsis (1993) refers to an 'unquantified number' of firms engaged in such activity, 'aiming more at distribution, commercial and other service activities and less at industrial ones' (1993: 167). He also asserts that this outward investment has a 'positive effect' although he does not explain and explore this assertion.

Accordingly our aim in this chapter is to begin to fill these gaps in the literature; we examine the extent and more importantly, in a sense, the potential impact of Greek outward investment in the Balkan countries. In so doing we are addressing fundamental issues concerning competitiveness, what this term means, and how the concept is related to social objectives; see also the chapters by Pat Devine and Johan Willner, for example.

Our particular concern is the impact on Greek international competitiveness and industrial development, our central question being: will outward investment help to achieve such competitiveness and development? In answering the question we challenge the presumed desirability of outward investment, suggest the need for a taxonomy of investments, and essentially warn against the dangers of either blindly accepting such investment or of assuming that it is part of some 'natural' development process. Both of these dangers are very real in the Greek case.

The plan of the chapter is as follows: in the second section we discuss preliminary evidence on the extent and nature of Greek outward investment and in the third and fourth sections consider its impact on Greek competitiveness and industrial development. When doing the latter we draw on the wider literature that has addressed the economic impact of outward investment on 'home' countries. A fifth section concludes by focusing on the design of industrial policies in the context of our earlier discussion. Before doing any of this, however, we will briefly comment on the meaning of competitiveness.

Following Pitelis (1994), the exact definition of competitiveness is a very thorny question. Porter, for example, suggests 'there is no accepted definition' (1990: xii). The most widely quoted definition of a country's competitiveness is the one adopted by the OECD: competitiveness is 'the degree to which a nation can, under free and fair market conditions, produce goods and services which meet the test of international markets while simultaneously maintaining and expanding the real income of its people in the long run'.[2] We find this vague (what is the test of international markets?) and unnecessarily restrictive (why free-market conditions, and why focus only on real incomes as the objective?). Pitelis (1994) suggests that the international competitiveness of a country is better defined as the degree to which the country can improve upon a (subjectively chosen) index of national welfare in a sustainable way, relative to other countries/nations.

Furthermore, in our view a nation's competitiveness is not the same as a (group of firms' competitiveness. In line with this we suggest that there need be no link between outward investment by Greek firms and Greek competitiveness as a nation. Although up to a point outward investment in the Balkans may arguably be seen as a sign of the existing competitiveness of Greek *firms vis-à-vis* Balkan host country firms,[3] competitiveness of Greek firms need not imply competitiveness of Greece *as a nation* – see also Pitelis (1993, 1994), Cowling and Sugden (1994) for more general discussion and analysis. This contrasts starkly with Porter (1990), who suggests that outward foreign direct investment is one of the best measures of international competitive advantage.

THE EXTENT AND NATURE OF GREEK OUTWARD INVESTMENT

Data selection for Greek outward investment in the Balkans is not readily possible at the aggregate level, because neither in Greece nor in the host countries is there a central authority to which investors are obliged to give all the relevant information. Thus, the only source where investments can be identified is in the local Chambers of Trade, where only legal data are available, with no relevant economic data.

Table 9.1 gives a full list of all Greek direct investments (including joint ventures) in Bulgaria, Albania and Romania, which are the major host countries of interest.

Various comments related to the numbers of establishments as presented in Table 9.1 are as follows.

1 Given the short time period that Greek manufacturing has had the opportunity to invest in the Balkan countries, the number of projects identified is considerable, in particular if it is compared to a virtually stagnating investment evolution within Greece itself for more than a decade.
2 By and large the sectoral composition of the investments is not surprising: services are well represented and the investments in manufacturing are concentrated in traditional sectors, where Greece has a relative specialization and where the Balkan countries are expected to represent interesting markets (food products and beverages, textiles, apparel and accessories).
3 In Romania it was not possible to break down investments by sector, because the majority of companies appear active in more than one and usually three or four sectors, totally unrelated with each other. The explanation offered for this, in our discussion with the local Chamber, was that companies are now able to register for a very small fee, and they try to assure their presence in the market before finalizing their feasibility studies. It is expected that several of these investments will never materialize. The same might be the case for the high share of investment classified as 'unknown' in Bulgaria.

Overall, while we suggest there is a pressing need for more detailed evidence to be collected and studied in the future, it is even clear from our preliminary evidence that outward investment from Greece is an important concern for immediate discussion and analysis.

Table 9.1 Greek direct investment in Bulgaria, Albania and Romania (number of establishments by sector)

Branches	*Bulgaria*	*Albania*	*Romania*
Animal farming	1	6	–
Growing of crops	–	3	–
Mining and extraction	–	1	–
Manufacture of food products and beverages	6	9	–
Tobacco	–	6	–
Textiles	2	12	–
Apparel and accessories	4	15	–
Leather dressing	2	1	–
Pulp paper and paper products	–	1	–
Non-metallic mineral products	–	1	–
Fabricated metal products, except machinery	1	1	–
Motor vehicles, trailers and semi-trailers	1	–	–
Furniture	4	–	–
Construction	1	1	–
Sales of motor vehicles	4	–	–
Wholesale trade	98	14	–
Retail trade	3	1	–
Hotels and restaurants	4	–	–
Land transport	17	2	–
Renting and business of computers	1	–	–
Other business activities	10	–	–
Education	2	–	–
Unknown	124	2	713
Total	286	76	713

THE IMPACT OF GREEK OUTWARD INVESTMENT: SPECIFIC ADVANTAGES AND DRAWBACKS

During the 1960s and 1970s the literature on transnationals gave quite a lot of attention to the arguments for and against outward investment – see, for example, Balogh and Streeton (1960), Frankel (1965), Hufbauer and Adler (1968), Dunning (1969, 1970), Gilpin (1976) and the text by Hood and Young (1979). Since then the arguments have received more sporadic attention, although see especially Dunning's (1992) recent contribution examining the impact of outward investment in the context of Porter's (1990) Diamond of Competitive Advantage. More generally the literature has focused on the impact of outward investment from various angles, including so-called 'home' and 'host' country concerns, the interests of consumers, capital and labour.

The particular perspective that is at issue for us is the impact on competitiveness and industrial development in the home country. More specifically, our concern is not whether or not outward investment is in some overall sense good or bad, but whether outward investment should be encouraged or discouraged as part of an industrial strategy to nurture competitiveness and industrial development at home: to the extent that outward investment is beneficial to these objectives, there may be a prima-facie case for including the encouragement of such investment as part of the home country's industrial strategy; to the extent that it is detrimental there may be a prima-facie case for discouraging such investment; and to the extent that it is neither beneficial nor detrimental there may be a prima-facie case for ignoring such investment in designing the home country's industrial strategy.

On the one hand this is a very specific concern which narrows our interests, although on the other hand this narrowing of concern is not as neat and clear cut as may at first appear. A particular problem is that it leaves open how industrial development is to be measured. We are assuming that the prime objective of industrial strategy in one fundamental sense should be to nurture industrial development,[4] but to the extent that this objective should be reduced to specific measures of development – to secondary objectives – these need to be identified. The precise identification of appropriate measures is not something to preoccupy out chapter; rather, we maintain an open and broad approach to thus feed into a wider debate. We are certainly interested in the impact on home output, employment, innovation, productivity and balance of payments, all of which can be seen as measures of industrial development.[5] But so too should we be interested in, for example, industrial structure: the mix between manufacturing, services and primary production; the mix within manufacturing, and so on.

With this in mind it is important to appreciate that existing literature identifies various potential pros and cons allegedly associated with outward investment. These include the following.

a) Outward investment in extractive industries may be argued to ensure stable and cheap supplies of raw materials (Hood and Young 1979). Such supplies may be deemed essential for industrial development. In fact in the Greek case our feeling is that this is not a significant issue, although we have not been able to test the point rigorously.
b) As a result of outward investment, arguably labour at home may be released from marginally productive jobs and transferred to jobs where productivity is higher (Kujawa 1974). However this argument loses some of its force in economies characterized by unemployment, and in Greece over 9 per cent of the civilian labour force was unemployed in 1992 (Tsipouri and Gaudenzi 1994).
c) Outward investment may be considered defensive, essential for the maintenance of a market (Hufbauer and Adler 1969; Hood and Young 1979). For instance, Dunning argues: 'Smaller European countries, such as the Netherlands, Sweden and Switzerland, could not have improved

or retained their competitive position without their companies' producing much of their output outside their home countries' (1992: 152–3). These considerations are an issue in the Greek case, as evidenced by the comment we received from one investor: 'Being small I am flexible enough to capture a big market share now. When my competitors come in two years, being slower in decision making, they will get a major share but I will keep at least something.'

d) In some ways related to point (c) but more generally, outward investment might be in warehousing and similar distribution facilities, judged to be essential to sell in the country in question. Such investment might be part of a proactive approach to explore and capture markets, anything but defensive. Again it is interesting to consider experience in other small economies. Thus Pedersen (1991) reports a survey based on questionnaires sent to all Danish firms with subsidiaries in different countries. Among 'production companies' 42 per cent of the foreign subsidiaries were 'production subsidiaries' whereas 58 per cent were 'sales/service subsidiaries'. Our tentative feeling from the Greek data is that as many as 90 per cent of outward investments (measured by numbers of establishments) may be sales/service subsidiaries. It is not clear precisely what the latter entail but there is a suggestion that warehouse-type investments may be an important aspect to Greek industrial economic development.

Some such investments are conceptually similar to incurring transport costs as an unavoidable part of international trade. As regards the design of an industrial strategy, however, whether they should be encouraged, discouraged or ignored depends upon a wider assessment; for example an investment essential to serve a firm's market is not worthwhile for a community as a whole if it is at the expense of another (perhaps domestic) investment with greater benefits for the community.

e) An outward investment may replace exports, with an adverse effect on the balance of payments (hence employment, etc.). However, the full impact of this would depend on the extent to which the overseas operation takes exports from the home country, and the extent to which there are lower order effects as a result of the overseas investment increasing economic activity overseas, hence causing a general rise in exports from the home country. The impact of the latter would depend upon the host country's aggregate propensity to import from the home country. (See Balogh and Streeton 1960; Dunning 1969; Kujawa 1974; Robertson 1986.) Moreover, it should also be recognized that there may be no real choice between domestic and overseas production. This is an issue raised with us in interviews we have had with major Greek investors.

As regards empirical assessment of the balance of payments effect, the Reddaway Report (Reddaway, Potter and Taylor 1968) concluded that the UK's balance of payments benefited from UK outward investment. However, this study has been much criticized; see for example Manser

(1967) and Bergsten, Hoorst and Moran (1978). One point of particular controversy is Reddaway's assumption that, in the absence of overseas production, the market would have been totally lost. The importance of this assumption is suggested by Hufbauer and Adler (1968). Their analysis of the US shows outward investment to have a negative impact on the home country's balance of payments when it is assumed that exporting from home is an alternative to overseas production. Unfortunately, as Bergsten, Hoorst and Moran (1978) point out, Hufbauer and Adler (1968) do not indicate that this assumption is reasonable!

What should we conclude from all this? First, there is a need to review the literature on this issue more closely and more thoroughly, and, perhaps, to consider Greek experience in empirical detail. Second, and at least pending this more extensive analysis, on the balance of payments count it would at least be sensible to monitor each proposed outward investment and not assume benefit to Greece.

f) Following Balogh and Streeton (1960), it may be argued that home country development requires investment to create a virtuous spiral leading to improved employment and productivity, rising income, hence increasing investment, and that outward investment is a diversion from this, see also Cowling (1986) on deindustrialization in Britain. Against this, it may be argued that if such a spiral is feasible it will attract funding in a free-market economy. However, some suggest that in practice free-market economies are unable to create the conditions for such success. Again following Balogh and Streeton (1960), one explanation of this may be in terms of a need for coordinated investment plans, absent in free market systems. Problems of short-termism also come into play here. Nevertheless in the Greek case it is hard to argue that the recent outward investment is in general a diversion from domestic investment, because Greece has been suffering a persistently low investment rate in manufacturing since the end of the 1970s (see the Chapter by Katsoulacos, Stogylopoulos and Kritsalis).

g) A long line of literature points to the possibility of a snowball effect, whereby one firm outwardly investing encourages others to follow suit, see for example Vernon (1971), Knickerbocker (1973) and more generally Dietrich and Schenk (1993) on 'bandwagon' effects. To illustrate, a firm that would decide against outward investment if it ignored some activity by others, might alter its decision if it took account of another firm investing overseas simply because of the risk that it would otherwise lose a valuable opportunity. For this reason, it is wrong to argue that each potential outward investment can be assessed in isolation *vis-à-vis* its costs and benefits for a community. Rather, a particular investment may spawn many more, thus an outward investment which, in isolation, may be desirable, may nevertheless be undesirable when assessed more fully. In a similar vein, it may also argued that, within a firm, an outward investment to pursue a particular opportunity may trigger a more general transnationalization process; it may create a transnationalization culture within a firm.

What seems to emerge from even this partial discussion of potential advantages and drawbacks is that outward investment is neither unambiguously good nor unambiguously bad. Thus at the very least we conclude that it is inappropriate to *presume* that Greek outward investment is ipso facto desirable for Greece.

THE IMPACT OF GREEK OUTWARD INVESTMENT: GENERAL CONCERNS

We would reinforce this conclusion by emphasizing two more general points which also emerge from the well-established literature. The first of these can be related to comments made by Dunning:

> In most circumstances, *there is likely to be a divergence between the private and social, or community, costs and benefits of overseas investment.* It seems to me an elementary but basic fact, that, in this particular sphere of economic activity, it is not *necessarily* true that what is the best course of action for businessmen to pursue (still less for any particular businessman) is the best for the community as a whole.
>
> (1970: 120)

This is clearly a fundamental issue.[6] Also interesting is Frankel:

> It is widely accepted, that investment is an engine of growth. Where investment occurs development takes place . . . If enterprises elect to invest abroad because the return to capital there is marginally higher than at home, then presumably the gains in development accrue to the foreign rather than the domestic economy . . . The domestic economy in effect trades the benefits of development . . . for slightly higher returns to capital.
>
> (1965: 412)

He continues: 'Foreign investment should not take place, it may be argued, simply because it offers a higher direct return to enterprises than is available from domestic investment. To be justified in terms of national well-being, it must yield a premium at least equal to development benefits which the national economy . . . forgoes' (1965: 413). In fact it seems to us that this latter argument is basically flawed. It is akin to the classic argument about Pareto efficiency and compensation (Kaldor's (1939) compensation principle, see Johannson (1991)): an alteration leaving some worse off and others better off will nevertheless be seen as Pareto-efficient if the gainers can compensate the losers yet still be better off themselves, which is not to say that such compensation should in fact be made. In the case of an economy that forgoes development in return for higher returns to its capital, can a price be put on the failure to develop – for instance given the view that people need to be involved in productive, socially useful activity for its own sake – and, if it can, can it be acceptable for this price to be left unpaid? We suggest not.

More generally, understanding the difference between the private and community costs and benefits of outward investment should be at the core of assessing the impact of such investment. For example, it might be argued that outward investment takes advantage of cheaper production costs in the host country, allowing Greek firms to improve or maintain their market shares. But the crucial issue *when focusing on Greek competitiveness and industrial economic development*, is: how does this activity help Greece? It may help Greek capital, improving its competitiveness in essentially free-market economies. Yet will it help Greece? Will it serve the objectives of communities in Greece? Will it help those communities meet those objectives in a socially efficient manner and in that sense improve Greek competitiveness (see also Johan Willner's Chapter)? Following Cowling and Sugden (1994), the reason outward investment takes place for a particular firm is, basically, because it benefits the strategic decision-makers (the capitalists) controlling the firm. Thus if we observe Greek firms investing in (say) the Balkans, we should not be surprised to see that this yields benefits; it *will* benefit Greek capitalists (unless they have made a mistake). But the objectives of firms need not coincide with those of people in Greece more generally; while firms may pursue profits, this need not lead to improved social well-being. Indeed this is particularly true for situations involving foreign direct investment, given such possibilities as transnationals not repatriating profits, not paying taxes in their home base, and exporting from their host nation to their home.

This leads us into an even more general point. It might be argued that the appropriate route to development for Greece is to copy alleged success in other countries – perhaps the US or even Britain – by, among other things, creating US or UK type transnational corporations.[7] We would caution against this on the basis of the impact of such firms in economies throughout the world: for example, re deindustrialization, industrialization under the terms of transnationals and not the communities involved, problems of product market monopolization, divide and rule of labour, etc.; see Pitelis (1993), and Cowling and Sugden (1994) for a discussion of this impact, stemming from the concentration of strategic decision-making power in the hands of an elite few within dominant corporations. This is not to deny the possibility that Greece and other smaller players could retain or even nurture some large (preferably monitored) companies which can serve the purpose of providing competition to existing giants and/or facilitate clustering (see Pitelis 1994). Moreover why simply copy? Do the people of Greece want development in directions that come out of their own history/culture/desires? Perhaps they want something characteristically Greek (which need *not* imply something either isolationist or nationalist).

GREEK STRATEGY TOWARDS OUTWARD INVESTMENT

We have explored issues relating to the impact of outward investment on Greek competitiveness and industrial development. In doing so we have referred to earlier literature and essentially identified various pros and cons, and we have considered the crucial importance of private versus community costs and benefits. Drawing on these two related strands in our discussion, we will now conclude the chapter by examining some tentative implications for a Greek industrial economic strategy.

As a general starting point, it should be emphasized that outward investment is relevant to a Greek strategy only insofar as such investment is a help or a hindrance to Greek competitiveness and industrial development; if outward investment has no (pertinent[8]) effect on development it should be no part of an industrial strategy. In practice, our discussion of the earlier literature suggests that in fact outward investment is likely to have an effect. However, we also suggest that our discussion reflects a consensus that outward investments may have desirable and undesirable consequences; en masse they are neither unambiguously good nor unambiguously bad. Hence on this basis we conclude that it is inappropriate for the Greek government to presume outward investment is unconditionally desirable and, as a minimum, it should attempt to design an industrial strategy which only facilitates outward investment beneficial to Greece. This might entail monitoring to determine both the actual and potential impact of outward investments and, where that impact is significant, to evaluate the possibility of influencing investment to the benefit of (communities in) Greece.[9] As part of this process it would be desirable to investigate the possibility of identifying generically beneficial types of investment in the uniquely Greek context. Thus a strategy might be evolved for handling different classes of investment in different ways. Within this, or if needs be more generally, it might be worthwhile evolving a case by case evaluation procedure which might attach appropriate conditions to particular investments.

The basic argument is *not* that Greece should never engage in outward investment. Rather there may be particular circumstances where it can benefit Greek industrialization. However, there are also cases where it is detrimental, and cases where it is perhaps irrelevant. Furthermore, if a form of monitoring is pursued, we suggest that it must be put in its proper context; it must be pursued in the context of an industrial strategy which among other things recognizes the possible distinction between private and community costs and benefits. This means assessing and, if appropriate, influencing outward investments only insofar as they serve Greece's interests. Thus policy-makers must ask if and how outward investment will serve (the wishes of communities in) Greece. Knowing this, some outward investments may be encouraged, others discouraged, and others ignored. Not knowing this, industrial policies may be fundamentally flawed, potentially harmful.

ACKNOWLEDGEMENTS

We would like to thank Stavros Thomadakis, Torben Pedersen, David Parker, Dimitri Deniozos, Ray Bowe and Renè Belderbos for comments and discussion. We would also like to acknowledge invaluable research assistance from Rachel Thomas and Ioanni Rossi.

NOTES

1 See for example the recent press reports, such as *To Vima* (28 August 1994) on investment by the Bikas Group in Bulgaria, *To Vima* (2 October 1994) on the Balkan extension of Hellas Can, and *Kathimerini* (2 October 1994) on the distribution network of MEVGAL in Bulgaria.
2 Quoted in, among others, UK Government White Paper (1994).
3 This need not imply competitiveness *vis-à-vis* firms from other countries.
4 This is not unanimously accepted; for a discussion of the meaning of industrial strategy, see Pitelis (1994).
5 There are real dangers in setting and measuring objectives in such terms. Ultimately, whether or not output growth, etc., matter for a particular community depends upon the wishes of that community, see Sugden (1990). Thus perhaps it would be more appropriate to set and measure objectives directly in terms of introducing and improving processes for economic democracy. This would be in line with the definition of industrial strategy suggested by Cowling and Sugden (1993, 1994), Pitelis (1994), and the explanation for why manufacturing matters in Sugden (1994).
6 One of the points that this raises is: what does international competitiveness *for a firm* cost the citizens of a country? The latter question is one of the points raised by Johan Willner in this volume.
7 We are not denying that, thus far, Greek outward investment has led to the creation of relatively small transnational corporations, not the sort of global giants that have originated from the US or UK.
8 Policy towards transnationals, hence towards the establishment and activities of Greek transnationals, should be derived from a coherent, wide-ranging industrial strategy. This strategy may imply the targeting of particular sectors. In this case, if outward direct foreign investment is in other sectors and has *no* impact on targeted sectors (including: it is not diverting scarce resources from the latter) then it can be ignored; it is coincidental and not part of an industrial strategy.
9 For a detailed discussion of the why and how of monitoring in a more general context, see Bailey, Harte and Sugden (1994).

REFERENCES

Amaral, L.M. (1994) 'Portuguese Industrial Policy. The Challenges of the 90s. Competitiveness and Internationalisation', paper presented at the *Lisbon Workshop on Objectives of Industrial Policy.*

Bailey, D., Harte, G. and Sugden, R. (1994) *Making Transnationals Accountable. A Significant Step for Britain*, London: Routledge.

Balogh, T. and Streeton, P. (1960) 'Domestic versus Foreign Investment', *Bulletin of Oxford University Institute of Economics and Statistics.*

Bergsten, C.F., Hoorst, T. and Moran, T.H. (1978) *American Multinationals and American Interests*, Brookings Institution: Washington. Page numbers in text refer to the excerpt in T.H. Moran (ed.) (1985) *Multinational Corporations.*

Cowling, K. (1986) 'Internationalisation of Production and Deindustrialization' in A. Amin and J. Goddard (eds) *Technological Change, Industrial Restructuring and Regional Development*, London: Allen and Unwin.

Cowling, K. and Sugden, R. (1993) 'Industrial Strategy: A Missing Link in British Economic Policy', *Oxford Review of Economic Policy*, 9(3): 83–100.

—— (1994) *Beyond Capitalism. Towards a New World Economic Order*, London: Pinter.

Dietrich, M. and Schenk, H. (1993) 'A Bandwagon Theory of the Firm', Sheffield University Management School Discussion Paper Series, No 93.29.

Dunning, J.H. (1969) 'The Foreign Investment Controversy', *Banker's Magazine.*

—— (1970) *Studies in International Investment.*

—— (1992) 'The Competitive Advantage of Countries and the Activities of Transnational Corporations', *Transnational Corporations*, 1(1): 135–68.

Frankel, M. (1965) 'Home versus Foreign Investment: A Case Against Capital Export', *Kyklos*, 18: 411–33.

Giannitsis, T. (1993) 'Globalisation, Technology Factors and Industrial Structuring in Southern Europe: The Greek Experience', in M. Humbert (ed.), *The Impact of Globalisation on Europe's Firms and Industries*, London: Pinter.

Gilpin, R. (1976) *US Power and Multinational Corporations*, London: Macmillan.

Hood, N. and Young, S. (1979) *The Economics of Multinational Enterprise*, London: Longman.

Hufbauer, G.C. and Adler, F.M. (1968) *Overseas Manufacturing Investment and the Balance of Payments*, Washington, DC: US Treasury.

Johansson, P.-O. (1991) *An Introduction to Modern Welfare Economics*, Cambridge: Cambridge University Press.

Kaldor, N. (1939) 'Welfare Propositions of Economics and Interpersonal Comparisons of Utility', *Economic Journal.*

Knickerbocker, F.T. (1973) *Oligolistic Reaction and Multinational Enterprises*, Boston: Harvard University Press.

Kujawa, D. (1974) *American Labor and the Multinational Enterprise*, London: Pall Mall Press.

Manser, W.A.P. (1967) 'The Reddaway Report – Not the Last Word on Foreign Investment', *Westminster Bank Review*, August. 14–22.

Pedersen, T. (1991) 'Main Types of Subsidiaries of Danish Companies and Their Effects on Export and Employment', paper presented at the *Danish Summer Research Institute.*

Pitelis, C. (1993) Transnationals, International Organization and Deindustrialization', *Organization Studies*, 14(4): 527–48.

—— (1994) 'Industrial Strategy: For Britain, in Europe, in the Globe', *Journal of Economic Studies*, 21(5): 3–92.

Porter, M.E. (1990) *The Competitive Advantage of Nations*, London: Macmillan.

Reddaway, W.B., Potter S.J. and Taylor C.T. (1968) *Effects of UK Direct Investment*

Overseas, Cambridge: Cambridge University Press.

Robertson, B. (1986) *The Multinational Enterprise: Trade Flows and Trade Policy*.

Sugden, R. (1990) 'Strategic Industries, Community Control and Transnational Corporations', *International Review of Applied Economics*, 4(1): 72–94.

—— (1994) 'The Structure of UK Industry: Does Manufacturing Matter?', forthcoming, *Economics Today*.

Tsipouri, L.J. and Gaudenzi, S. (1994) 'Industrial Policies for Latecomers', paper presented at the Conference on Industrial Policies for Small, Less Favoured Countries in the European Union, Athens.

UK Government White Paper (1994) *Competitiveness: Helping Business to Win*, London: HMSO.

Vernon, R. (1971) *Sovereignty at Bay: The Multinational Spread of US Enterprises*, London: Basic Books.

10

THE EUROPEAN COMMISSION'S FRAMEWORK PROGRAMME SUPPORT: IMPACT ON GREEK ORGANIZATIONS

Y. Katsoulacos, G. Strogylopoulos and P. Kritsalis

INTRODUCTION

The objective of this chapter is to examine the impact of the European Commission's Framework Programmes (FPs) I (1984–7) and II (1988–91) on Greece. It is based on a research project undertaken by Planet SA, the Institute for Economic Policy Studies (IMOP) and Logotech SA, which lasted for eight months (from May 1993 to December 1994). The title of the project was 'Evaluation of the impact of the Community's RTD policy in Greece', and was undertaken for PRAXI KP, an initiative of the Greek Confederation of Industries (SEB) and the Greek Foundation for Research and Technology (FORTH), and funded by the Commission's Stride programme. In more detail, the study analyses the impact of the FPs on:

- the participating organizations,
- the overall Greek R&D environment and
- the National Research and Technology policy.

The present chapter illustrates the impact of the FPs on Greek organizations participating in the Community Framework Programmes and pays some special attention to the impact on the participating Greek firms. Additionally it presents some results concerning the relevant impact on the Greek R&D environment, which may be seen as a significant determinant of Greek competitiveness. However, the effect on competitiveness will usually manifest itself after a long lag so no claim can be made concerning the magnitude of this effect at present.

In the following pages we start with a presentation of the main characteristics of the Greek economy and of the Greek R&D activities. This presentation is followed by an analysis of the data and the methodology used. Finally, the findings of the research as well as some conclusions are presented.

Table 10.1 Selected economic development indicators (annual percentage change)

	GNP		*Fixed investment*			
			Total		*Machinery & equipment*	
	1960–79	*1979–91*	*1960–79*	*1979–91*	*1960–79*	*1979–91*
Greece	5.6	1.3	6.7	–0.8	9.1	1.4
Portugal	5.6	2.9	5.2	3.3		
Spain	5.6	2.8	6.7	4.3	6.9	-6.6
EC	4.0	2.1	3.9	2.3	5.1	3.8
OECD	4.2	2.6	4.6	2.6	5.9	4.8

	Labour productivity		*Exports (% of GDP)*				*Per capita income OECD = 100*			
	1960–79	*1979–91*	*1960*	*1979*	*1980*	*1991*	*1960*	*1970*	*1979*	*1991*
Greece	6.6	0.8	9.1	17.5	20.9	22.7	30	41	47	44
Portugal	5.0	1.8	17.5	27.1	27.4	32.1	33	42	47	52
Spain	5.3	2.4	10.1	14.6	15.4	17.0	50	64	65	72
EC	3.7	1.6	19.0	26.7	26.5	28.1	87	89	90	92
OECD	3.0	1.4	11.2	18.5	19.4	18.8	100	100	100	100

Source OECD Economic Surveys, 'Greece', OECD 1993

Table 10.2 Basic fluctuations of the output of various manufacturing sectors

	Turning point	*Average annual change* (%)			*Total change* (%)		
		1951–90	*1951–80*	*1981–90*	*1950*	*1980*	*1990*
Food, beverages, tobacco	1979	5.9	7.3	1.8	23.3	19.0	22.0
Textiles	1979	5.0	6.8	–0.4	20.0	17.6	16.5
Clothing, footwear	1979	3.5	5.4	–2.4	20.0	8.9	6.2
Wood and furniture	1979	4.7	7.1	–2.6	5.9	4.0	2.9
Paper, printing	1979	6.8	8.2	2.4	4.1	4.0	4.9
Chemicals	1979	10.6	13.1	3.1	3.7	12.8	16.9
Non ferrous metals	1980	7.2	9.6	–0.1	6.6	8.8	8.4
Basic metal-lurgical	1980	15.2	20.3	–0.3	0.4	6.1	5.7
Products	1981	6.6	9.4	–2.0	10.4	11.8	9.3
Machinery	1982	9.4	12.0	1.4	2.4	4.6	5.1
Transport	1977	4.9	6.9	–1.0	3.2	2.4	2.1
Other	1980	8.2	8.2	0.2	100.0	100.0	100.0

Source: (1994) 'The Greek Economy 1994', *Annual Economic Review*, Athens: Epilogi.

Table 10.3 Number of industrial companies and licensing agreements signed during the period 1960–87

Year	*Number of companies*	*% annual change*	*Number of contracts*	*% of total*	*% annual change*
1960–63	86	–	95	13.1	–
1964–67	79	–8.1	86	11.8	–95
1968–71	130	64.6	155	21.3	80.2
1972–75	146	12.3	151	20.8	–2.6
1976–79	128	–12.3	140	19.3	–7.3
1980–83	56	–56.3	71	9.8	–49.3
1984–87	27	–51.8	29	4.0	–59.2
1960–87	652		727	100.0	
Average annual change					
1960–87		–2.22			–2.09
1960–80		+1.60			+1.57

Source: Giannitsis *et al.* (1993).

THE GREEK ECONOMY

Greece is a country with some special characteristics relating to its technological and industrial evolution. It enjoyed remarkably high growth rates during the 1960s and 1970s but its economy has been characterized by stagnation during the 1980s and 1990s (Tables 10.1 and 10.2).

The growth and transformation of the Greek economy from a solely agricul-tural to an industrialized one was mainly based on technology imports in the form of capital goods, direct foreign investment and licence agreements (Table 10.3). The latter were mainly between mother companies (multinationals) and subsidiaries or through commercial local representatives of capital goods (suppliers). The aforementioned 'types' of technology transfer led to the development of an industry based on traditional sectors producing mainly consumer goods.

As is also indicated in the tables, despite the significant importance of the manufacturing sector for the Greek economic transformation, there was a serious reduction of its contribution (%) to GDP after the end of the 1970s, a fact that was accompanied by an almost analogous fall in labour productivity. Many studies have been carried out in order to identify the reasons for this shift in the Greek economic performance. The majority of them point to the following factors:

- Domination of traditional industries and production of low added value products. Food, beverages textiles and clothing have a share of 45 per cent of the total Greek industrial output.
- Small number of large companies. Greece is characterized by a large number of SMEs. Companies employing more than 100 and 500 people are not more than 700 and 80 respectively.[1]

Table 10.4 Research and development expenditure in the business enterprise sector (BERD)

	EC shares (%)		
	BERD		*GDP*
	1980	*1990*	*1985*
Germany	36.8	35.0	24.5
France	20.3	21.9	20.7
UK	24.8	20.3	18.2
Italy	7.7	10.7	16.5
Netherlands	4.5	4.2	5.3
Spain	1.7	3.3	6.2
Belgium	3.1	2.9	3.2
Denmark	0.8	1.2	2.3
Ireland	0.2	0.3	0.7
Portugal	0.1	0.1	0.8
Greece	0.05	0.1	1.3[a]

	Greek BERD 1989	
	US$ million	*% of value added*
Sector		
Manufacturing	46.8	0.56
Electronics	5.8	. . .
Chemicals	4.0	} 0.54
Rubber and plastics	1.8	
Petroleum refining	0.8	
Non-ferrous metals	1.4	. . .
Stone, clay and glass	2.3	0.37
Fabricated metals	10.4	1.33
Food, beverages and tobacco	1.5	0.01
Textiles and clothing	0.4	0.02

Note: [a] Greece's share in the EC GDP was 1 per cent in 1990

Source: OECD (1993).

- Difficulty in adopting new technologies and designing new products which is strongly related to the low percentage of R&D spending.
- Low productivity and low ROI which is also related to the small size of the Greek market and the reduced possibility of large investments.
- Instability of the tax system and high cost of money for investment.
- High level of protectionism for Greek products (up to 1981).[2]

The above factors led to a weakening of Greek competitive advantages and difficulties for Greek industry to modernize.

Table 10.5 Classification of the sectors of Greek industry according to their technological and structural characteristics

	Participation (1988) in:			*Expenses*	
	Employment	*Added value*	*Exports*	*R&D*	*Royalties*
Sectors of low technological intensiveness	23.9%	21.6%	24.3%	6.2%	5.4%
Tobacco					
Textiles					
Wood					
Publications					
Leather					
Sectors of low/medium technological intensiveness	34.4%	25.9%	26.7%	21.7%	21.9%
Food					
Footwear, clothing					
Furniture					
Paper					
Machinery					
Sectors of medium/high technological intensiveness	4.0%	10.6%	25.7%	3.7%	14.7%
Metallurgy					
Oil products					
Sectors of high technological intensiveness	6.1%	8.7%	3.5%	29.4%	21.1%
Chemicals					
Rest of the cases	31.6%	33.2%	19.7%	39.0%	36.9%

Source: Giannitsis *et al.* (1993).

Additionally, the low percentage of R&D spending by both industry and the public sector (Table 10.4) did not create significant opportunities for either the internal technological modernization of the firms or the overall development of new science based on medium and high technology industries (Tables 10.5 and 10.6).

The lack of R&D activities led the Greek government to institute a number of changes and to establish new infrastructures in order to promote R&D collaboration (technology push). These infrastructures include new government-funded research institutes, five sectoral companies, eight technology parks, four business innovation centres, new departments at Greek universities, the reorganization of existing research centres and also the promotion of mechanisms for funding research activities. These new infra-

Table 10.6 Revealed comparative advantage[a]

	1970	*1979–81*	*1990*
Food, drink and tobacco	298	255	310
Textiles, footwear and leather	230	403	574
Petroleum refining	81	368	352
Stone, clay and glass	118	379	289
Basic metal industries	295	151	207
Ferrous metals	286	122	167
Non-ferrous metals	313	218	271
Low-technology industries	174	210	252
Medium-technology industries	60	37	33
High-technology industries	15	21	18
Resource-intensive industries	221	251	250
Labour-intensive industries	115	198	294
Scale-intensive industries	96	42	39
Specialized supplier industries	10	18	18
Science-based industries	35	26	18

Notes: Revealed competitive advantage is calculated by taking the ratio of product *i* to the total countries' manufactured exports and dividing it by the ratio of total OECD exports of product *i* to the total OECD manufactured exports.

[a]Only commodity groups with above average competitive advantage are shown.

Source: OECD(1993)

structures have been developed since the mid-1980s and almost in parallel with the participation of Greek firms and organizations in general in the Framework Programmes.

DATA USED AND METHODOLOGY

Two of the strongest propositions established in economic science in the last 30 years or so are the following:

1 First, technological progress has been shown to be the main factor in economic growth and promoting social welfare.
2 Second, unhindered market forces may not generate the rate and extent of technological progress that would be required to attain optimum benefits to the economy and society.

We need not at present go into the details of why the second proposition is true. We should note that while this proposition provides a rationale, it does not provide a justification for government (or supra-governmental) intervention in the process of technical change, since such intervention often results in inefficiencies that may override the benefits of intervention. Nevertheless, in practice, the proposition has been used by national governments, and in the last ten years or so by the Commission of the European

Union, to provide the basis of active interventionist policies in supporting the process of generation and diffusion of new technologies. The cornerstone of these policies are the Framework Programmes (FPs).

At the Community level the huge growth in support of the Research and Development activities of European firms and academic and research institutions has led especially in the last five years to a parallel growth in the area of evaluation of CEC support programmes. Such evaluations may be 'horizontal', that is concerned with the impact across Europe of a specific CEC Programme (e.g. ESPRIT), or country-specific, that is concerned with the effects of Framework Programmes in general on a specific country.

In the rest of this section of the chapter we describe the main data used for our evaluation of the Greek case as well as the dimensions on which the methodological approach was made.

The study involved a questionnaire-based survey of Greek organizations that participated in the first two Community framework programmes. The working team clustered the participants into three main categories: Private firms (including industrial companies), Research Institutes and Universities. Overall, 238 participants, corresponding to 795 projects, have been identified. Among them are 108 private firms (257 projects), 34 Research Institutes (215 projects) and 96 University departments (323 projects) (Table 10.7).

More specifically, the data were collected on a basis of interviews using a structured questionnaire. Overall, 224 interviews were conducted, 94 of them with firms (covering 233 projects), 39 with research institutes (covering 208 projects) and 91 with university departments (covering 300 projects). Additionally, a number of interviews (around 50), based on semi-structured questionnaires, were conducted, so as to obtain the additional qualitative information concerning the impact of the FPs and the opinions of national representatives, Greek opinion leaders, Commission officials and representatives from other EU countries, were asked.

As was mentioned in the introduction, this chapter concentrates on a part of the dimensions analysed in the relevant study. These dimensions are related mainly to the direct impact on the firms participating in FPs and are the following:

1 The picture of participation
2 The technological impact

   a) Extent of technology transfers
   b) Research outputs

3 The impact on co-operative behaviour

   a) Relations with partners
   b) Importance of the partners
   c) Co-operation after the project(s)

Table 10.7 Project allocation

Number of projects	%	
Firms	257	32
Universities	323	41
Research Institutes	215	27
Total	795	100

4 Additionality

a) New research activities
b) New co-operation
c) Changes in R&D budget
d) Changes in research/scientific staff

5 The overall picture, benefits and barriers
6 Conclusions

All the tables presented in the following pages (unless indicated differently) are included in the relevant study under the title 'Evaluation of the impact of the Community's RTD policy in Greece'.

PRESENTATION AND ANALYSIS OF THE RESULTS

A picture of the participation

We start the presentation of the results by mapping the overall participation of the Greek organizations in the first two Framework Programmes.

As mentioned in the previous section, universities participated in 41 per cent of the projects, research institutes in 27 per cent and firms in 32 per cent. Table 10.8 shows the regional allocation of the projects. As can be clearly seen, the vast majority of the participating organizations (70 per cent) and of the projects (67 per cent) are concentrated in the area of Athens. Concerning firms, 30 per cent are located in the area of Athens. The relevant figures for research institutes and universities are 71 per cent and 48 per cent respectively.

Although universities have participated in the majority of the projects, the largest part of the funding was allocated to companies (Table 10.9). Additionally, there was a significant rise of the total Greek participation in FPs, from 0.7 per cent of the Community budget in the first FP to 1.7 per cent in the second.

The research areas where the majority of the organizations have participated are those of information technologies and telecommunications and also

Table 10.8 Regional allocation of the projects

	Firms		*Research institutes*		*Universities*		*Total*	
Town	*No.*	*Projects*	*No.*	*Projects*	*No.*	*Projects*	*No.*	*Projects*
Athens	97	239	24	102	46	190	167	531
Thessaloniki	4	4	3	12	23	57	30	73
Patras	2	3	2	25	18	56	22	84
Crete	2	2	5	76	3	7	10	85
Ioannina	–	–	–	–	3	7	3	7
Volos	1	4	–	–	–	–	1	4
Xanthi	–	–	–	–	3	6	3	6
Drama	1	1	–	–	–	–	1	1
Chalkida	1	4	–	–	–	–	1	4
Total	108	257	34	215	96	323	238	795

Table 10.9 Concentration of projects and funding per category of organization

Organizations	*% of projects*	*% of funding*
Firms	32.3	38.6
Research institutes	27.1	29.2
Universities	40.6	32.2
Total	100.0	100.0

of industrial technologies. Figure 10.1 presents the concentration of the projects in each research area.

Firms participated mainly in projects related to information and telecommunications (IT) technologies; universities in IT, environmental technologies and life sciences; and research institutes participated, mainly in industrial and materials technologies.

The participation of Greek organizations in the first two FPs had a number of effects. In the following sections we present the impact of this participation on the organizations through the use of their own opinions.

The technological impact

We start the presentation of the results by analysing the technological impact. The study examines mainly the effects relating to technology transfer actions as well as to the research output such as publications, new products or production methods, patents, licences, royalties, etc.

According to Table 10.10 technology transfer was relatively important for all participating organizations including the Greek firms. Technology transfer

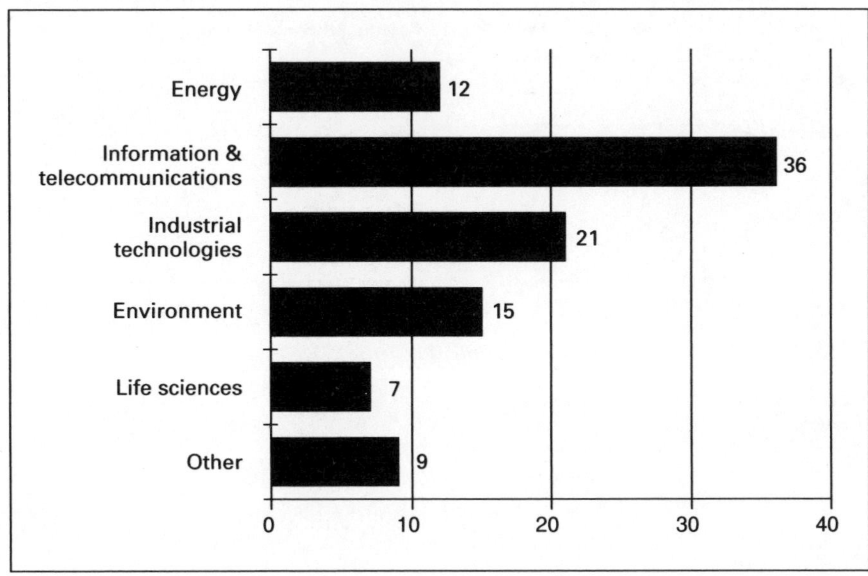

Figure 10.1 Concentration of projects in research areas

Table 10.10 Significance of technology transfer (%)

Level of significance	*1*	*2*	*3*	*4*
F	4.4	35.6	41.1	18.9
RI	0.0	23.3	53.5	37.2
U	3.3	22.0	40.7	35.2
T	3.1	27.7	43.3	29.0

1 No technology transfer at all.
2 There was but not important for the organization.
3 There was and was important for the organization.
4 There was and was important for both the organization and the external environment.

to the external environment of the organization is important for research institutes and universities, but not for the firms. However, the latter is an expected result due to competition.

Concerning the 'type' of the transferred know-how, Table 10.11 shows that for the firms, knowledge about software and hardware was most significant. The same type was also important for the universities, but scored below the 'scientific results' (Scientific Methods and Research Results). Research institutes show an interesting performance concerning new production methods and creation of prototypes.

Table 10.11 Type of transferred know-how (%)

What was the type of the transferred know-how	*1*	*2*	*3*	*4*	*5*	*6*
F	25.0	27.3	9.1	59.1	27.3	6.8
RI	33.3	30.3	6.7	10.0	43.3	26.7
U	4.0	14.7	5.3	24.0	81.3	0.0
T	16.1	21.5	6.7	31.5	57.7	7.4

1 New production methods.
2 Creation of prototypes.
3 Energy-saving and environmental-protection methods.
4 Software – hardware.
5 Scientific methods – research results.
6 Others.

Table 10.12 Research output/publications

Research work as documented in:	*F*	*RI*	*U*	*T*
Postgraduate thesis	64	130	247	441
Scientific publications	256	887	1006	2149
Communications	238	617	1234	2089
Scientific work under publication	154	260	334	748
Other	2	21	97	120

Table 10.12 shows the significant impact of the projects on the research output. Although the total number of Greek participations is relatively small, the total number of the publications and communications is high but their relative scientific importance is not obvious since it depends on the quality level of the scientific journals where they were published.

It has to be mentioned here that the number of publications produced by Greek scientists was always high. A comparison (for the year 1988) between Greece, Spain, Portugal and Italy, for publications per 100 scientists and engineers reveals figures of 34.48, 21.7, 8.44, 14.8 respectively. These findings support the argument that the quality of the research output of Greek scientific work was always significant despite the lacks of infrastructure facilities.

A very interesting result is the number of new products or production methods as an outcome of the participation to research projects. The results shown in Table 10.13 are rather disappointing, especially for the firms.[3] Only in 31 per cent of the cases was there one product or production process potentially capable of exploitation/commercialization.

Table 10.13 Research output/new products and production methods

How many new products or production processes resulted from your participation to FPs?	*F*	*RI*	*U*	*T*
0	42.2	41.9	62.6	50.4
1	31.1	41.9	20.9	29.0
2	17.8	7.0	13.2	13.8
3	3.3	9.3	2.2	4.0
4	2.2	0.0	0.0	0.9
5	3.3	0.0	1.1	1.8
After how many years they will be probably commercialized?				
Up to 3	87.0	61.1	13.0	59.9
4–5	8.7	27.8	35.2	20.3
6+	0.0	2.8	37.0	11.5
Never	1.1	0.0	0.0	0.5
DK/NA	3.3	8.3	14.8	7.7

Table 10.14 Research output/patents and licences

	E	*RI*	*U*	*T*
How many patents did you buy either in Greece or abroad?	3	0	0	3
For how many patents did you aquire the property rights?	28	17	7	52
How many licences/ royalties have you acquired?	18	5	40	63

The picture is completely opposite when analysing patents and licences. Table 10.14 shows that companies have a better success rate than the research institutes and universities. This result was more or less expected since companies, through their collaborations with foreign and local partners, found new dimensions for possible development of their production range. However, the results presented in Table 10.14 cannot be further analysed due to the lack of information concerning the overall activities of these organizations beside the Community projects.

Co-operative behaviour

One of the most important areas of the Community's technology policy is the support of co-operation activities among European organizations (see also the chapter by Christine Oughton and Geoff Whittam). Such co-operative efforts are promoted mainly for two reasons:

1 They often lead to the increase of investment activities
2 They facilitate the diffusion of new technologies and technological know-how.

This part of the chapter examines various dimensions of co-operative behaviour of the Greek firms resulting from their participation in FPs. Table 10.15 shows the relation of the participating organizations with their partners. It is clearly illustrated that many of the Greek organizations knew their partners either through previous collaborations in EC programmes or through research and technological collaborations outside FPs. Personal contacts of the scientists and engineers have proved very important. At the same time EC events and lists have not been found to be very effective concerning the promotion of Greek participation.

Table 10.16 examines the economic relation between the Greek organizations and their partners. As in the majority of the European countries, co-operation between direct competitors is rare. More often we observe co-operation between indirect competitors (those who produce similar products but for regionally different markets). The most common relation is that of organizations which show complementarity in their activities. Economic theory supports the argument that organizations showing that kind of complementarity co-operate successfully. As a result the Community's technology policy, implemented through FPs, does not influence the aforementioned general behaviour of firms. The behaviour of research institutes and universities was similar but the word 'competition' cannot be translated the same way in their case.

Another interesting finding is how the organizations feel about the importance of the role of their partners relative to the success of the projects and the fulfilment of the research goals. Table 10.17 shows that, in general, partners played a significant role. All partners are important for the universities and research institutes. The important finding from this table is that the other collaborating companies are very substantial partners for the firms.

The findings shown in Table 10.18 are very encouraging and compatible with the results of a recent European survey. The table shows that half of the participants usually co-operate with their partners after the end of the project(s) in relevant research activity. Percentages are quite high for the research institutes (68 per cent) and Universities (65 per cent) and less high for the firms (40 per cent). The percentage of organizations that continue

Table 10.15 Co-operative behaviour/relations with partners

How did you find your partners?	*Never*				*Rarely*				*Often*				*Always*				*MA*			
	F	*RI*	*U*	*T*	*F*	*RI*	*U*	*T*	*F*	*RI*	*U*	*T*	*F*	*RI*	*U*	*T*	*F*	*RI*	*U*	*T*
From other EC projects	34.4	23.3	33.0	31.7	22.2	18.6	13.2	17.9	31.1	44.2	45.1	39.3	7.8	7.0	5.5	6.7	2.1	2.3	2.2	2.2
Outside EC projects	12.2	2.3	8.8	8.9	21.1	4.7	5.5	11.6	41.1	67.4	46.2	48.2	20.0	20.9	38.5	27.7	2.7	3.1	3.1	2.9
From EC events	45.6	25.6	60.4	47.8	14.4	34.9	19.8	20.5	33.3	32.6	11.0	24.1	3.3	2.3	3.3	3.1	1.9	2.1	1.5	1.8
From EC lists	63.3	51.2	76.9	66.5	15.6	25.6	17.6	18.3	12.2	16.3	0.0	8.0	2.8	2.3	0.0	1.3	1.5	1.6	1.1	1.4
Other	1.1	2.3	9.9	4.9	0.0	0.0	0.0	0.0	7.8	2.3	3.3	4.9	7.8	0.0	6.6	5.8	3.3	2.0	2.3	2.7

Table 10.16 Cooperative behaviour/economic relation with partners

How often were your partners:	*Never*			*Rarely*			*Often*			*Always*			*M.A.*		
	F	*RI*	*T*	*F*	*RI*	*T*	*F*	*RI*	*T*	*F*	*RI*	*T*	*F*	*RI*	*T*
Direct competitors?	52.2	60.5	54.9	23.3	23.3	23.3	17.8	11.6	15.8	3.3	0.0	2.3	1.71	1.48	1.64
Indirect competitors?	40.0	55.8	45.1	24.4	16.3	21.8	27.8	20.9	25.6	3.3	2.3	3.0	1.94	1.68	1.85
Involved in complementary activities?	20.0	25.6	21.8	11.1	11.6	11.3	44.4	34.9	41.4	16.7	23.3	18.8	2.62	2.58	2.61
Your customers or suppliers?	52.2	79.1	60.9	18.9	0.0	12.8	21.1	11.6	18.0	3.3	0.0	2.3	1.74	1.25	1.59

Table 10.17 Co-operative behaviour/importance of partners

How important was the work of your partners for your research goals?	*Unimportant*				*Almost unimportant*				*Almost important*				*Very important*				*M.A*			
	F	*RI*	*U*	*T*	*F*	*RI*	*U*	*T*	*F*	*RI*	*U*	*T*	*F*	*RI*	*U*	*T*	*F*	*RI*	*U*	*T*
F	12.2	11.6	2.2	8.0	12.2	16.3	13.2	13.4	44.4	27.9	29.7	35.3	20.0	18.6	17.6	18.8	2.81	2.71	3.0	2.85
U	7.8	2.3	0.0	3.6	11.1	11.6	6.6	9.4	43.3	53.5	42.9	45.1	26.7	27.9	41.8	33.0	3.0	3.12	3.38	3.18
RI	11.1	2.3	0.0	4.9	13.3	9.3	4.4	8.9	38.9	53.5	42.9	43.3	23.3	23.3	35.2	28.1	2.85	3.10	3.37	3.10

Table 10.18 Co-operative behaviour/after the project(s)

How often did you continue your co-operation with your partners after the end of a project?	*Never*				*Rarely*				*Often*				*Always*				*M.A.*			
	F	*RI*	*U*	*T*	*F*	*RI*	*U*	*T*	*F*	*RI*	*U*	*T*	*F*	*RI*	*U*	*T*	*F*	*RI*	*U*	*T*
In related research	27.8	7.0	15.7	19.0	17.8	23.3	10.8	16.2	36.7	53.5	39.8	41.2	4.4	14.0	25.3	14.4	2.2	2.7	2.8	2.56
In irrelated research	35.6	23.3	38.6	34.3	20.0	55.8	18.1	26.4	26.7	18.6	26.5	25.0	2.2	0.0	8.4	4.2	1.9	1.9	2.0	1.9
In commercial activities	45.6	76.7	78.3	64.4	27.8	14.0	4.8	16.2	11.1	0.0	2.4	5.6	0.0	0.0	1.2	0.5	1.5	11.	11.	1.3
In EC funded activities	42.2	20.9	42.2	38.0	16.7	20.9	7.2	13.9	21.1	46.5	27.7	28.7	3.3	4.7	14.5	7.9	1.8	2.3	2.1	2.07
No contin-uation	23.3	32.6	45.8	33.8	25.6	41.9	13.3	24.1	14.4	16.3	4.8	11.1	18.9	2.3	8.4	11.6	2.3	1.8	1.6	2.05

Table 10.19 Additionality/new research activities

How did FPs work? Were they the starting point of new research programmes or were they embodied in already existed research activities?												
	1	2	3	4	5	6	7	8	9	10	DK/NA	M.A.
F	16.7	10.0	10.0	5.6	11.1	7.8	12.2	5.6	6.7	12.2	2.2	5.14
RI	2.3	2.3	9.3	4.7	7.0	11.6	7.0	7.0	18.6	25.6	4.7	7.19
U	9.9	1.1	6.6	5.5	22.0	3.3	8.8	11.0	7.7	24.2	0.0	6.43
T	11.2	4.9	8.5	5.4	14.7	6.7	9.8	8.0	9.4	19.6	1.8	6.06

Notes: 1 FPs as the starting point.
10 Embodied to already existing research activities.

their collaboration in irrelevant research activities is quite low. The encouraging point is that the percentage of R&D co-operation without EU funding (after the finalization of the projects) was significant, implying that potential co-operative effects were initiated by FP projects.

Additionality

Additionality is one of the most important parameters. In this part of the chapter we examine if the participation of Greek firms led to results (such as increase in R&D expenses) that would have never occurred without this participation.

Table 10.19 presents the level of additionality, concerning new research activities. As is evident, additionality is quite high in the case of the participating firms and less important for universities and research institutes. For the latter, the percentage of projects of which EU funding was a starting point of new activities is very low.

The additionality concerning research collaborations is shown in Table 10.20. Here the increase of collaborations for all categories of participants is the dominant element. Table 10.21 shows that for the larger part of participating organizations, including firms, R&D budgets increased either as absolute figures or as percentages of turnover.

Significant increase was also seen in the number of research and technical staff of the participants. The most important result of this is that many of the new scientists and technicians remained in their positions after the finalization of the projects (Table 10.22). This is the case for the firms and research institutes, and not for the universities.

Table 10.23 points to the suggestion that a large number of projects would have not been completed at all without Community support (22 per cent). Some 27 per cent would have been completed only if they were funded by another source. Table 10.23 indicates that FPs led to a significant increase of the research activities of the participating organizations.

Table 10.20 Additionality/co-operation before and after funding

How often did you co-operate with a university, research institute or a firm before your participation in FPs?																				
	Never				*Rarely*				*Often*				*Always*				*M.A.*			
Before	*F*	*RI*	*U*	*T*	*F*	*RI*	*U*	*T*	*F*	*RI*	*U*	*T*	*F*	*RI*	*U*	*T*	*F*	*RI*	*U*	*T*
U	26.7	4.7	17.8	18.8	21.1	14.0	22.2	20.2	40	46.5	48.9	44.8	8.9	30.2	7.8	12.6	2.32	3.07	2.48	2.53
RI	31.1	7.0	18.9	21.5	25.6	18.6	25.6	24.2	32.2	44.2	44.4	39.5	7.8	23.3	7.8	10.8	2.17	2.9	2.42	2.41
F	27.8	44.2	41.1	36.3	14.4	30.2	26.7	22.4	38.9	14.0	21.1	26.9	14.4	4.7	7.8	9.9	2.4	1.7	1.9	2.1
After																				
U	6.7	7.0	2.2	4.9	11.1	7.0	1.1	6.3	5.0	34.9	19.8	34.8	30.0	51.2	74.7	52.2	3.0	3.3	3.7	3.3
RI	17.8	7.0	8.8	12.1	14.4	9.3	8.8	11.2	45.6	51.2	24.2	37.9	21.1	32.6	56.0	37.5	2.7	3.09	3.3	3.02
F	10.0	25.6	33.0	22.3	10.0	14.0	6.6	9.4	40	39.5	18.7	31.3	37.8	18.6	39.6	34.8	3.07	2.52	2.66	2.80

Table 10.21 Additionality/changes in R&D budget

	Increase				*Reduction*				*N/A*			
	F	*RI*	*U*	*T*	*F*	*RI*	U	*T*	*F*	*RI*	*U*	*T*
Budget	80.0	86.0	—	87.9	3.3	4.7	—	2.2	16.7	9.3	—	9.8
%	75.6	88.4	—	86.2	6.7	4.7	—	4.0	17.8	7.0	—	9.8

Table 10.22 Additionality/changes in the number of research and scientific staff

How many people are employed as research staff in your unit?	*Researchers*				*Technicians*[a]			
	F	*RI*	*U*	*T*	*F*	*RI*	*U*	*T*
Before the participation	46.7	15.65	7.0	7.57	2.05	12.16	1.38	3.43
During	9.34	25.89	12.72	13.76	3.35	16.24	1.60	4.85
After	9.24	26.74	9.13	12.63	3.64	17.31	1.11	5.27

Note: M.A. per category of positive answers.

Table 10.23 Additionality in the implementation of the research works *If you were not funded by FPs will you have carried out the specific research project(s)?*

	1	*2*	*3*	*4*	*5*	*6*	*7*	*8*
F	21.1	33.3	3.3	11.1	8.9	0.0	28.9	1.1
RI	30.2	39.5	11.6	2.3	11.6	0.0	16.3	0.0
U	30.8	46.2	0.0	5.5	13.2	1.1	16.5	3.3
Total	26.8	39.7	3.6	7.1	11.2	0.4	21.4	1.8

1 Only if there was another funding mechanism targets
2 Yes, but at a lower level
3 Yes
4 Yes, but with different research
5 Yes, but the duration would
6 Yes, other
7 No
8 D/K-N/A

Overall, FP projects led to a significant increase of the research activities of the Greek participating organizations compared with their previous performance.

The overall picture, economic benefits and barriers

Table 10.24 shows the major benefits from the participation. For all organizations the most essential benefit is the enhancement of research activities. Firms do not seem to believe that the financial benefits were important, but attach significant importance to the acquisition of know how and marginal importance to the improvement of the staff's expertise and the development of stronger co-operations with research institutes and universities.

When we look at the barriers to exploitation and commercialization of research results (Table 10.25), firms believe that the availability of funds is not enough and thus their scarcity is a major barrier.

In general, 88.4 per cent of the participating organizations declared that cost was equal to the benefits[4] or benefits were more. The latter is the case mainly for the research institutes. According to Table 10.26 we could assume that either the firms were not ready to benefit by participating in the European projects, or the conditions and/or the results from their participation were not satisfactory. The latter is better explained by the results presented in Table 10.27, see p. 195.

According to Table 10.27, firms and industry were less happy concerning the success of the initial goals[5] of their projects. Again, Table 10.27 implies the same assumption made for Table 10.1 concerning the participation of the firms.

Table 10.24 Benefits from the participation

	Unimportant				*Almost unimportant*				*Almost important*				*Very important*				*M.A.*			
	F	*RI*	*U*	*T*	*F*	*RI*	*U*	*T*	*F*	*RI*	*U*	*T*	*F*	*RI*	*U*	*T*	*F*	*RI*	*U*	*T*
Know-how	4.4	0.0	5.5	4.0	12.2	9.3	17.6	13.8	42.2	46.5	46.2	44.6	37.8	44.2	29.7	35.7	3.17	3.34	3.0	3.14
Enhancement of R&D activities	4.4	0.0	0.0	1.8	17.8	11.6	3.3	10.7	46.7	37.2	33.0	39.3	27.8	51.2	62.6	46.4	3.0	3.39	3.6	3.32
Economic benefits	20.0	4.7	3.3	10.3	38.9	18.6	4.4	21.0	28.9	46.5	18.7	28.1	7.8	30.2	73.6	38.8	2.25	3.02	3.62	2.97
Skills improvement	4.4	0.0	1.1	2.2	16.7	4.7	4.4	9.4	47.8	53.5	46.2	48.2	27.8	41.9	48.4	38.8	3.02	3.37	3.41	3.25
New markets	25.6	25.6	61.5	40.2	22.2	23.3	8.8	17.0	35.6	27.9	7.7	22.8	13.3	11.6	3.3	8.9	2.37	2.28	1.41	2.0
Better relations with R&D organizational	2.2	0.0	1.1	1.3	22.2	7.0	5.5	12.5	52.2	41.9	29.7	41.1	18.9	51.2	62.6	42.9	2.91	3.44	3.55	3.28
Increased competitiveness	15.6	14.0	5.5	11.2	16.7	18.6	4.4	12.1	37.8	20.9	36.3	33.9	23.3	37.2	48.4	36.2	2.73	2.89	3.34	3.01
Other	0.0	2.3	0.0	0.4	0.0	0.0	0.0	0.0	0.0	0.0	1.1	0.4	0.0	2.3	3.3	1.8		2.5	3.75	3.33

Table 10.25 Barriers to exploitation/commercialization of research results

	Unimportant				*Almost unimportant*				*Almost important*				*Very important*				*M.A.*			
	F	*RI*	*U*	*T*	*F*	*RI*	*U*	*T*	*F*	*RI*	*U*	*T*	*F*	*RI*	*U*	*T*	*F*	*RI*	*U*	*T*
Industrial property rights (NL)	71.1	72.1	57.1	65.6	12.2	18.6	4.4	10.3	6.7	2.3	5.5	5.4	2.2	2.3	3.3	2.7	1.34	1.31	1.35	1.34
Industrial property rights (CL)	71.1	74.4	53.8	64.7	15.6	18.6	6.6	12.5	5.6	4.7	4.4	4.9	1.1	0.0	4.4	2.2	1.32	1.28	1.41	1.34
Availability of funds	28.9	44.2	36.3	34.8	8.9	7.0	9.9	8.9	37.8	37.2	20.9	30.8	16.7	9.3	13.2	13.8	2.45	2.11	2.13	2.26
Strategy of the organization	53.3	72.1	64.8	61.6	6.7	9.3	6.6	7.1	18.9	7.0	6.6	11.6	12.2	9.3	2.2	7.6	1.89	1.52	1.32	1.60
Propriety status of the organization	65.6	79.1	69.2	69.6	6.7	2.3	2.2	4.0	8.9	14.0	3.3	7.6	8.9	0.0	0.0	3.6	1.56	1.31	1.11	1.35
Communication problems between R&D and production	67.8	62.8	53.8	61.2	16.7	11.6	12.1	13.8	7.8	11.6	15.4	11.6	3.3	7.0	6.6	5.4	1.44	1.60	1.71	1.57
Actions of the partners	48.9	72.1	47.3	52.7	23.3	7.0	19.8	18.8	16.7	14.0	9.9	13.4	6.7	2.3	6.6	5.8	1.8	1.43	1.71	1.69
Existence of more advanced technology elsewhere	53.3	55.8	59.3	56.3	16.7	18.6	14.3	16.1	18.9	11.6	8.8	13.4	5.6	7.0	1.1	4.0	1.75	1.67	1.42	1.61
Lack of training of the potential users	40	53.5	34.1	40.2	15.6	18.6	13.2	15.2	21.1	14.0	26.4	21.9	13.3	4.7	9.9	10.3	2.08	1.66	2.14	2.02
Other	3.3	9.3	1.1	3.6	0.0	0.0	1.1	0.4	2.2	0.0	2.2	1.8	3.3	4.7	3.3	3.6	2.62	2.0	3.0	2.57

Table 10.26 General evaluation of the participation cost-benefit (%)

How do you evaluate your participation in FPs in relation to the cost and benefits?	*Large cost small benefits*	*Cost benefit equal*	*Large benefits small costs*
Firms (F)	11.1	60.0	23.3
Research institutes (RI)	2.3	44.2	53.5
Universities (U)	8.8	52.7	36.3
Total (T)	8.5	54.0	34.4

Table 10.27 Success on the goals set (%)

Did you succeed in your goals?	*All*	*Some*	*None*
Firms/industry	38.9	52.2	1.1
Research institutes	67.4	32.6	0.0
Universities	65.9	33.0	0.0
Total	55.4	40.6	0.4

Conclusions

The general picture of Greek participation shows that the vast majority of the participating organizations are located in the area of Athens. As a result organizations close to the sources of information were found to be more likely to be the first participants of FPs. Additionally Athens has a large concentration of research institutes and also of high-/medium-technology companies. Firms participated mainly in IT projects, and this implies that this category or firms (including also a number of consulting companies) was more ready and more technologically capable in meeting the needs of these Community Research areas.

The technological effects are quite important according to the opinions of the participants. Transfer of know-how was found to be significant for the organizations and in many cases led also to diffusion to the external environment. The type of transferred know-how was software and hardware for the firms and scientific results and methods for RIs and universities. This effect is expected from the aforementioned overall participation of firms in IT projects. Although technology transfer was relatively important to the large part of the participants, the picture is not encouraging, when analysing the potential products or methods for exploitation as an output of their participation. Only in one third of the cases is there a potentially new product or process for commercialization.

If the above result is correlated with the large participation of RIs and universities, an argument that could be supported is that the development of products and processes might not always be the priority of the participants (RIs and universities). A clear positive outcome was the production of publications and communications, since their total number is relatively impressive and justifies the traditionally successful performance of Greek scientists in these types of research output. But the same argument cannot be supported for patents and licences since their numbers were limited.

Overall, the impact on the co-operative behaviour of Greek organizations is positive. It has surely facilitated the diffusion of new technologies and knowledge but it is doubtful if there was any impact on further investment in R&D activities. It is evident that partners played an overall significant role for the fulfilment of the goals set. Additionally, research work in many cases continued with partners after the end of the project, indicating that Community support had a dynamic impact on research activities. However, the percentage of collaborations on commercial activities was very small and co-operation between companies existed mainly in the case of complementary activities and not when direct or indirect antagonism existed.

Finally, partnerships were promoted mainly through personal contacts (either through or outside FP projects) and Community events and short lists were not found to influence the search for partners and the creation of consortia. An argument justifying this is that the effort of a small country like Greece to participate in a new research system organized mainly, at its initial stage, by other countries was not an easy thing to do. So personal contacts of the Greek research staff (who were well known abroad) played a very important role.

The overall picture is that FPs also led to a significant enhancement and enrichment of the R&D activities of the participants. Almost 22 per cent of the projects would have not been carried out without Community support and especially for the case of firms, where the percentage is almost 30 per cent. A substantial rise has been noticed concerning the research staff and technicians involved in R&D. In the case of firms and research institutes, the number has remained unchanged after the finalization of the projects. Universities, due to their reduced flexibility concerning the management of their human resources, faced a reduction of this personnel. Additionally, involvement in new research areas was very important for the firms but less for the research institutes. As a result RIs found their activities more compatible with EC initiatives. Finally, additionality is also identified through the improvement of management skills, the ability to prepare better proposals, the enhancement of scientific skills and the acquisition of scientific instruments and equipment.

According to the participants the enhancement of the research activities and of the skills of research personnel has led to a significant increase of the competitive position of Greek R&D units. This fact led to greater optimism concerning future participation. The benefits of the firms are not very important except in the cases of software and hardware producing companies.

The major barrier concerning the exploitation and commercialization of the results is the scarcity of funds. This barrier is very important – especially for the companies. Other significant barriers are the lack of skills of potential users, the actions of the partners, the weaker position of the Greek partners, the small size of the Greek market, etc.

Overall, research institutes have proved more ready to deal with EC programmes. This was an expected result since RIs are more flexible schemes than universities and EC funding is vital for their survival. However, the majority of the participants were happy concerning their participation and the fulfilment of their initial goals except for firms which show a little scepticism concerning their future participation.

Community support in the form of Framework Programmes I and II took place during a reorganization phase of the Greek RTD infrastructure. The overall impact of these programmes can be characterized as important since they led to the development of significant expertise relating to the realization of large-scale projects, the enhancement of the research skills of the participating researchers and technicians as well as of the quality of research.

The Greek RTD system has found itself in the middle of a development and restructuring process during the 1980s and 1990s. As a result, participation in FPs was a kind of test for the new infrastructure and a challenge for the Greek firms which are still characterized by a low level of R&D activities and spending.

Although the overall output concerning the exploitation of the results cannot be found as important, the two first FPs should act as a guide in order for Greece to continue to improve the networking of its RTD infrastructures, to promote R&D collaboration with the industry and to identify the potential entrepreneurs in order to exploit successfully the research output.

APPENDIX I

The basic dimensions of the study were:

1 Efficiency of the implementation of FPs

a) Adequacy of awareness of programme
b) Barriers to participation
c) Applications procedures
d) Selection procedures
e) Management and administration
f) Monitoring and evaluation
g) Dissemination of research results

2 Impact and effectiveness of CEC RTD support
   a) Participant level
      (i) Additionality of support
      (ii) Economic impact
      (iii) Impact on non-selected applicants
      (iv) CEC RTD support and non-participants
      (v) Dynamic implications – sustainability
      (vi) Impact of support in relation to characteristics of participants
   b) Broader effects/national effects – macro-economic level and sectoral level effects
3 Appropriateness of CEC RTD support for Greece – implications for Greek technology – industrial strategy

NOTES

1 ESYE (1988), National Statistical Agency.
2 Giannitsis *et al.* (1993).
3 We should note at this point that a further analysis should be made concerning the outcome of the industrial companies only. The aforementioned percentages (31.1 per cent for 1 product) include all kinds of firms.
4 It has to be noted that the terms 'cost' and 'benefit' do not imply solely financial conditions but the overall idea of the participants concerning their participation (all inputs and outputs).
5 The term 'goal' implies the scientific and the technological goals set in the projects.

REFERENCES

Annual Economic Review (1994) 'The Greek Economy 1994', Athens: Epilogi.
EU (1994) 'Evaluation of the impact of the Community's RTD policy in Greece', report funded by the EU Commission's Stride Programme.
Giannitsis T. *et al.* (eds) (1993) *Technological Infrastructure and Technology Transfer in the Greek Industry*, Athens: Gutenberg.
OECD Economic Surveys (1993) *Greece*, Paris: OECD.

11

EU STRUCTURAL POLICIES AND INDUSTRIAL DEVELOPMENT

Application of the subsidiarity principle in the Italian case

Piera Magnatti

INTRODUCTION

It is a fact that the current stage of European integration is based on a substantial U-turn in the policy-making approach of the Community. The Single European Act represents the transition from a centralized model of public intervention to an approach mainly based on the co-operation of the various national and local authorities, (see also Patrizio Bianchi in Chapter 3).

Although Community funds have rapidly increased over the last few years, the most important element of this 'new phase' is that the new approach is greatly influencing the industrial policies adopted by the single member states. In particular, the new EU approach has started a process of change affecting the old practice of the national governments of providing subsidies for individual firms to compensate for structural disparities. The aim is that of fostering progressive structural adjustment, by reinforcing the local network of productive and service relations in order to stimulate endogenous market forces in the less favoured areas of the European Union.

Italy represents a significant example of this change; in fact, it is necessary to point out that:

- after forty years, the Special Intervention in the *Mezzogiorno* has finished. However, the 'post-intervention' is still not too clear; the pronouncement of general principles such as 'it is necessary to return to formal administration actions' has not been accompanied by clear operational references;
- the local/regional level of intervention (in other words, the actions promoted not only *for* the regions, but also *by* the regions) is still moving from 'national neglect' (the regions with ordinary statutory powers have

not been granted any of the power needed to deal with industry) towards the 'EU legitimation' (the EC considers the regional authorities to be significant actors in the definition and implementation of regional development policies); and
- in general terms, the role of the public development interventions is going to be revised.

But it is also necessary to point out that:

- the new policy-making approach adopted by the EU is still in an evolutionary phase; if some elements characterizing the new approach are already stable and clear, others are still emerging (the new approach cannot be considered as a 'definitive model' since it is learning from its operational experiences);
- the failure of many EU regional interventions implemented in Italy raises a number of questions; is the new policy-making approach inadequate in general terms or is the Italian situation substantially different from the other member states? As a consequence, should the new EC approach be redesigned or should the Italian context be made more 'receptive' as regards the new EC scheme?
- the role of the Commission is not still completely clear. Is the Commission:
    1 a 'distributor' of financial resources on the basis of European rather than national parameters?; or
    2 a 'source of inspiration' for the definition of new policy-making approaches?; or, finally,
    3 an authority that can force the member states to introduce new ways of intervening?

In this perspective, the main objective of this chapter is to reflect on:

1 the effectiveness of the new approach and the needs in terms of industrial policy within the EU;
2 the conditions for the implementation of such policies; and
3 the role of the Commission within this context.

Since Italy represents an interesting example of 'complexity' among the member states (Objective 1, 2 and 5b areas, significant internal unbalances, etc.), the Italian case will be used as a 'case study' for such a reflection, paying particular attention to the generalization of the conclusions drawn to the other member states.

THE NEW EU INDUSTRIAL POLICY APPROACH

In recent years the European Community has implemented a policy-making approach based on the possibility of creating conditions for industrial co-operation among small and medium-sized firms (see also Christine

Oughton and Geoff Whittam, Chapter 4). This approach has been pioneered by several specific programmes promoted by the Commission, and finally embodied in the Treaty of Maastricht.

This new approach stresses that industrial adjustment has to be supported by the creation of a positive environment for inter-firm co-operation, the promotion of entrepreneurship and innovation, the full development of innovative opportunities and the development of human capabilities.

Analysing the Treaty of Maastricht, and looking at the programmes launched by the Commission, it is evident that the Community considers industrial innovation and, in general, economic dynamics to be the results of a collective, systemic, cumulative effort. In this perspective, industrial policy at Community level is not simply the transfer of the old idea of industrial policy from the national level; it is the entire range of macro and micro intervention of all the levels of policy-making to create the conditions to promote that industrial adjustment which is necessary to sustain efficiently the process of economic integration inside the EU and support the process of opening the internal market to global competition.

The adoption of the Single European Act by Community member states has reaffirmed and consolidated the idea of solidarity already implicit in the Treaty of Rome and which poses, as an objective, economic and social cohesion over the whole Community territory. In order to pursue this objective it is necessary to reduce the disparities in the various areas, on the basis of an increasingly regional level of intervention.

With the Reform of the Structural Funds, established by the Single European Act, another aspect has been further accentuated; that is, the necessity to provide interventions aimed at 'appropriate' territorial areas. This idea of the 'relevant geographical level', introduced by Regulation 2088 on 23 July 1985 concerning the Integrated Mediterranean Programmes, was taken up in the regulation of the Funds which defines, according to the objectives pursued, relevant actions for each region. There is, therefore, a recognition of the necessity for geographically differing interventions according to the objectives pursued.

This point carries implications of particular importance as regards the approach to policy-making outlined by the Community, above all concerning the bodies which should be considered as government authorities carrying out actions promoting economic development. In this sense, the application of the *principle of subsidiarity* becomes fundamental.

Four levels of government come into play in the Community: local, regional, national and supra-national. The essential criteria for evaluating the most efficient level of government for given actions are the incidence of the costs and benefits of the specific actions; and the most appropriate level of government for public benefit is, in principle, that which includes the majority of these benefits. The principle of subsidiarity is substantially this, in that the highest levels of government should only exercise functions which guarantee public benefits that cannot be provided in an efficient way by lower levels.

This principle therefore essentially demonstrates the necessity to identify the most efficient correlation between the competent government authorities and the proposed initiatives. What is more, this point should not be defined in general terms, but by paying particular attention to the specific area involved. In this sense, it is possible to state that the principle of subsidiarity recognizes the organization and the territorial dimension of the economy.

The request for *partnership* between many different bodies for following common objectives is strictly tied to the principle of subsidiarity described above. This rule is applied with reference to all the possible fields of economic intervention. However, in the case of regional policies it is considered a fundamental aspect of the present position, as it is potentially capable of influencing the whole range of innovations introduced during the process of programming, implementing and evaluating initiatives. This partnership is obviously realized at different levels according to the territorial context.

The principle of the partnership, apart from establishing the direct involvement of all those indicated in the various phases around which the realization of the activities is based, also identifies the regions as an integral part of the administrative process of policy-making. Although the importance of the role of regional governments varies from state to state, according to the powers and privileges of the sub-national governments involved in each of these, this principle highlights the fact that the Community is evolving towards the creation of inter-governmental 'management' of regional policy which involves Community bodies, the state and the interested regions. The new strategy for European integration therefore hopes to overcome the dominating role previously played by most of the national governments, by identifying the regions as primary subjects in the process of policy-making.

In general terms, the new EU industrial strategy can be considered as twofold:

1 on the one hand, it is applied at a territorial level to favour the endogenous growth of the less-favoured areas (regional policies, aimed at creating a positive environment in which to develop new industrial and service activities); and
2 on the other hand, it is used for innovation policy and human resources development in education and research policy (public support for innovation, especially for very innovative sectors, and for the development of small companies through the promotion of a network of innovators).

The first approach (regional policies) enacted by the Commission is to overcome the previous dominant role of the national government, bringing into play the regions as primary actors of the policy-making and implementation processes. Regional governments try to create a favourable local environment for industrial development through direct involvement of all the local public and private actors for the definition of common development programmes; these programmes have to be supported by the integrated use of complementary policy instruments offered by regional, national and Community authorities to promote industrial development and innovation, such as training programmes, export consortia, service centres, common research and application technology projects.

Local partnership is therefore the key issue of the Structural Funds reform. This principle is crucial because it outlines that development of the less favoured areas can result from a variety of complementary projects, activated by different levels of public authorities, with the direct involvement of private sector, entrepreneurial associations, local clubs, aimed at redefining not just the production sites, but to act on the local community and environment itself. This approach assumes that the basic externality for the development of local forces is given by the civic society itself, that is the local community, with its history, traditions, collective norms, which can establish the collective trust that is necessary for the growth of the economy.

The second approach (public support for innovation) implemented by the Commission has been influenced by the impressive growth of industrial districts and remains beyond the specific fortunes of the individual areas. At present, the main interest is not so much how these industrial networks are working, but to what extent it is possible to favour the agglomeration of such a network of innovators and if so, how.

This approach is based on the possibility of favouring the aggregation of firms, research institutes and universities, framed in their own national contexts, but forced to co-operate in producing innovation. The positive result is not limited to the innovation *per se,* such as a patent or a book, but it is the capacity to induce individuals and institutions to modify the existing routines in order to 'work together' with individuals and institutions rooted in different frameworks.

This idea is clearly based on an evolutionary view of economic dynamics: because the interaction between people creates norms for collective action, which induces subjects, which are rooted in different institutional contexts, to come together to work on a specific project.

Until now, these two parts of the overall EU strategy have evolved in parallel, with quite:

1 different objectives:
   a) cohesion at regional level for the first;
   b) efficiency at EU level for the second;
2 different interlocutors:
   a) national and regional authorities for the first;
   b) 'points of excellence' for the second;
3. different ways of implementation:
   a) by acting on the local environment for the first;
   b) by creating transnational networks for the second.

The main results of this 'twofold approach' have been that:

1 On the one hand, the regional policies have mainly focused their attention on 'traditional factors' (the Structural Funds have so far tried to promote regional capabilities in the field of science and technology normally through the strengthening of RTD infrastructures).
2 On the other hand, the problem of the diffusion of innovation has been managed following criteria of efficiency, so excluding *de facto* the participation of the 'weak bodies' belonging to the less favoured areas (problems of receptivity).

As already stated in the Introduction, from recent evolution (e.g. the *Regional Technology Plans* project promoted, jointly, by DG XIII and DG XVI or the linkages between the Fourth Framework Programme and the new Community Support Frameworks 1994–9) it seems that the strict division of labour between regional development and diffusion of innovation is going to be overcome in order to better achieve the final objective of reducing the disparities between the member states and the regions of the Community.

DISPARITIES BETWEEN THE MEMBER STATES AND THE REGIONS OF THE COMMUNITY

The economic situation confronting the regions of the Community in 1993/1994 is different from that which prevailed when the Commission produced the *Periodic Report on the Social and Economic Situation and Development of the Regions in the Community* at the end of 1990. Then, economic growth was averaging 3–4 per cent per annum, jobs were being created at a record rate and unemployment was falling steadily even in the face of an expanding labour force.

Now the Community's economy is at the end of a relatively deep recession – output seems to have fallen slightly in 1993 for the first time since 1975 – and unemployment has risen to 11 per cent, slightly above the level a decade earlier when it was at its highest in the Community's history. Although signs of improvement are visible, they have not provided the ideal circumstances for a reduction in interregional disparities, as pointed out in previous Periodic Reports.

More detailed analysis of the trends at member state and regional levels reveal a mixed picture in terms of their capacity to generate income (defined in terms of Gross Domestic Product and expressed per head of population). At member state level, the net effect of the differences in performance over the past decade can be summarized in terms of a period of slight widening in disparities in GDP (in per capita terms) between 1980 to 1984 followed by a steady narrowing (real convergence).

Disparities between the regions of the Community show a more varied trend than between member states. The overall tendency seems to have been

Table 11.1 Disparities in GDP per head (PPS) in the Community, 1980–91 (EUR 12=100)

	Average 10 weakest regions	*Average 10 strongest regions*	*Average 25 weakest regions*	*Average 25 strongest regions*	*Disparity*[a]
1980	44.0	145.8	54.9	135.3	26.6
1981	44.0	149.2	53.7	137.7	28.4
1982	44.7	149.4	53.8	138.5	28.2
1983	43.8	151.0	53.5	138.2	28.3
1984	42.6	150.6	52.8	138.5	28.6
1985	43.2	152.1	52.6	139.3	29.0
1986	42.6	151.4	51.9	138.3	28.5
1987	41.7	151.9	52.1	138.7	28.2
1988	41.0	152.4	52.7	137.5	28.2
1989	41.1	152.8	53.5	138.0	27.9
1990	40.5	150.6	53.1	137.4	27.9
1991	41.8	151.6	54.4	137.0	27.9
1992[b]	33.4	151.6	42.9	137.0	30.6

NUTS 2: French Overseas Departments, Azores and Madeira not included.
[a]Disparity is the standard deviation weighted by the size of the population in each region.
[b]Including the new German Lander.

Source: European Commission, (1994), *Competitiveness and cohesion: trends in the regions. Fifth periodic report on the social and economic situation and development of the regions in the Community.*

one of slightly widening disparities during the slow growth years over the first half of the 1980s and a gradual narrowing over the second half of the decade which levelled off in the 1990s.

This trend of regional convergence refers to all the Community's regions (defined at the NUTS 2 level) aggregated together in a single statistical measure. It is also instructive to examine the position of the regions situated at the extremes and to compare, for example, the 25 richest regions with the 25 poorest regions. Here there was no change over the 1980s, with the 25 richest regions having in 1991 an average GDP per head some 2½ times higher than the average for the 25 poorest regions, the same as in 1980. Narrowing the focus to compare the 10 regions at the two extremes suggests a slight deterioration in the situation. The top 10 regions had an average GDP per head some 3.3 times higher than the bottom 10 regions in 1980 but 3.6 times higher in 1991.

In summary, there is evidence of real economic convergence in regional economic performance over the recent past. Many of the weakest member states and regions have been able to sustain rates of growth above the Community average over much of the period since the mid-1980s. This has been a slow and gradual process, however, and major reductions in the wide disparities between the richest and the poorest regions remain a long-term challenge. Within this general trend, there have been member states and regions showing significant improvement while certain others have experienced a relative decline. These latter regions are those which present the biggest challenge to national and Community cohesion policies.

With regard to unemployment rates, disparities which narrowed at the end of the 1980s widened again in 1992 and 1993. Unemployment in 1993 in the 10 worst-affected regions averaged 25.3 per cent, some 7 times higher than the 10 least-affected regions where the rate averaged 3.6 per cent. The 10 worst affected regions are located entirely in the Community's less develped areas: Spain and South of Italy.

Regional variations in unemployment rates at the Community level are mirrored at the national level, though the extent of differences is, of course, less. Nevertheless the variation in rates in Spain and Italy in particular is considerable. In Italy the gap between the most and least affected regions was equivalent to around 20 percentage points.

The challenge for the rest of the decade is not only to raise general rates of growth to above $2\frac{1}{2}$ per cent but to ensure that the regions of high unemployment perform better than the rest.

Faced with the on-going challenges of the Single Market and the new challenges posed by economic and monetary unification, the Commission's medium-term budgetary proposals covering the period 1993 to 1999 (the Delors II package) have called for another significant increase in structural expenditure to promote economic and social cohesion. In consequence, the funds devoted to structural policies will increase by 41 per cent from over ECU 21 billion in 1993 to ECU 30 billion in 1999, including the new Cohesion Fund. Structural funds in 1999 will, therefore, be three times their real value in 1989.

INDUSTRIAL POLICY IN ITALY

Regional policies in member states: recent trends

The past five years have been a period of considerable uncertainty and upheaval in the regional policies of member states. Major geopolitical developments, economic fluctuations and almost continuous structural change have combined to create a difficult environment for regional policy. These changes are reflected in northern member states in a decline in large-scale, automatic support to business in favour of a more selective approach with more emphasis than in the past on developing the business environment and small enterprises.

In southern member states and Ireland, expenditure on regional incentives has increased and is now among the highest in the Community in relation to GDP. These countries have maintained relatively extensive geographical coverage in their regional incentive schemes whereas in northern member

Table 11.2 Regional incentive expenditure indicators

	Population coverage in assisted regions (% national Popul.)			*RIE per head of population in assisted regions (ECU 1990 prices)*			*RIE (% national GDP)*		
	1980	*1986*	*1992*	*1980*	*1985*	*1990*	*1980*	*1985*	*1990*
Belgium	39.50	33.10	33.10	38.15	49.67	44.71	0.13	0.14	0.11
Denmark	27.00	24.00	19.90	9.82	10.62	5.40	0.02	0.02	0.01
France	38.20	39.00	40.00	16.85	11.73	7.57	0.05	0.04	0.02
Germany	36.00	35.00	27.00	30.07	28.38	33.15	0.08	0.07	0.07
Greece	65.00	58.00	58.00	7.13	36.28	52.47	0.07	0.35	0.49
Ireland	28.00	28.00	28.00	117.00	57.46	58.14	1.66	0.75	0.63
Italy	35.60	35.60	35.60	185.19	238.72	404.63	0.60	0.72	1.04
Luxembourg	100.00	100.00	79.70	63.97	23.72	70.91	0.51	0.17	0.41
Netherlands	27.40	25.00	19.90	58.45	42.10	33.09	0.13	0.08	0.05
Portugal	—	100.00	100.00	—	—	27.35	—	—	0.38
Spain	—	58.60	58.60		—	31.93	—	—	0.19
UK	49.50	36.80	36.80	70.61	62.27	36.92	0.30	0.20	0.10
EUR9	37.90	35.50	33.40	—	—	—	—	—	
EUR12	—	41.00	39.10	—	—	—	—	—	

Notes: [a]For Greece the figure for population coverage under 1980 is for 1981; the figures for RIE under 1980 are for 1982 and under 1990 are for 1988.

Source: European Commission (1994).

Table 11.3 Major policy changes in regional incentive policy since 1980 in Italy

1986	New legislation for the *Mezzogiorno* introduced. Eligibility for aid extended. Three-year rolling programmes implemented. *Mezzogiorno* divided into three grades of area and discrimination in rate of support introduced. Rates of maximum support increased.
1988	Under Commission pressure, certain parts of the North *Mezzogiorno* de-designated as from 1990 and others from 1992.
1990	Discrimination on rates of support increased.
1992	'Special intervention' for the *Mezzogiorno* abolished as from 1993.

Source: European Commission (1994).

states such coverage has been reduced. This has tended to reduce differences in expenditure on regional incentives across the Community when expressed per head of population. The major exception is Italy, where expenditure per head remains substantially ahead of the rest of the Community.

The shift in regional policy objectives to focus more on structural adjustment, with increasingly limited resources in many member states, is evident in the design of incentives to attract new productive activity. A common theme in the composition of incentive packages, their administration, spatial coverage, the conditions for eligibility and the rates of support is a more selective approach to promote indigenous regional development.

Over the past decade, both the number and form of regional incentives used by member states have become more limited. The diversity of incentives, common in most Community countries during the 1970s, is disappearing (particularly as regards fiscal concessions and interest-related subsidies), and most incentive packages are now heavily grant-based. The diversity that remains tends to be greatest in the less developed countries: Greece, Italy, Ireland and Portugal typically have more numerous and varied incentives, including labour-related subsidies, than other member states.

The institutionalization of the regions

Since 1970, when the regions with an 'ordinary' statute were created, regional decentralization has become a 'game' open to new players and new rules. The Presidential Decree N. 616 of 24 July 1977 activated the institutionalization of the Regions and the decentralization of state competences according to Article 117 of the Constitution.

With the exception of the border regions, those with special ethnic characteristics, and the islands (Sicily and Sardinia), the regions with ordinary status have not been granted any of the power needed to deal with industry. They do have powers concerning local area improvements, craft industries and professional training, and are, in addition, empowered by article 10 of

Law No. 281 of 16 March 1970, to set up financial agencies which can, in certain cases, by special provisions in their founding charter, be entitled 'Development and Promotion Boards'.

The above-mentioned distinction between the regions with an ordinary statute and the regions (or provinces) with a special statute is significant also in financial terms. In this regard it is important to note the distribution of the 'free' revenue (not tied to a particular purpose). This revenue grants the regions considerable autonomy in expenditures. A comparison between the regions with an ordinary statute and the regions with a special statute also gives significant results: in 1991 the free revenue of the former represented about 13 per cent of the total revenue while for the latter it constituted over 50 per cent. This discrepancy becomes even more marked when the volume of free revenue is considered per capita.

The regions with an ordinary statute therefore have to rely above all on the revenue destined and usable only for certain sectors or subsectors and, in some cases, only using predetermined procedures. This has particular results on the co-financing of EU policies on the part of the region and on financial flexibility as regards default or delay on the part of the EU or national funds.

Since the beginning of the 1980s, there has been a growing conviction in almost all the regions, especially those with single-sector spatial concentrations of small and medium-sized companies, that established companies should be consolidated and strengthened. The formulation of local government policies designated to encourage the development of the economic structure of the territory has indeed become a very important part of Italian industrial policy, hitherto characterized by a centralized approach to public intervention given, among other things, the lack of authority granted to local bodies. This phenomenon has some rather interesting characteristics in so far as a variety of initiatives have been tried, which, in contrast to the tradition at the national level, have favoured approaches that do not involve a direct transfer of financial resources to companies.

The national and regional levels of intervention

The Italian approach to industrial policy has been based mainly on direct transfer from the central government to individual companies. State aid to industry has been a constant element of Italian industrial policy. Throughout the post-war period, the Italian government has provided subsidies (on a sectorial basis and on a national scale) in order to promote the development of the less favoured regions and to favour the innovative efforts of small and medium-sized enterprises.

The most significant tools promoted by the Italian government for the regional development of areas affected by industrial decline, rural areas and less favoured regions, are the following:

Law	Object
Presidential Decree 902/1976	Restructuring of Northern SMEs
Law 64/1986	Extraordinary intervention for the South
Law 44/1986	Promotion of youth entrepreneurship
Law 488/92	Financial support to firms setting up new productive investments in disadvantaged areas

Other interventions (destined for the entire Italian territory, without specific territorial references) have been set up at the national level; the list of the main industrial policy laws includes:

Law	Object
Law 1329/1965	Acquisition of new machines by SMEs
Law 675/1977	Industrial restructuring: revision of all the laws on industrial intervention
Law 46/1982	National Fund for technological innovation
Law 696/1983	Acquisition of new machines by SMEs
Law 399/1987	Acquisition of machinery by SMEs
Law 317/1991	Technological innovation and development of SMEs

The basic concepts were:

1 first, that small firms and companies working in the marginal areas were financially disadvantaged in securing loans from the banking system; and
2 second, that the only innovation considered was the acquisition of new machinery (in fact, looking at the list of the main laws concerning public aid it is possible to note that most of the laws provide subsidies for the acquisition of new machinery).

The high level of aid testifies to a rigid, central bureaucracy, which provides subsidies to compensate for operating disadvantages simply because it is not able to initiate a real process of institutional change. The main example of such rigidity is provided by the case of the public support of investment in the *Mezzogiorno*.

In recent years, there has been an extraordinary growth in intervention launched by local governments, business groups and, less frequently, by large firms, aimed at reorganizing and strengthening the production systems of the local community.

Exploiting the powers available to them, regional governments have developed a wide range of interventions, by employing different instruments which, although under their supervision, are not directly managed by them.

Since the beginning of the 1980s, almost every region has come to the conclusion that existing industrial systems have to be consolidated and strengthened. This was to be achieved by setting up centres which would provide services to local firms mainly by transferring new technologies or by supplying specialized services with high value added. This conviction has been influenced by a combination of several factors: first, by the need to identify new means by which to implement innovation policies in order to reduce the almost exclusive role played by grants. Second, by the importance of awarding a fundamental role to production-related services during the structural readjustment phase of production cycles; and, third, by the increasing difficulties encountered by small firms in responding to the challenges presented by technological revolution, in the absence of environmental conditions which favour the assimilation by the entrepreneur of the innovative stimuli present in the system.

A lively debate has developed in Italy concerning the relevance of the initiatives in terms of industrial policy in the field of services to manufacturing companies, generally named '*servizi reali*' (structural services). This category involves an undefined mix of services covering information technology, databases, technology transfer, research and development, standard certification, professional training, management consulting, and so on, but also often refers to basic infrastructures. *Servizi reali* can be considered to be those activities whose provision modifies in a structural, non-transitory way the firm's organization of production. In other words: the inclusion of these services in the production process allows a structural change, e.g. the reshaping of processes, or the differentiation of products, or a change in market coverage.

If by industrial policy we mean the set of interventions aimed at inducing structural change in the productive system, the *servizi reali* may well be considered as an instrument of industrial policy.

In conclusion, it is possible to say that, despite the current Italian legislative framework and the consequent network of institutional responsibilities, the local initiatives set up over the past few years have demonstrated not so much the importance of an organized system with clearly defined responsibilities, but rather the primacy of those many participants operating at various levels who have each been able to meet specific needs of the industrial system while another considerable financial intervention can only come from central government, at the same time local government – even without legislative and financial autonomy – can play an important role in modernizing the industrial system through initiatives which do not require vast sums of money but which identify and meet specific local needs thereby filling any gaps present in the industrial system.

Regional policies in Italy: the extraordinary intervention in the *Mezzogiorno*

As already stated in the previous paragraph, the extraordinary intervention in the *Mezzogiorno* represents the typical example of regional policy in Italy. The economic and industrial development in Italy has always been

Table 11.4 GDP Per head: *Mezzogiorno*/Centre-North (%)

1951	*1990*	*1993*
66%	56%	59%

Table 11.5 Unemployment rate (%)

	1990	*1993*
Mezzogiorno	16%	17%
Centre-North	6%	7%
Italy	11%	10.4%

characterized by significant disparities between the Centre-North and the South, both in terms of GDP per head and employment (Tables 11.4 and 11.5).

The *Mezzogiorno* has been considered a special intervention area since the post-war period: a central agency was created (*Cassa per il Mezzogiorno*) to manage all the interventions directly, because local administrators were not considered capable of driving the industrialization process.

After the closure of the *Cassa* in 1986, the intervention was still managed through a restricted number of central agencies, despite the fact that constitutional reform established regional governments in 1977.

The basic assumptions behind this special intervention were:

- the *Mezzogiorno* is a homogeneous area, with common problems;
- the local authorities have neither the technical capacity nor the political legitimation to intervene in these problems, thus a central intervention is required.

According to these assumptions, central government has for decades given public subsidies to relocate industrial plants to the Southern regions of the country. Money was also given to individual companies through the banking system to acquire machinery, without any attempt to create networks of relations. The result has been a large proportion of firm failures.

Public shareholding companies that were ordered to invest in the Southern regions in order to create new jobs invested in capital-intensive sectors, which were seen as the core of the rapid industrialization process.

The economic crises of the 1970s had a very negative impact on most of these new plants, inducing a further decline of these depressed areas. In the second part of the 1980s, unemployment in the South grew, while the Northern regions were close to full employment; Italy was thus the only country in Europe to have increased internal regional disparities in terms of unemployment.

At the beginning of the 1990s there was a rethinking of the special intervention for the *Mezzogiorno*: the old Law 64 was cancelled and a new law (488/92) regulating regional interventions (not only in the South) was issued.

The predisposition of the new law was greatly inspired by the main principles of the EU structural approach; in fact, the main characteristics of the Law 488/92 are:

1 The responsibilities in terms of policy-making and policy implementation have been assigned to the ordinary administration (the Ministry of the *Mezzogiorno* has been abolished); more specifically, the Ministry of the Budget has been appointed with co-ordinating functions concerning all interventions aimed at regional development (not only for the South);
2 The areas of intervention do not belong only to the Southern part of the country; they are now indicated as 'areas of crisis', since they represent the most problematic (in terms of unemployment, industrial decline, etc.) territories of the whole country;
3 The significant role of the local authorities within the policy-making and implementation process was stressed.

THE APPLICATION OF THE NEW EU APPROACH TO ITALY

Through the observation of the implementation of the EU 'twofold approach' mentioned above within the Italian context, some preliminary considerations can be drawn.

As regards the application of EU regional policies in Italy, the most significant (and worrying) emerging factor – apart from the 'quality' of some of the interventions proposed by the Italian government and disputed by the Commission because they were still based mainly on subsidies – is that the new structural approach proposed by the EU has not been implemented.

In several cases, in particular in the South of Italy, the Integrated Mediterranean Programmes and the actions promoted under Objective 1, which require an active role from local authorities, has not worked, so that the Commission redirected part of IMPs' grants from Southern Italy to France. Checking the different IMPs, it is also evident that some regions (Molise, Abruzzi and Puglia, like the Northern regions), have managed their programmes well and have therefore received Community subsidies. The least-favoured areas have not been able to organize a local network of productive partnership, and therefore they missed the opportunity because prolonged dependency on the central government reduced their capacity to promote endogenous development.

It has to be noted that regional governments are not equally active. In all the European countries, the most active regional governments are those that administer the most favoured areas. In contrast, the economic ills of the less-favoured areas are usually accompanied by a weak local administration, which is traditionally dependent on the central authority and used to dealing with local problems by claiming support from the national government rather than directly implementing new development projects.

As regards the implementation of the structural funds in Italy, despite the fact that the national level has had exclusive responsibility for relations with the EU, ever since the establishment of the Integrated Mediterranean Programmes, the role of the regions has been significant.

It should be noted that there has been a 'division of labour' rather than a proper collaboration between the two institutional levels; the national level has often refused to co-operate with the regions (considered to be antagonists rather than partners) during both the policy-making and implementation processes.

In some cases (e.g. IMPs) the national level has maintained a marginal position during the overall process; in others it directly took part in the initiatives without involving the regional bodies (within the 1989 Report on the Structural Funds, the Commission states that the regions have often been kept in a very marginal position during the negotiation process).

In the case of the IMPs, the regions were responsible for the definition and implementation of the Programmes which were submitted for approval to a specific Committee (composed of representatives of the ministries and regions involved) and then to the '*Comitato Interministeriale per la Programmazione Economica*' (Interministerial Committee for Economic Planning) (CIPE). The Department for the Co-ordination of Community Policies was in charge of transmitting the IMPs to the Commission, through the Ministry of Foreign Affairs.

During the policy-making process, many informal contacts were set up between some regions and the national level (Department for the Co-ordination of the Community Policies). Some regions have also set up informal contacts with the Community to discuss the content of the programmes as well as to secure up-to-date information; several trilateral meetings (Commission, member state, region) have been organized (either at the Commission or in Italy) to analyse each programme presented.

In several cases the active (even if not institutionalized) role covered by some of the social and economic bodies, in particular at the regional level (Provinces, *Comunità Montane*, Trading and Professional Associations, etc.) in the definition of the content of the programmes and in the proposal of specific measures has been particularly evident.

The IMP experience has demonstrated how the consideration of the specific local needs in the formulation of the programme had positive effects in the phase of implementation, in particular for 'open' actions. 'Open' actions are those in which:

a) the programme only defines the contents of the measure/project in general terms and therefore requires a feasibility study to define the contents and the rules in detail before implementation;
b) the programme does not identify the organizers and/or the beneficiaries of the financing and therefore a selection of the latter is necessary before the project gets under way for which seeking consensus becomes an indispensable condition for obtaining effective results.

The participation of the national and regional level in the formulation of the Development Plans (1989/1993) or Single Programming Documents (1993/1999) differs according to the Objective involved.

As regards the Objective 1 1989/1993, the centralist approach which distinguished the national intervention for the *Mezzogiorno* has also been prevalent during the definition of the Development Plan.

In contrast with, for example, France which has proposed five different Development Plans (one for each region involved), Italy has presented a single Development Plan for all eight regions of the *Mezzogiorno*. The Commission has pressed for an effective participation of eight regions in the policy-making and implementation process by modifying, for example, the amount of financial resources devoted to the two levels (from a share of 50 per cent to the multi-regional level proposed by the member state within the Development Plan to a share of 45 per cent to the multi-regional level and 55 per cent to the regional level proposed by the Commission. The final result has been that of 49 per cent for the multi-regional level – 51 per cent to the regional level).

As far as the implementation of EU research and innovation policies is concerned, recent studies have examined the geographical patterns of RTD activity in the Community. The most striking finding is that laboratories and enterprises which are involved in the RTD projects are highly concentrated in comparatively few 'Islands of Innovations'. These islands are relatively small, mostly urban areas, with a dense network of enterprises and research laboratories interacting in the development of new products and processes of production, (see Chapter 10 of this volume, on Greek experience).

A limited number of such islands in the Community stand out from the rest: Greater London, Rotterdam/Amsterdam, Ile de France, the Ruhr area, Frankfurt, Stuttgart, Munich, Lyon/Grenoble, Turin and Milan.

Up to three quarters of all public research contracts, including those funded by the Community, are estimated to be concentrated in these few places. They also tend to work closely together as part of highly exclusive network. The large majority of science-based innovative activities in the Community, therefore, involve laboratories and enterprises located in this innovative core. By contrast, laboratories and enterprises located in peripheral regions of the Community only participate in 5–8 per cent of the networks.

An additional aspect of geographical diversity concerns the type of agency engaged in these networks of co-operation. The further the distance from the central Islands of Innovation, the more partners tend to be laboratories rather than enterprises and the smaller and more specialized the projects become.

Finally, RTD activities in the Community's weakest member states are often concentrated in a few regions, normally around capital cities. In Italy, only 3 per cent of industrial research undertaken by the private sector takes place in the South and, in 1989, barely 9 per cent of public sector research.

As regards Italy in particular, we could observe that, as already stated above, since the favourite interlocutors for the Commission have been the bodies representing qualified reference points for their local economic systems, the presence of participants belonging to Objective 1 areas has been very scarce. It is possible to say that, in this context, the Commission has paid attention to the 'national presence' (the balanced participation of all the Member States to the Programmes) rather than the regional one.

In this perspective, the effects of the research and innovation policies on cohesion have been very scarce.

CONCLUSIONS

Recent literature stresses that industrial development is the systemic, evolutionary result of an interaction of social relations, so that individual competitiveness is largely affected by the organization of the institutional setting, which frames the firm's environment: the richer the institutional environment, the lower the need of the firm to internalize activities having high economies of scale and 'sunkness' (such as education and research).

In this perspective, new issues are emerging from the above considerations:

- There are two relevant levels of policy design and implementation: the macro level, which defines the normative system which governs the behaviour of all actors and sanctions free-riders and abuses of dominant positions; the micro level, which establishes the capabilities with which the actors take part in the economic arena. Together, policies on both levels must be integrated to create the positive externalities needed for growth in order to avoid the formation of regressive coalitions to resist change.
- Since policy-making in an open context is an evolutionary process, it requires continuous readjustment of top–down interventions to define the institutional environment for firms' reorganization and of bottom–up actions to test local experiences of industrial reorganization (through, for example, the application of evaluation procedures).
- It is necessary to overcome the traditional approach to industrial policy based on national laws for funding individual firms and a centralized bureaucracy to administer the funds. The new approach requires

numerous policy implementors, whose role is to design and manage local or sectorial interventions. This body of implementors must operate in the local and national administrations, but also in the entrepreneurial associations, in the universities and research centres and international organizations.

- It is necessary to favour the aggregation of local forces, using a variety of programmes where municipal, regional, national and supra-national authorities can work together for defining the different project oriented to re-establishing the sense of local community.
- Finally, the development of less favoured areas can result from a variety of complementary projects, activated by different levels of public authorities, with the direct involvement of the private sector, entrepreneurial associations, local clubs, aimed at redefining not just the production sites, but to act on the local community and environment itself. This approach assumes that the basic externality for the development of local forces is given by the civic society itself, that is the local community, with its history, traditions, collective norms.

All these general prescriptive considerations should now be translated into operational propositions by taking into account the diversity of social, economic and cultural factors within the European regions.

The process of implementation of such relevant concepts will represent the subject of further necessary steps of research.

ACKNOWLEDGEMENTS

The content of this paper draws extensively on the results of an intense research activity committed to Nomisma by the Commission of the European Communities and carried out by the author since 1990. The research activity has regarded mainly studies and research works on industrial and regional policies within the European Union and, in particular, the evaluation of regional and innovation policies promoted by the Commission, DG I, VI, XIII, XVI. The author would like to thank Patrizio Bianchi for his help and encouragement during the elaboration of this paper.

REFERENCES

Bellini, N., Giordani, M.G. and Pasquini, F. (1990) 'The Industrial Policy of Emilia Romagna: the Business Service Centers' in R. Leonardi and Nanetti R. (eds) *The Regions and European Integration. The Case of Emilia Romagna*, London, New York: Pinter.

Bianchi, P. (1992) 'Industrial Strategy and Structural Policies', in K. Cowling and R. Sugden, (eds), *Current Issues in Industrial Economic Strategy*, Manchester and New York: Manchester University Press.

—— (1993a) 'An Industrial Strategy for Small and Medium-sized Enterprises in an Opening Economy. An European Perspective', paper presented at BID Workshop on 'Small Firms' Development', Washington, 18–19 November.

—— (1993b) 'Industrial Districts and Industrial Policy: the New European Perspective', in *Journal of Industry Studies*, I, October: 16–29.

Bianchi, P. and Bellini, N. (1991) 'Public Policies for Local Networks of Innovators', *Research Policy*, 20: 487–97.

Bianchi, P. and Giordani, M.G. (1993) 'Innovation Policy at the Local and National Levels: the Case of Emilia Romagna', *European Planning Studies*, I.

Bianchi, P. and Miller, L.M. (1994) 'Innovation, Collective Action and Endogenous Growth: An Essay on Institutions and Structural Change', *Birmingham Workshop on Industrial Economic Strategies for Europe,* revised version of a paper presented at the 1993.

Buresti, C. and Marciani, G.E. (1991) 'L'esperienza dei Programmi Integrati Mediterranei', *Rivista Economica del Mezzogiorno*, V, 1: 7–53.

Commission of the European Communities (1990) *The Evaluation of the Integrated Mediterranean Programmes*. Papers presented at the International Workshop promoted by DG XVI, Brussels, 20 and 21 September.

Cowling, K. and Sugden, R. (eds), (1992) *Current Issues in Industrial Economic Strategy*, Manchester and New York: Manchester University Press.

D'Antonio, M. (1990) 'The Tortuous Road of Industry Through the *Mezzogiorno*', *Rivista di Politica Economica*, V: 189–237.

European Commission (1994) *Competitiveness and Cohesion: Trends in the Regions. Fifth periodic report on the social and economic situation and development of the regions in the Community*, Luxembourg: EC.

Leonardi, R. (1990) 'The regional revolution in Europe: the Single European Act and the Regional Fund', mimeo. European University Institute, Florence.

Magnatti, P. (1989) 'The Evaluation of Industrial Policy at Local Level', paper presented at the 29th Regional Science Association European Congress, Cambridge.

Marino, M. (1993) 'Le Regioni del *Mezzogiorno* d'Italia e l'integrazione europea nella prospettiva dei nuovi regolamenti dei fondi strutturali', *Rivista Giuridica del Mezzogiorno*, VIII, 3: 663–75.

Moro, F. (1992) 'Legge per le piccole impresse, aree di crisi Industriale e *Mezzogiorno*', *Rivista Economica del Mezzogiorno*, VI, 4: 787–800.

Nomisma, (1991a) *The ex ante evaluation in objective 5b areas: Trento and Toscana*, research study commissioned by EC-DG VI.

—— (1991b) *The evaluation of the initiatives in the field of industry and services carried out within the EC support framework (1989–1993) to Italian regions included in the Objective 1 Group*, research study commissioned by EC-DG XVI.

—— (1991c) *Evaluation of EEC SPRINT actions on transnational networks of industrial research organisations*, research study commissioned by EC-DG XIII.

—— (1992) *Evaluation of the EEC SPRINT Specific Projects Action Line*, research study commissioned by EC-DG XIII.

—— (1993a) *Technical assistance to the science and technology sector reform programme in Slovenia*, research study commissioned by EC-DG I.

—— (1993b) *Ex ante evaluation of the industrial initiatives of the Regional Development Programme 1994–1999 for the Italian regions – Objective* 1, research study commissioned by EC-DG XVI.

—— (1994a) *Evaluation, Audit and Benchmarking of Research and Technology Organisations*, research study commissioned by EC-DG XIII.

—— (1994b) *Survey on Consultant Engineering Services*, research study commissioned by EC-DG XIII.

—— (1994c) *Transnational evaluation of the MINT Programme*, research study commissioned by EC-DG XIII.

—— (1994d) *Industrial innovation, diffusion and technology transfer policy developments*, research study commissioned by EC-DG XIII.

—— (1994e) *The ex-post evaluation of objective 5b areas: Lazio*, research study commissioned by EC-DG VI.

—— (1994f) *The ex ante evaluation of six Italian Single Programme Documents presented by the EU Member States under the Objective 2 framework*, research study commissioned by EC-DG XVI.

—— (1994g) *Regional Technology Plans. Constitution of a secretariat for the network of participating regions*, research study commissioned by EC-DG XIII.

Prodi R. (1993) 'The Single European Market: Institutions and Economic Policies', *European Planning Studies*, 1, 1.

Prodi, R. and De Giovanni, D. (1991) 'Forty-Five Years of Industrial Policy in Italy: Protagonist, Objectives and Instruments', *Rivista di Politica Economica*, V: 31–57.

Vaccaro S. (1993) 'Tra due riforme. L'utilizzazione dei Fondi strutturali comunitari in Italia in relazione alla revisione dei Regolamenti del 1988' in ANIDE, Associazione Nazionale per l'informazione e la Documentazione Europea, *Fondi strutturali e direttive communitarie. Una sfida per il sistema Italia,* SIPI: 75–111.

12

ECONOMIC CONVERGENCE OR CRISIS MANAGEMENT?

Subsidiarity and local economic strategies in the UK

Steve Martin

INTRODUCTION

Recent years have witnessed a marked change in some UK local authorities' perceptions of their role within Europe. While the phrase 'Europeanization' perhaps implies a far greater degree of cultural change than has occurred in most areas, there has undoubtedly been a growing awareness of the new challenges and opportunities which result from closer European integration and some authorities have undergone radical organizational and structural changes as part of a pro-active, corporate approach to maximizing the benefits which it offers.

The achievements of these authorities in beginning to determine local and regional priorities and gain resources to implement them may be seen as particularly significant given the way in which national economies are being submerged in the new globalized, economic order by complex processes of integration, and local economies have become increasingly vulnerable to the strategic decisions of transnationals with little or no allegiance to the communities in which they locate (Cowling and Sugden 1994; see also Pitelis, Sugden and Tsipouri (Chapter 9 in this volume). Furthermore, the relative weakness of sub-national government in the UK makes it one of the member states in which one might, a *priori*, least expect to observe such developments. However, the emergence of local and regional economic strategies linked to EU funding and going beyond traditional concerns with rectifying market failure, hints at the possibility of increasingly dispersed decision making.

RESPONSES OF SUB-NATIONAL GOVERNMENT IN THE UK

There are considerable variations between the responses to closer European integration of British local authorities. While the most pro-active have welcomed the opportunities afforded by closer European integration seeing in them a chance to increase their resources, enhance their political significance and validate attempts to tackle local economic problems, others have continued to regard EC directives/regulations and policy initiatives as an unwelcome burden and EU assistance as irrelevant.

The range of responses was highlighted by an Audit Commission survey undertaken in 1991–2 which analysed the level of resources and effort devoted to 'European issues' by approximately 50 per cent of British local authorities. It found that expenditure varied by a factor of ten and that there were wide variations in the number of specialist 'European staff' employed. Only a third of authorities had developed a 'European strategy' and just 13 per cent had a strategy document. The most active authorities were those in metropolitan areas, whilst many shire districts employed no 'European staff' at all (Audit Commission 1992).

These variations have been classified by John (1994) in terms of a continuum from 'EC minimal' to the 'fully Europeanized authority'. At the lower end of his 'Ladder of Europeanization' John places activities such as responding to EU directives and regulations and developing formal means of disseminating information about European legislation and potential sources of EU assistance. At the next 'step' up he recognizes a group of 'financially orientated' authorities whose strategic emphasis is upon maximizing receipts of EU funding. Third, he recognizes 'EC networking authorities' that have sought to develop links with partners in their areas and joined transnational networks. Fourth, John identifies a small group of 'fully Europeanized' authorities. These have adopted the 'European dimension' as a corporate priority which is taken into account by all their departments and sought to influence the 'European' policy.

While this framework is clearly oversimplified, it provides a useful summary of the key areas of local authority activities to date and serves to highlight four key areas: managing information, the development of corporate strategies to respond to European issues, forming links with other authorities and partners and securing EU funding.

'Information managers'

Much current EC legislation is 'of direct concern to local authorities, not only as monitoring, enforcing and licensing bodies, but also as employers and property owners' (LGIB 1991) and sub-national government has assumed greater responsibilities for the implementation of a range of primary and secondary European Union legislation (including issues such as public procurement, environmental protection and health and safety standards). In addition pro-active local authorities have moved beyond a narrow focus on their statutory duties and sought to inform not only their own departments but also local businesses about the implications of 'European policies'.

The Single Market was seized upon as a key issue by a wide range of authorities which regarded it as a threat to the prosperity of their areas. The Audit Commission survey showed that, in the early 1990s, most UK local authorities regarded this as by far the most important 'European issue' (Audit Commission 1992). Their concerns stemmed from a view that Cecchini's (1988) forecasts of the benefits of the Single Market were over-optimistic and that such benefits as might arise were unlikely to accrue to their areas. Baimbridge and Burkitt (1991), for example, claim that Cecchini's estimates of the potential cost savings which would result from the abolition of legal barriers, increased competition and economies of scale were exaggerated, while Begg (1989) highlighted the way in which the long-term beneficial impacts of the Single Market will be distributed unevenly within and between Member States. Cutler *et al.* (1989) suggest that strong centripetal tendencies within the Union will mean that freer trade will benefit the economies of the core areas while placing many peripheral regions at a disadvantage. Grahl and Teague (1990) also maintain that most peripheral regions will suffer as a result of lower productivity, their isolation from markets, lack of infrastructure and low skill levels. Research into the determinants of regional competitiveness, sponsored by the European Commission (CEC 1991a), heightened concerns by highlighting the vulnerability of local economies which are heavily reliant on traditional industrial sectors (including most large UK city regions).

In the light of these macro-analyses, a growing number of local authorities have undertaken 'audits' of the likely impacts of the Single Market on their local economies. Many of these have shown that whilst traditional urban areas seem particularly vulnerable to new competition, rural areas will also suffer as a result of their remoteness within the Single Market, and from the effects of reforms of the CAP and reductions in subsidies associated with settlement of the GATT (Martin 1993a). Analyses have suggested that regular farm based employment in some regions will decline by up to 7 per cent between 1993 and 1997 and that average farm incomes in some upland areas may fall to less than ECU 170 per week (Askham Bryan 1991).

In response to these threats, many authorities staged so-called '1992 events' designed to raise awareness of the Single Market and to assist local business to 'gear up' for it. These included seminars, exhibitions, conferences, information leaflets and 'Europe weeks'. A few authorities also provided on-going advice to local employers about the implications of new legislation, ranging from information leaflets and generalist seminars to specialist advice on marketing and legal issues. Some authorities have also sought to strengthen trading links between local companies and those in other European regions by arranging and/or sponsoring visits by local firms to trade exhibitions and to 'twinned' authorities in the EU, Eastern and Central Europe and the former Soviet Republics.

'European strategists'

John's analysis suggests that 'fully Europeanized authorities' require a corporate strategy for dealing with 'European issues'. However, some of the most 'active' authorities have no documented strategy and it is clear that the existence of a strategy is not of itself a guarantee of success in attracting EU funding and/or facilitating more effective networking. Nevertheless, in some areas, strategy formulation has helped to raise awareness of 'European' issues, to increase the commitment of key elected members to responding to them and to clarify local economic priorities (Martin 1993b).

'Networkers'

While some areas were able to operate successfully on their own in the 1980s, this is now seen as being unworkable by a growing number of UK local authorities which have therefore sought to become involved in 'networks'. There has been increasing emphasis on intra-authority co-operation at the sub-regional and regional levels and a growing recognition of the benefits to be gained from pooling resources and information. Most UK authorities now operate through informal regional fora in order to counteract the problems associated with the lack of a regional tier of government. This has received strong support from the Commission which has placed considerable emphasis on involving a wide range of economic and social partners in the preparation of joint strategies for securing EU funding (Martin and Pearce 1993).

The perception that closer European integration offers the chance for them to gain greater influence over EU policy making has also contributed to the mushrooming of interest in local authority networks (Benington 1994). The Treaty on European Union made explicit reference to a role for sub-national government in Community affairs and established the Committee of the Regions with a right to comment on a wide range of legislation including education, vocational training, economic and social cohesion, trans-European networks, public health and crime. In particular, the Treaty's emphasis of subsidiarity or the 'nearness principle' is seen as holding out the prospect of local authorities gaining a stronger bargaining position *vis-à-vis* national government, particularly if they join with other local and regional authorities in order to lobby EU institutions. Links with local and regional governments through transnational networks have therefore become increasingly important. These provide a means of sharing experiences, learning from other areas, joint lobbying and of securing short-term funding (for example under Article 10).

'Big grant hunters'

By far the largest number of authorities which have responded actively to 'European' issues lie somewhere between the minimalist approach of simply processing information about 'Europe' and those which have pro-actively formed networks and sought to shape the policy agenda. Much of the interest in 'European' issues has been prompted primarily by the search for additional funding.

Most bids for Structural Fund assistance in the early and mid 1980s were one-off applications targeted at alleviating particular problems associated with specific economic setbacks. Examples include substantial assistance to Corby District Council to alleviate the effects of steel closures in the early 1980s; South Glamorgan County Council's 'blue book' strategy which bid for assistance following the announcement of the closure of East Moors steel works; Birmingham's highly publicized use of the ERDF to finance city-centre regeneration; and substantial EC investment in 'hard' infrastructure projects (particularly roads and harbours) in the Highlands and Islands region of Scotland.

The 1988 reform of the Structural Funds led to the adoption of a more formal, standardized approach. Community Support Frameworks and Integrated Development Operations in many parts of the UK presented very similar cases for assistance, with a large proportion of ERDF continuing to be devoted to infrastructure projects, particularly road building. However, the same authorities which had cultivated links with the Commission during the 1970s and early 1980s tended to secure the highest levels of assistance because their familiarity with the 'Brussels bureaucracy' enabled them to lobby more successfully for eligibility, to launch opportunist bids at short notice for funding from the increasingly important Community Initiatives and to take up underspend from other areas (particularly in the case of ESF).

By 1993 the bidding process was taken extremely seriously by a large number of authorities. More than twenty London boroughs launched bids (focused on five areas – the Lee Valley, Park Royal, Camden/Islington, Lambeth/Southwark and the East Thames Corridor) for Objective 2 status, a large number of rural areas lobbied for Objective 5b and Merseyside secured Objective 1 funding. Whereas the 1988 bidding process went largely unnoticed by those outside specialist 'European' and Economic Development Departments, the formulation of regional and sub-regional strategies in 1993 involved a much wider range of partners, complex strategic alliances between neighbouring authorities and intensive lobbying on behalf of their areas by local authorities, MPs, MEPs and businesses, both at national and transnational levels. The quality of bids was somewhat improved, with signs of a shift away from the formulaic dependence on infrastructure projects which characterized the period 1988 to 1993, and there were signs that local authorities were embracing genuine local partnerships and a wider perspective on local economic regeneration.

LOCAL AUTHORITY CAPABILITIES

The increasingly pro-active approach to economic development and regeneration of many British local authorities in the early 1990s resulted at least in part from the severity of the UK's relative economic decline over the previous two decades, manifested in a range of socio-economic problems at local level including persistent, unprecedented high levels of unemployment, pockets of extreme deprivation (particularly in inner urban areas and on peripheral housing estates), rising crime, continuing racial tension and sporadic outbursts of social unrest. During the 1980s many Labour-controlled local authorities in traditional manufacturing areas began to develop economic strategies. However, the recession of the early 1990s demonstrated the vulnerability of service industries and commerce based in the traditionally prosperous region of South East England. Combined with the effects of the decline of the defence industry and continued decreases in agricultural employment, these developments sparked new interest in local economic initiatives among previously inactive, Conservative-controlled authorities (Chester and Martin 1994). Large numbers of local authorities formed Economic Development Units/Departments and the role of sub-national government in economic development was eventually recognized under section 33 of the 1989 Local Government and Housing Act, which granted local authorities new powers to engage in economic development activities and formulate economic strategies for their areas. In addition to these new powers, many local authorities built up particular expertise in formulating strategic frameworks for regeneration and bringing together diverse interest groups and agencies to implement these.

While some of their traditional activities have been fragmented and they have faced severe financial constraints imposed by central government, local authorities continue to play a key role in promoting local economic strategies. They are the only agencies with a local democratic mandate and the professional and managerial expertise required to formulate and implement economic regeneration strategies. Furthermore, they are able to form links with local and regional governments in other member states in order to lobby the European Commission and are often the only local agency with the necessary expertise and networks to bid effectively for central government and European financial assistance. They often therefore take the lead in:

- co-ordinating bids for assistance from a large number of potential applicants (including local employers, trades unions, Training and Enterprise Councils (TECs)/Local Enterprise Companies, voluntary organizations, education institutions and a wide range of other public bodies);

- analysing the needs of the local economy and developing strategies for addressing them;
- managing information flows about 'European' policies; and
- representing and lobbying for the interests of their areas at regional, national and supra-national levels.

CONSTRAINTS ON UK LOCAL AUTHORITIES

The ability of local authorities to take a leading role is likely to be a key determinant of the success of local economic strategies in most areas. They have however faced a growing number of constraints. Not all of these are unique to UK sub-national government. However, many stem from the centralization of power in Westminster and central government's ambivalence both to economic strategies and to closer European integration.

In particular, local authorities see their lack of resources as a key constraint. As central government's own regional and urban policies have been downgraded, many local authorities have come to depend upon the EU's Structural Funds to finance local economic strategies. However, the lack of additionality (especially regarding ERDF) has lessened the value of any EU assistance which they secure. Furthermore, because of more than a decade of tight control of public spending and the Treasury's continuing unwillingness to grant supplementary credit approvals, they frequently lack the resources to match the contributions made by the Commission.

The original ERDF regulations stated that 'the Fund's assistance should not lead member states to reduce their own regional development efforts but should complement these efforts' (CEC 1975) and should have a 'genuine additional economic impact in the regions concerned' (CEC 1991b). However, critics claim that the British government (in common with some other member states) has failed to comply with this and deducted from local authorities' approved borrowing programmes equivalent amounts to that which they have received from the ERDF (Comfort 1987; Armstrong 1989). As a result ERDF financed projects have led to few, if any, *additional* benefits to localities, except to the extent that they have lessened loan charges (Thomas 1992).

The loss of some local authority powers and functions has been a further constraint, militating against a co-ordinated action. Some TECs and local authorities, for example, employ separate 'European staff' and Brussels consultants. The process of local government review (outside of metropolitan areas) has also diverted attention and energies from strategic issues and fractured relationships between county and district councils which have been locked in an increasingly hostile 'battle for survival' (Martin and Pearce 1994). Thus in 1994, Nottinghamshire County Council and TECs sponsored a separate Brussels Office from that which was funded by the district councils, and the two worked largely in isolation from each other.

Moreover, in the longer term there are doubts about the ability of smaller unitary authorities, which are to be created in some parts of the country, to operate effectively in 'Europe' (AMA 1992; Martin 1994) and growing evidence that the continuing lack of a regional tier hampers the efforts of UK authorities in their dealings with the Commission and attempts to link up with regions in other member states (Barber and Milins 1993).

CONCLUSIONS

The Commission places considerable emphasis on achievement of economic and social convergence between member states. Thus the Single Act specified that the achievement of cohesion was a major objective of Community policy and Article 130B envisaged that a combination of the Structural Funds and the activities of the European Investment Bank would assist the economic restructuring of less competitive regions. The Structural Funds and the increasingly important 'Community Initiatives' are, however, seen very differently in the UK. At the local level they are regarded primarily as a means of compensating for the reductions in central government's regional policy measures. At national level, central government, which is ideologically opposed to large scale public sector intervention, wishes UK regions to receive the maximum possible allocations of EU assistance in order that Britain 'recoups' as much as possible of its (increasingly contentious) net contribution to the EU budget.

The contribution which the Structural Funds actually make to convergence is unknown because of the lack of rigorous evaluation studies (McEldowney 1991). Both the 'audit-based' approach adopted by European institutions and the ex post evaluations commissioned by UK central government focus almost exclusively on immediate impacts, such as the length of road built or hectares of land reclaimed (see, for example, PIEDA 1992). Since the degree of linkage between these impacts and net additional investment leading to convergence is unclear, it is impossible to judge the ultimate effectiveness of EU policies. Furthermore, because of the additionality problem, many of the outcomes ascribed to EU assistance may in fact have occurred in the absence of funding 'from Brussels'. It is clear, however, that given the relatively small scale of EU assistance it cannot be expected to have more than a marginal affect on the major structural problems currently facing 'declining' regions – even if it is fully additional. In spite of the assistance they have received many local authorities expect their areas to continue to experience long-term, mass unemployment and continued dis-investment in traditional sectors and, in this context, EU intervention may be seen as little more than a short-term palliative which has more to do with crisis management than convergence.

It might therefore be argued that the most significant, long-term impact of EU assistance will be the way in which it has revitalized local economic strategies and encouraged local agencies to embrace new approaches (see also the chapter by Katsoulacos, Stagylopoulos and Kritsalis). The incentive of EU funding has already led to greater intra-regional co-operation, encouraging a more pluralist approach which embraces new social and economic partners. There are also signs that it is encouraging the adoption of a more strategic framework for the long-term recovery of sub-regional economies. The success of such moves will depend crucially upon the ability of local authorities to embrace new roles based on enabling rather than providing economic development/regeneration. This will require a willingness to stand back from short-term measures, such as provision of social and economic 'safety nets', to develop a longer-term, more integrated, holistic approach that promotes sustainable economic regeneration and is concerned with the social and environmental (as well as economic) well-being of local citizens.

Given the UK's lack of a tradition of civil society, such an approach will require a redistribution of power not only to but also within local communities in order to promote fully participative community decision-making (see Devine this volume), and ultimately a redefinition of the constitutional role of local and regional government to give it powers to oversee the activities of a wide range of locally based agencies. To date the involvement of key players such as trades unions in local economic and industrial strategies has often been minimal and the potential of more pro-active local authority responses to compensate for a democratic failure/deficit at national and EU levels has been constrained by the lack of any real attempt to empower local people. Public participation in the formulation of Economic Regional Development Strategies, prepared as part of the 1993 bids for Structural Funds, was for example almost non-existent. Instead the programmes were devised by consultants and/or local authority officers with little input from local politicians and almost no meaningful contribution from community groups.

As such the achievement of genuine subsidiarity in the UK falls well short of the 'European' ideal as defined by Norton (1992). In practice a 'top–down' fixing, at EU level, of regulations regarding competition policy and regional policy continues to have marked impacts at local/regional level and there remains only limited scope for local determination of priorities and self expression. The absence of regional banks and the weakness of trade associations, combined with the lack of democratic regional structures, militates against integrated regional policy-making.

In the context of local economic development there are therefore few signs, within the UK, of the emergence of Marks's (1993) 'multi-level governance' whereby continuous negotiations occur among 'nested government at several territorial tiers'. Neither is there much evidence of Benington and Harvey's (1994) notion that increasing connections between sub-national governments and pluralistic styles of European decision-making are leading to the displacement by new 'spheres of influence' of traditional 'tiers' of government. National government continues to act as the 'gatekeeper' of regional policies through the Council of Ministers and has a major role in the designation of eligible areas and formulation of Single Programming Documents submitted to the Commission (Anderson 1990).

The reality of the British situation is therefore much closer to Duchacek's (1990) concept of 'perforated sovereignty' and the inter-governmentalist scenario identified by Mitchell (1994). The 'Whitehall by-pass', whereby the role of national government is superseded by sub-national government and the Commission, is not a realistic prospect. Indeed the creation of new integrated regional offices of central government departments has been seen by some as moving in the opposite direction, signifying an attempt by central government to 'seize the vacant regional ground' (Morphet 1993). According to this view new regional directors may act in effect as 'commissars' who are portrayed by central government as the true representatives of the 'regions'; an interpretation which reflects UK government's initial proposals for non-elected UK 'representatives' to sit on the Committee of the Regions.

However, even within existing constraints, local authorities are beginning to play an increasing role as catalysts and co-ordinators of local strategies. There are therefore signs that, whilst it may not lead to economic convergence, EU assistance has begun to act as an incentive for local policy makers to adopt more coherent, participative (more 'European') approaches to regional and sub-regional economic planning. In spite of the continuing problems and limited progress to date, such a convergence of policy perspectives and approaches to local economic problems may in itself represent a form of 'cohesion' which, given the deep-seated rivalry between local stakeholders and the UK's history of *ad hoc*, market driven initiatives, will come to be seen as a considerable achievement. There is though a need for a considerable strengthening of the formal powers of sub-national government within EU policy making before we will see the emergence of 'action promoted not only *for* the Regions, but also *by* the Regions' (see Magnatti this volume). Only when this is achieved will it really be possible to claim that meaningful subsidiarity has been achieved within the UK in relation to local industrial and economic strategies.

ACKNOWLEDGEMENTS

This paper is drawn from the preliminary findings of a two year study funded by the Economic and Social Research Council which is being undertaken by the author with Tanya Crook and Graham Pearce.

REFERENCES

Anderson, J.J. (1990) 'Skeptical reflections on a Europe of the regions', *Journal of Public Policy* 10: 417–47.

Armstrong, H. (1989) 'Community regional policy', in J. Lodge (ed.) *The European Community and the Challenge of the Future*, J. London: Pinter.

Askram Bryan Agricultural College (1991) *Survey of Farm Incomes in North Yorkshire*, North Allerton.' North Yorkshire County Council.

Association of Metropolitan Authorities (1992) *The New Europe: Implications for Local Government*, London: HMSO.

Audit Commission (1992) *A Rough Guide to Europe*, London: HMSO.

Baimbridge, M. and Burkitt, B. (1991) 'The Cecchini Report and the impact of 1992', *European Research*, September.

Barber, S. and Millns, T. (1993) *Building the New Europe*, London: Association of County Councils.

Begg, I. (1989) 'The regional dimensions of the 1992 proposals', *Regional Studies*, 23, (4): 368–75.

Benington, J. (1994) *Local Democracy and the European Union: The Impact of Europeanisation on Local Governance*, London: Commission for Local Democracy.

Benington, J. and Harvey, J. (1994) 'Spheres or tiers: the significance of transnational local authority networks' in P. Dunleavy and J. Stanyer (eds) *Contemporary Political Studies*, Exeter: PSA.

Bryden, J. (1990) *Rural Change in Europe: Research Programme on Farm Structures and Pluriactivity*, London: Arkleton Trust.

Cecchini, P. (1988) *The European Challenge 1992: The Benefits of a Single European Market*, Luxembourg: European Community.

Chester K.B. and Martin, S.J. (1994) *The Local Authority and Economic Regeneration in the Mid-1990s: Co-ordination, Community Involvement and Partnership*, Luton: Local Government Management Board.

Comfort, A. (1987) 'The principle of "additionality" in regard to the ERDF and its application in some member states', *European Parliament Research and Documentation papers, Regional and Transport Series No. 15*, Strasbourg: European Parliament.

Commission of the European Communities (1975) Regulation (EEC) No 724/75, *Official Journal* L 73/1, 21.3.75.

—— (1991a) *Europe 2000: Outlook for the Development of Community's Territory*, Luxembourg: DGXVI.

—— (1991b) *Annual Report on the Implementation of the Reform of the Structural Funds* Luxembourg: Office for the Publication of the European Communities.

—— (1992) *From the Single Act to Maastricht and Beyond: The means to match our ambitions*, COM (29) 2000 final, 11.2.92.

Cowling, K. and Sugden, R. (1994) 'Industrial strategy: guiding principles and European Contex' in P. Bianchi, K. Cowling and R. Sugden (eds) *Europe's Economic Challenge*, London: Routledge.

Cutler, C., Haslam, C., Williams, J. and Williams, K. (1989) *1992 – The Struggle for Europe: A critical evaluation of the European Communinity*, New York: Berg Publishers.

Duchacek, I. (1990) 'Perforated sovereignties: towards a typology of new actors in international relations', in H. Michelman and P. Soldatos (eds) *Federalism and International Relations*, Oxford: Clarendon.

Grahl, J. and Teague, P. (1990) *1992 – The Big Market: The Future of the European Community*, London: Lawrence and Wishart.

John, P. (1994) *The Europeanisation of British Local Government: New Management*

Strategies, Luton: *Local Government Management Board.*

Local Government International Bureau (1991) Responding to the Challenge of EC Law, Paper No. 9, London: LGIB.

McEldowney, J.J. (1991) Evaluation and European Regional Policy, *Regional Studies,* 25(3): 261–6.

Marks, G. (1993) 'Structural policy and multi level governance in the EC' in A. Cafruny, and G. Rosenthal (eds) *The State of the European Community Vol. 2: The Maastricht Debates and Beyond,* Boulder, CO: Lynne Rienner.

Martin, S.J. (1993a) 'The Europeanisation of local authorities: challenges for rural areas,' *Journal of Rural Studies,* 9 (2): 153–61.

—— (1993b) 'European Regional development Strategies: new opportunities for public–private partnership', *European Business and Economic Development,* 2: 84–90.

—— (1994) 'The prospects for unitary authorities in the New Europe: will Tonto really be better off if the Lone Ranger is shot?', *Local Government Policy Making,* 21 (3): 63–5.

Martin, S.J. and Pearce, G. (1992) 'The Europeanisation of local authority economic development strategies: Birmingham in the 1980s', *Regional Studies* 26 (5): 499–503.

—— (1993) 'European regional development strategies: strengthening meso-government in the UK?', *Regional Studies,* 27, (7): 681–86.

—— (1994) 'Prospects for new unitary authorities in the New Europe: the demise of the Lone Ranger', *Local Government Policy Making,* 27, (5): 14–20.

Mitchell, J. (1994) 'The articulation of regional interests in the European Union', paper presented to the PSA Annual Conference, Swansea.

Morphet, J. (1993) 'Mandarins lay strategy to seize the regional ground', *Planning,* 989.

Norton A. (1992) *The Principle of Subsidiarity and its Implications for Local Government,* Luton: Local Government Management Board.

PIEDA (1992) *Ex Post Evaluation of Birmingham Integrated Development Operation,* London: PIEDA.

Thomas, I.C. (1992) 'Additionality in the distribution of ERDF grants to local authorities', *Local Economy,* 6, (4): 292–310.

INDEX

Note: Italic page numbers refer to information in tables.

Adams, W. and Brock, J.W. 14
additionality 189, *190–1*, 192, 196, 226, 227
Adenauer, Konrad 57
agglomeration economies 66–7
Al-Agraa, A.M. 49
Amaral, L.M. 159
AMICE 99
Amsterdam School 100
Andersen, E.S. and Lundvall, B.A. 80
Anderson, J.J. 229
Anglo-Saxon model 3, 4
Armstrong, H. 226
Arrington, B. and Haddock, C.C. 25
Askham Bryan Agricultural College 222
aspirations/goals 126–8, 143
Audit Commission 221–2
Audretsch, D. and Vivarelli, M. 62, 76
Austria, application of concept of competitiveness to 137–8; crisis and new credibility 130; discriminating between sectors 131–2; economic preconditions/development 128–9; governance structures in 136–7; nationalized industries in 134; and price liberalization129; relevance of the future 130–1; rules for foreign capital 134–5; Topinvestitionen 132–4
Austrian Institute of Economic Research (WIFO) 133
Axelrod, R. 68

Baden-Württemburg 59, 61, 63, 67, 68, 71, 72
Bailey, D. *et al.* 169
balance of payments 2, 164–5
Balogh, T. and Streeton, P. 162, 164, 165
bandwagon effects 165
Bangemann Report 60
banking system 71–2, 95, 136, 137, 228
bargaining xxi, 83–5, *86–7*, 88, 91, 93, 94, 100; American *97*; British 96, 98–9; Dutch 95, *97*; effort 24–5; French 94–5, *96*; German 95, *96*; Italian *96*, 98; Japanese 97; Swedish 95, *96*, 98
Bartlett, W. *et al.* 14
Bayer, K. 136
Beck, B. 143
beggar-my-neighbour policies 2, 4
Benington, J. 223; and Harvey, J. 228
Bennett, J.T. and Johnson, M.H. 28
Bergsten, C.F. *et al.* 165
Bessa, D. 151
Best, M. 5
best practice 71, 74
Bianchi, P. 6, 10, 31, 69, 74; and Miller, L.M. 13
Binnenmarkt 140
Boardman, A. and Vining, A. 17, 28, 35
Bode, R. 100n
Borcherding, T.E. *et al.* 29
Bös, D. 17, 18, 21, 22, 34
Boyd, C.W. 28
Braverman, H. 81
Bretton Woods system 2, 4

BRITE 99
Brusco, S. 77

Cable, J.R. and Machin, S.J. 22
Calvo, G.A. 130
capital 21–2, 98, 116, 117, 134–5, 148; formation *155*; transfers 153, 154, 156, 158
Cassis de Dijon 49
CDU/CSU 118
Cecchini, P. 222
Central and Eastern Europe (CEE) *see* transition economies
CEPR 47
Chester, K. B. and Martin, S.J. 225
CITER (Centro Informazione Tessile Emilia-Romagna) 71
Clark, A. 24
Club of Rome 122
co-operation xvii, xix, xxiv, 6, 31, 58, 200–1; among SMEs 67–9, 70, 71–3, 75–6; and competition 13–14, 74–5; inter-firm 201; promotion of 75–6, 77
Cohen, R. and Zysman, J. 100
cohesion 91, 95, *96–7*, 98, 99, 203, 229
Cohesion Fund 206
Comfort, A. 226
Commission of the European Communities (CEC) 49, 56, 59, 60, 61, 69–70, 74, 76, 222, 226
Community Initiatives 227
competition 12–13, 75–6, 184; artificial 15; and co-operation 13–14, 74–5; and costs 29; free 60; insitutional 50; not always feasible 30–1; perfect 13; role of xv; strategy 14, 55–6; unworkable 14–15
competitive advantage 5, 61; dynamic 1–2; static 1, 5; weakening of 175
competitiveness, ambiguities in xxiii; application of concept xxii, 125–8, 137–8; between regions 6–7; as capability to compete 17; community-centred 149; defined xiv-xv, xvii, 1–2, 58–9, 124, 125–8, 141–2, 147–50, 157, 160; economy level 149; encouragement of 19; in EU 115; in Europe 140–1; factors of 124, 143; firm level 123; formula for 125; in Germany 115–16; industrial 148; inter-community 2; in Japan 122, 140; level playing field 8, 74, 118; national level 123–5, 148, 149; Portuguese 150–6; in post-war Austria 128–38; priority action 60; promotion of accelerators/multipliers 136; quest for 93, 101; routes to 2–5; state-societal arrangements 3–5; in Switzerland 138–9; timing 121–2; in USA 122, 139–40
Competitiveness Policy Council (USA) 148
concepts of control 79, 81, 83, 98; defined 100–1; and EU 99–100; industrial democracy 82; macro-Fordism 82; micro-Fordism 82; networks 81–2; Toyotism 82–3
Confederation of Industries (SEB) 172
Confraria, J. 153, 157
convergence xvii-xviii, xxii, 118–19, 141, 153, 156, 205, 227
core firms 80, 100; bargaining relationships 82; and competitiveness 93; and concepts of control 81–3; defined 84; and policy objectives 91, 94; and subsidiarity 91, 93
costs, comparisons 30, 35; and competition 29; and effect on quality 25–8; effect on quality 25–8, 35; fixed 59, 67–8, 74, 77; high 29; influence of ownership on 28–9; marginal 22; permissable range of inefficiency 19–21; public/private 19–27, 167; reductions in 26, 35; unit 22, 26–7, 124
Council of the Heads of State 45
Cowling, K. and Sugden, R. 8, 9, 14, 161, 167, 169, 220
Cullis, J.G. and Jones, P.J. 34
Cutler, C. *et al.* 222

Dahl, R. 83
Davies, S. *et al.* 13
De Banville, E. and Chanaron, J-J. 91
De Fraja, G. 21; and Delbono, F. 14
decision-making 9–10, 99; decentralized xix, 13–14, 54; levels of 31; processes of 4–5, 44–7, 56, 144; strategic 167
Delbono, F. and Denicolò, V. 13
Delors, Jacques 54
demand elasticity 19–20, 27

dependency relations 81, 85, 88, *90*, 91
Deprins, D. *et al.* 28
deregulation 4, 25–6, 31
Devine, P. 7, 143
Diamond of Competitive Advantage 162
Dias, J. 157
Dietrich, M. and Schenk, H. 165
direct foreign investment xvi, 113, 169; in CEE *106–8*, 110; cumulative 105, 107; implications for CEE 116–17; implications for western Europe 117–18; and international trade 104–5; main host countries 105, *106*; motivations for 114; pattern of 105; role of Germany in 114–16; *see also* investment; outward investment
divergence 118–19
division of labour 5, 7, 9, 10, 93, 95, 116
Dodgson, J.S. and Katsoulacos, Y. 26, 35
Dohse, K. *et al.* 82
Dorman, P. 13
DOWC 115
Duchacek, I. 229
Dunning, J.H. 162, 163, 164, 166

Eaton, B.C. and White, W.D. 24
Economic Community (EC), disparities between member states/regions 204–6
Economic and Social Committee 46
Economic Union (EU), new industrial 'twofold' approach 199–204, 213–16
economies of scale 62, 77, 83, 216; internal/external 59, 64–9, 71, 73, 74, 75–6
economies of scope 83
The Economist 95
Edwards, F.R. and Stevens, B.J. 35
efficiency xxi, 59, 140, 203; defined 25, 143; managerial 21–2, 35; as measure of progress 55–6; and ownership xv, 21–25; Pareto 12, 25, 166; in private/public sector 32–4; static/dynamic 61; wages 24
endogenous growth theory 61–2
enlargement 118–19
enterprise networks 60, 61
environment 16, 54
equilibrium 61, 66
Erhard, L. 17
ESPRIT 99, 178
Estrin, S. and Hughes, K. 114
European Coal and Steel Community (ECSC) 44
European Commission 45–6, 99; inter-governmental 46, 47; role of 200; supra-national 46, 47
European Company Councils 99
European Free Trade Association (EFTA) 147, 152
European Recovery Programme (ERP) 131–2, 133
European Research and Development Fund (ERDF) 226
European Roundtable of Industrialists (ERT) 99
European Single Act (ESA) xxiv, 31, 42, 44–50, 54, 56, 60, 98, 153, 201, 227
European Union (EU) xxiv-xxv, 42, 58, 62, 69, 75, 79, 94, 100, 147, 200; convergence, divergence and enlargement 118–19
Europeanization 220, 221
Eurosclerosis 99
exchange controls 2, 3
exports 141, 150, 152; enough 126
external economies 59, 137; co-operative 59, 67–9, 71, 73, 74, 75–6; competitive 59; defined 64; exogenous 67, 71, 75

Farrands, C. and Totterdill, P. 10
federal states 45, 46–7, 52, 54
flexible specialization 82–3, *89*, *92*, 93, 94, 96, 98, 100
Fordism 81; automated/ultra 83; macro- 83, *89*, *92*, 94, 95, 96–7, 98, 99, 100; micro- 83, 84, *89*, *92*, 93, 94, *96–7*, 98, 100; neo- 83
Foundation for Research and Technology (FORTH) 172
Framework Programmes (FPs) xvii, xxiii-xiv, 172, *173–4*, 204; additionality 189, *190–1*, 192, 196; benefits and barriers 192, 193–4, 195, 197; co-operative behaviour 184, *185–8*, 189, 196; data collection and methodology 177–9, 197–8; impact of 172, 196–7;

organization participation 179–80; technological impact 180–3, 195–6
Frankel, M. 162, 166
free trade market 6, 7, 53, 60, 135, 160, 165
French model 44–5
Frenkel, J.A. 130
Fujitsuism 84
full employment xix, 4, 25, 59

Galtung, J. 79
GATT 8, 222
GEP 152
German Basic Law 53
Geroski, P. 67
Giannitsis, T. *et al.* 198
Gilpin, R. 162
global social contract 101
globalization 4, 138
Goodwin, P.B. 25
Goto, A. 13
governance structures 135–7
government, infra-national 4; local xviii, 201, 228, 229; national 201, 226, 227, 229; regional 201, 226, 228–9; sub-national 220–5; supply-side policies 5; supra-national 4, 46, 47, 201, 226
Grabher, G. 95
Grahl, J. and Teague, P. 222
Gramsci, A. 82
Gravelle, H. 22; and Rees, R. 20
Greece, and additionality 189, *190–1*, 192, 196; benefits and barriers of FPs 192, *193–4*, 195, 197; co-operative behaviour in 184, *185–8*, 189, 196; economy 174–7; impact of FPs on 172; participation in FPs 179–80; and technology transfer 180–3, 195–6
Growth, Competitiveness, Employment (1993) 58, 62, 73, 76
Gunderson, M. 23, 24

Handl, V. 117
Hannequart, 227
Hargreaves Heap, S. 76
Hart, J. 3
Haskel, J. and Szymanski, S. 23, 26
hierarchies 83
Hood, N. and Young, S. 162, 163
Hufbauer, G.C. and Adler, F.M. 162, 163, 165
Hughes, A. 72
Hughes, K. 115, 116, 117, 157

IMF 12
import substitution 151
incentive schemes 21, 152, 208
income/s xx, 16, 30, 128, 140; aspirational factor 126–7, 143; disparities in 60–1
industrial complex xxi, 100; bargaining relationships 80; characteristics 79–80; defined 80
industrial democracy 81, 89, 92
industrial strategy 58–9, 75–6, 136, 164, 169; aggregation of local forces 217; barriers to 79; and co-operation/competition 71–5; development of less favoured areas 217; foundations for 151–2; funding 216–17; inter-community negotiation 9; internal/external economies of scale 64–9; in Italy 206–13; macro/micro levels 216; market failure 8; new EU approach 200–4; protectionism 8–9; public support for innovation 202, 203; recent developments 59–64; regional 202–3; Scandinavian model 9–10; and subsidiarity 69–70; top–down/bottom–up approach 59, 216; twofold approach 199–204, 213–16; underlying tensions 7–8
influence 83
innovation 61, 62, 140, 202, 203, 215–16
Inotai, A. 111, 117
Institute for Economic Policy Studies (IMOP) 172
institutional economics 61
Integrated Mediterranean Programmes (IMPs) 213–14
Integrated Programme in Favour of SMEs and the Craft Sector (1994) 63–4, 69–70, 73, 76
integration xxi-xxii, 47, 99, 220; normative 47–50; UK responses to 220–5; vertical 83
inter-community exchange 2, 5
Interministerial Committee for Economic Planning (CIPE) 214
internal economies 59, 64–9; defined 64–5

international trade 148, 149; flows 110–11, *112*, 113; and foreign direct investment 104–10; motivations for 114
internationalization 94, 95, 116
intervention 31, 54; geographical level 201; Italian national/regional levels of 209–11; local/regional 199–200; in *Mezzogiorno* 211–13; policy 177–8; Special xxiv, 199; top–down 216
investment 59, 95, 98, 135, 140, 144, 156, 157, 210; attracting 152–3; *see also* direct foreign investment; outward investment
Islands of Innovation 215–16
Italy, application of new EU approach to xxiv, 213–16; institutionalization of regions 208–9; intervention in *Mezzogiorno* 211–13; national/ regional levels of intervention 209–11; regional policy trends 206, 207, 208

Jacquemin, A. and Slade, M. 149
Japanization 84
Johannson, P.-O. 166
John, P. 221, 223
Johnson, G.E. 24

Kaldor, N. 166
Kapteyn, P.J.C. 53, 54
Katsoulacos, Y. and Newell, E. 13
Katz, L.F. and Summers, L.M. 22
Kay, N. 58
keiretsus 3, 135
Kenney, M. and Florida, R. 83
Kitchen, H. 35
Knickerbocker, F.T. 165
Kramer, H. 118
Krugman, P. 5, 153
Kujawa, D. 163, 164

labour 21–4, 98; mobility of 148, 150, 153; organized 3
Ladder of Europeanization 221; Big grant hunters 224; European strategists 223; information managers 221–2; networkers 223
laissez-faire policy 14
Lashmar, P. 18
Lazonick, W. 65
Leijonhufvud, G. 35n
LGIB 221
Local Government and Housing Act (1989) 225
Lorenz, E.H. 72–3
Lundvall, B. 80, 91

Maastricht Treaty 69, 99, 138, 153, 201
McCrone, G. 77n
McEldowney, J.J. 227
Machin, S.J. 22; and Stewart, M.B. 22
MacPherson, D.A. 22
Manser, W.A.P. 164–5
Marks, G. 228
Marshall, A. 64–5, 66–7
Martin, S.J. 58, 157, 222, 223, 227; and Parker, D. 30, 36n; and Pearce, G. 223, 226
Meihsi, D. 129
mergers xix-xx, 31
Michalski, A. and Wallace, H. 118
Milgrom, T. and Roberts, T. 62
Millward, R. 16, 28
Mitchell, J. 229
mixed, economy 9; oligopoly 14, 16, 27
Møjset, L. 82
mode of conflict management 91
Morphet, J. 229
Moura, F. 151
multi-speed Europe 100
multinational enterprises 116, 135
mutual recognition 49, 53, 54–5, 56; and qualified majority 50–51

Nash bargaining 23
nation-states 45, 47
nationalized industries 15, 16, 134, 136, 144
negotiated economy 9–10
Nelson, R.A. 29, 91
network externalities 14–15
networks xxiv, 82, 223; formal/ informal 71–3, 74; of innovators 203; inter-firm 61
Neves, J. 153
new right 4
Nielsen, K. and Pedersen, O. 9
normative concept 127–8
North, 61
Norton, A. 228

Nugent, N. 46, 47
Nuti, M. 118

objectives 1–2, 4–5, 7, 31, 91, 94; of equity and stability 55; of managers 157; of public sector 15–17; setting and measuring 169
OECD 111, 130, 147, 157, 160
Oliver, N. and Wilkinson, G. 82–3
Olson, 137
open actions 214–15
Organization for European Economic Cooperation (OEEC) 44
Orlowski, 124
Oughton, C. 118; and Whittam, G. 68, 71, 76
outward investment 159–61; costs and benefits 167, 168; effect on balance of payments 164–5; extent and nature 161; Greek strategy 168–9; impact of 162–8; pros and cons 163–6; *see also* direct foreign investment; investment
Overbeek, H. 101
ownership, cost (in)efficiency 19–25; effect on technical efficiency 29–30; influence of 28–30; and social justice 20–5; and wage bargaining 23–4

papal encyclicals 53, 77
Parker, D. and Martin, S. 23
Parris, H. *et al.* 28, 34
Parsons, T. 83
partnership 202, 203
Pateman, C. 83
Pedersen, T. 164
Pedip *(Programa Especificio para o Desenvolvimento da Indústria Portuguesa)* 152
Perelman, S. and Pestieau, P. 28
performance 124; good 148–9, 150; macro 139, 140; in protected markets 151–2
Periodic Reports 204
Pestoff, V. 9
Pettigrew, A. 84
Pfeffer, J. 84
PIEDA 227
Pint, E.M. 21
Piore, M. and Sabel, C. 77, 81
Pitelis, C. 2, 160, 161, 167, 169
Planet SA 172
Porter, M.E. 5, 123–4, 143, 157, 160, 161, 162
positive concept 127–8
power 83–5, 88, 91, 167; monopoly 65, 142–3; national/regional harmonization 8;
redistribution of 10
Praten, C. 77
PRAXI KP 172
'Preis- und Lohnkommission' 129–30
Principles of Economics (Marshall) 64
private sector 4, 15, 16–17, 22; cost (in)efficiency 19–27; relative efficiency of *32–4*; under natural monopoly 19–20
privatization xx, 22, 30, 149–50; adverse effects 26; aims of 18; reasons for 17–19
production 116, 182, 211; cheap 124; cost of 151; influence of ownership on 28–30; internationalization of 4
productivity concept 124
profit 13–14, 16, 22, 23, 30, 35, 91, 139, 151, 167
public sector 12, 14, 18; cost (in)efficiency 19–27; objectives 15–17; relative efficiency of *32–4*; under natural monopoly 19–20

qualified majority 50–51

RACE 99
Radice, H. 116
Ramanadham, V.V. 34
Ramsay, 14
reciprocal recognition 6, 54–5
Reddaway, W.B. *et al.* 164
Rees, R. 35
Regional Technology Plans 204
resources, (re)allocation of 1, 7, 8, 149
Robbins, Lord 52, 56–7
Robertson, B. 164
Rodrigues, F. *et al.* 152
Roemer, P. 61
Rosen, A. 24
Rothschild, K. 84
RTD system xxiv, 197–8
Ruigrok, W. and Van Tulder, R. 100, 101

Sabel, C. *et al.* 72
Sachverständigenrat 124
Salazar, O. 152

Scandinavian model 9
Schafer, G.F. 53, 54
Schenk, H. 14, 64, 76
Schioppa, P. 50, 51–2
Schriver, J.S. 122
Schumpeter, J. 66
Sengenberger, W. *et al.* 76
service industries 100
Shapiro, C. and Stiglitz, J.E. 24
Silva, A. 151
Sinclair, P. 7, 8
Singh, A. 1, 2, 28, 34, 143
Single European Act *see* European Single Act (ESA)
small and medium enterprises (SMEs) xvi, xxi, 59, 174, *210*; and co-operation 67–9, 70, 71–3, 75–6; Collective Service Centres 71; disadvantages 63, 67; and economies of scale 64–9, 71, 73, 74, 75–6; finance for 71–2; and innovation 62; and *Integrated Programme* 63–4, 69–70; networking arrangements 71–3, 74; promotion of 74–5; role of 62; as source of employment creation 62; and subcontracting 72–3
Smith, A. 52
Social Chapter 5, 31
Social Charter 99
sovereignty 55
Sraffa, P. 66
Stackelberg model 22, 123, 142
START 99
state 3, 9, 15, 54
state-owned enterprises (SOEs) 12, 15, 16, 17–18, 34; commercial performance of 18–19; relative efficiency of 28–30
Stigler, G. 148
structural funds xxv, 55–6, 61, 118, 201, 204, 206, 214, 224, 226, 227–8
subcontractors 72–3, 116
subsidiarity xv, xviii, xix, xx, xxv, 2, 5, 31, 56, 91, 93, 99; achievement of 228–9; application of 201–2; and community objectives 7; defined 51–2; in federal states 47; framework for 6–7; and industrial policy 68–71, 74; origins of 51–5, 77; principle of 5–6, 42–3; top–down/bottom–up approach xvi
Sugden, R. 169
Sutton, J. 77

tariff/s 56; barriers 48, 49
Technology Policy 184
Third Italy 59, 61, 63, 67, 68, 71
Thomas, I.C. 226
Thurow, L. 122
Tirole, J. 14
Tispouri, L.J. and Gaudenzi, S. 163
Toyotism *89*, *92*, 93, 95, *97*, 98–9, 100
trade balance 150
trade flows, barriers to 111; differences in 111; German role 110–11; main partners 111, *112*, 113
Training and Enterprise Councils (TECs) 225, 226
transition economies 122, 128; direct foreign investment in 104–10; future of 119; implications for 116–17; and integration 119; role of Germany in 14–16, 119
transnational corporations 6, 150, 166, 167
Treaty of the European Union (TEU) 42–3, 44, 70
Treaty of Rome 42, 43–4, 45, 49
Tyson, W.J. 27

UNCTAD 98
unemployment 2, 204, 206
unitary states 52
United Kingdom, achievement of subsidiarity in 228–9; constraints on local authorities 226–7; local authority capabilities 225–6; responses to integration 220–5
Urwin, D.W. 44
user-producers 80

Van der Pijl, K. 100
Vandermerwe, S. and Rada, J. 100
Vernon, R. 165
Vickers, J. and Yarrow, G. 18, 21, 28, 29, 30, 34, 35
virtuous growth cycles 81
Vitols, S.I. 72

Wade, R. 136
wages 22–4, 61, 115, 128, 135, 137, 139, 143
Wallensteen, P. 79, 84

wealth 125
welfare 21–2, 23, 26–7, 30, 31, 35, 150
White Book 45, 49, 50–1
White, P.J. 26
Whitehall by-pass 229
Wijkman, P.-M. 118
Williamson, O. 83–4; and Ouchi, W. 83
Willner, J. 8, 14, 22, 25, 27
Winckler, G. 130
Winters, L.A. 111

Yarrow, G. 28, 34

zero-profit 123, 142
zero-sum 13, 149
Zetterberg, J. 24